PUBLICATIONS OF THE AMERICAN JEWISH ARCHIVES · NO. I

JACOB R. MARCUS, PH.D., *Editor*

EVENTFUL YEARS
AND EXPERIENCES

THE GENEROSITY OF

MR. LAWRENCE R. WECHSLER

HAS ENABLED

THE AMERICAN JEWISH ARCHIVES

TO PUBLISH THIS VOLUME

IN THE CONSECRATED MEMORY

OF HIS BELOVED WIFE

TOBELEAH

EVENTFUL YEARS AND EXPERIENCES

STUDIES

in Nineteenth Century American Jewish History

BY BERTRAM WALLACE KORN, D.H.L.

THE AMERICAN JEWISH ARCHIVES

Cincinnati • 1954

Library of Congress Catalog Card Number: 54–10965

———

COPYRIGHT, 1954, BY

THE AMERICAN JEWISH ARCHIVES
*On the Cincinnati campus of the Hebrew Union College -
Jewish Institute of Religion*

———

PRINTED IN THE UNITED STATES OF AMERICA

PRESS OF *Maurice Jacobs* INC.

224 N. 15TH ST., PHILADELPHIA 2, PENNA.

For RITA

AND I WILL BETROTHE

THEE UNTO ME FOREVER

Preface

As AMERICAN JEWRY stands upon the threshold of the fourth century of Jewish life on this continent, it well behooves us to attempt to appraise our past. This volume is intended to serve as a modest contribution to the knowledge of those who would seek to understand the contemporary problems and achievements of the American Jewish community against the background of the experiences of foregoing generations.

Although these studies deal largely with the same period in the nineteenth century and with the same *dramatis personae*, they do not trace a coherent, connected story. For, truly, the range of American Jewish history is as broad and as deep as life itself . . . and trained scholars have been working for too brief a time to permit anything more than an investigation of limited areas of that life. Not in our time can a definitive history of American Jewry be written; not, I am so bold to think, until hundreds of fragments and excerpts such as these have been researched and published and corrected and modified and criticised and rewritten and republished. Six of these studies have had the benefit of this process; they were first published in the learned journals and annuals and have been modified and added to, before republication in this form.

Excerpts though they may be, I believe that these studies will cast some illumination upon certain phases of the American Jewish story which are of significance to students of Jewish and general American history alike. These are not petty details but, in some cases at least, decisive events and experiences during those formative years of the nineteenth century when the present pattern of American Jewish institutions and attitudes was being hammered out of chaos. Here are described the integration of a specific group of German-Jewish immigrants into American life; the tedious but challenging work of attempting to create a structure for the new Jewish life in an atmosphere of freedom and voluntarism unmatched in the European experience of our forebears; the reaction of American Jews to a political party's bigotry against Roman Catholics and immigrants; the indifference of a great American Jew to his ancestral heritage; the first sign of recognition by Congress of the equality of Judaism with Christianity as an American faith; the editorial policy of a distinguished rabbinical journalist during the Civil War; the birth and slow death of the first American Jewish rabbinical seminary; the response of American Jewry to the religious needs of military personnel who served during the Spanish-American War.

Every historian is dependent upon hosts of helpers — predecessors, teachers, colleagues, librarians, directors of historical societies, students, descendants of yesteryear's colorful personages. Acknowledgement cannot here be made to every person who rendered assistance in the research stage of these studies, but the notes, wherever possible, indicate the sources of information, persons as well as books and pamphlets and newspapers. I am grateful to hundreds whose kindness made the work develop with greater speed and ease, but especially to the chief librarians and staff members of the libraries of the Hebrew Union College - Jewish Institute of Religion, the Jewish Division of the New York Public Library, the Library of Congress, the Dropsie College for Hebrew and Cognate Learning, the American Jewish Historical Society, and the American Jewish Archives. My particularly affectionate appreciation must be recorded to Dr. Jacob R. Marcus, Director of the last named repository, for his unfailingly resourceful counsel, guidance and informativeness in the preparation and writing of each of these studies, and for his cooperation in sponsoring this volume for final publication.

Every book, physically, is the product of the talent and faithfulness to duty of artists and technicians. For the physical attractiveness of this volume, I am deeply indebted to my long-time friend and associate, Dr. Maurice Jacobs, and his capable press staff, led by Mr. David Skaraton.

My appreciation must also be recorded for faithful and accurate secretarial assistance during a long period of research and writing. To Miss Mathilde Belfield, Miss Imelda McGonigle, Miss Hattie Jacobs and Mrs. Sylvia Dunsker: my sincere gratitude for such wonderful help.

Ideally, the person to whom a book is dedicated ought to receive the book as a total surprise, a present. My dear wife to whom this is dedicated knows it so well that she will never have to read it in published form. She not only suffered the pangs of long periods of enforced silence and neglect during research and writing stages, and patiently endured the necessity of serving as historical judge and literary critic, but also earned the permanent appreciation of every reader who consults the Index, which is truly the devoted work of her hands, eyes, time and tolerance.

Words can hardly serve to speak my warm regard for Mr. Lawrence R. Wechsler of my congregation, whose generous friendship has made the hope of publishing this volume the present reality. His dear wife Tobeleah, to whom this is a memorial, was a talented and sensitive woman and artist whose untimely passing was genuinely a deprivation not only to her three splendid children and her adoring husband, but to many friends in all walks of life to whom she was a breath of graciousness and charm in an ofttimes cold age of frustration and competition. She was no stranger to these studies: I discussed them with her frequently, and I am happy that she is associated with them in this manner.

B.W.K.

Philadelphia,
Thanksgiving Day, 1953.

NOTE: Sources referred to most frequently in the notes are abbreviated as follows:

AJCW	Bertram Wallace Korn, *American Jewry and the Civil War*, Philadelphia, 1951.
ASM	*The Asmonean*, New York, 1849–58.
DAB	*Dictionary of American Biography*, 22 vols., New York, 1946.
HL	*The Hebrew Leader*, New York, 1862–80.
ISR	*The (American) Israelite*, Cincinnati, 1854–
MESS	*The Jewish Messenger*, New York, 1857–1903.
OCC	*The Occident and American Jewish Advocate*, Philadelphia, 1843–69.
PAJHS	*Publication(s) of the American Jewish Historical Society*, Baltimore, New York, 1893–
UJE	*The Universal Jewish Encyclopedia*, 10 vols., New York, 1939–43.

Table of Contents

EVENTFUL YEARS
AND EXPERIENCES

I

Jewish "Forty-Eighters" in America*

DURING the century and more since the first "refugees" fled to America after the failure of the Revolutions which swept through Central Europe in 1848, the appellation "Forty-Eighter" has undergone a confusing development. Originally applied only to those persons who had participated in the European Revolutions and who then migrated to America because of personal disillusionment or the fear of governmental reprisal, the term has frequently been used so loosely that some commemorative articles published during 1948 regarded as "Forty-Eighters" certain intellectuals who came to America as early as 1833 and almost anyone who left Germany between 1848 and 1860. It is essential, however, that a study of any group of immigrants define the nature of that group clearly and exactly.

The most authoritative students of the subject have agreed that the total number of political refugees who came to America following the wreckage of the Revolutionary efforts was much smaller than has customarily been estimated. Professor Marcus Hansen, writing in 1940, believed that "taken altogether, the political refugees who emigrated to America numbered only a few thousand." [1] Dr. A. E. Zucker assembled detailed data on something more than three hundred "Forty-Eighters," but believes that a conservative estimate of the total number might

* Read at the annual meeting of the American Historical Association in Washington, D. C., December 30, 1948, published in original form in the *American Jewish Archives*, Vol. II, No. 1 (June, 1949), pp. 3–20, and, in German translation of excerpted portions, in *Aufbau*, Sept. 23, 1949, Sept. 30, Oct. 14 and Oct. 28.

be four thousand. [2] Dean Carl Wittke, on the other hand, while agreeing that there is no authentic foundation to the over-enthusiastic statistics discussed by certain writers, concludes that it is impossible to posit a reliable figure because the sources are lacking in information concerning the humbler folk who did not make a mark for themselves in American life. [3]

A number of reasons may be presented to explain the comparatively small group of political refugees who came to America. Many of the supporters of the Revolutions were not compelled to flee their native countries; unwilling to give up hope, they determined to remain and, perhaps, outlive the reactionary regimes. Others, including some who served out prison sentences or who fled to exile in nearby European havens, could not be diverted from their objectives by one failure; they were determined to stay at home, or at least in Europe, to continue to work for the triumph of liberal principles. Yet another reason which deterred many from making the trip to America was a fairly common conception of America as an uncultured outpost of civilization. And, finally, there were the natural inertia and reluctance to pull up stakes which characterize most people.

It cannot be denied, of course, that the failure of the Revolutions was responsible for increased emigration to America in the years after 1848. Hundreds of thousands of persons who had taken no active role in the fighting were completely disillusioned with life in Europe after the return of the reactionaries to power; a factor which contributed to that disillusionment was the post-1848 economic slump which served as a damning indication of the weakness of autocracy. But these individuals, Jews and Christians alike, who decided to emigrate for personal economic, social and political reasons, ought not be regarded as "Forty-Eighters" in the strict interpretation of the term.

In our study of Jewish "Forty-Eighters," therefore, it is necessary that we learn to distinguish between those who left Europe because they were determined to seek the personal opportunity, economic freedom and political equality which were denied to them in Europe, and those who felt compelled to leave because of their own personal participation in the Revolutions.

Outbreaks of anti-Semitism during and after the Revolutions were a signal for a summons to mass emigration of Jews to America. Isidor Busch and Leopold Kompert, writing in the *Oesterreichisches Central-Organ für Glaubensfreiheit,* urged Bohemian and Austrian Jews to pack up their belongings, gather their families together, and set out for America, in order to escape the violence of European hatred of the Jews. [4] Lewis A. Levy of Houston, Texas, wrote an enthusiastic letter which was published in the *Asmonean,* calling upon the Jews of Central and Eastern Europe to leave their homes and to come to America, particularly to Texas, where "thousands of acres of land can be bought, within the settled portions of the State, for the small sum of from 25 cents to $1 per acre; good arable, fertile land, where a man can make his living to his liking, and more independent than the Autocrat of Russia, or the Emperor of Austria themselves." [5]

But those who responded to these appeals were not necessarily "Forty-Eighters." Indeed, the failure of the Revolutions, and the anti-Jewish outbreaks which occurred during 1848, were almost routine experiences for the Jews of Central Europe. They suffered repression, discrimination, and hostility all through the years, and needed no special political motivation for emigration. The year of their departure was, more often than not, purely coincidental. One of those who came to America in 1848, for instance, was Mayer Lehman, the founder of the great cotton and banking firm and father of Justice Irving and Senator Herbert Lehman. But it might just as well have been any other year, for his decision was based not on the status of the Revolution, but on the fact that his brothers Henry and Emanuel, who had preceded him to the United States, had now successfully established themselves and were therefore able to pay for his ocean passage. [6] Lazarus Straus, founder of a prominent American-Jewish family famous for government service and the development of that great institution known as Macy's, also left Bavaria for economic reasons. He despaired of any future in his home, and so set out in 1852 for the land of opportunity across the sea. [7] The Brandeis-Wehle clan, whose story has been told so well, were by no means "Pilgrims of '48" in the sense of being political refugees. Economic opportunity in the new world was undoubtedly the most important reason for their decision to leave Prague. [8] And so also with the Prussian family named Sutro who brought with them a twenty-year old son named Adolph who was to build a tunnel called after his name and become Mayor of San Francisco and own a sizeable portion of that city's real estate. The Sutro family had been in the cloth-manufacturing business, but the severe depression after the Revolution drove them into bankruptcy and forced their departure. [9]

These folk and their motivations were typical of the more than fifty thousand Jews who left Central Europe between 1848 and 1860 to come to the United States. Had the Revolutions achieved political and economic opportunity for the Jews, they might not have emigrated. The events of 1848–9 for the most part, however, merely reinforced a prior decision to seek new horizons.

But what of the Jewish Revolutionaries themselves, those who through political or military participation in the liberal revolts declared themselves active enemies of long-established governments? It has commonly been thought that large numbers of Jewish "Forty-Eighters" came to the United States. But research into the background of literally thousands of German-Jewish immigrants does not support this conclusion. Only forty have come to light during an exhaustive search of the available sources.

4

That there were so few is indicated, negatively, by the silence of the American-Jewish periodical press of the times. These periodicals commented on every significant development in European and American Jewish life. Had any large numbers of political refugees arrived in the United States, they would have been the first to publicize the fact among their readers. Indeed, the only extended Jewish commentary on the "Forty-Eight" refugees which we have been able to discover, fails to indicate that there were more than a handful of Jews among them.

In 1850, a Committee in Aid of the German Political Refugees, composed of three non-Jews and two Jews, E. Eichhorn and Dr. M. Mayer, adopted the procedure of holding mass meetings in churches of various denominations for the purpose of raising funds. The first such meeting was held on July 21, 1850, at the Anshi Chesed Synagogue of New York City. Dr. Max Lilienthal delivered the major appeal, entitled, "Love the Stranger." Nowhere in that address did Lilienthal, speaking to a Jewish audience, imply that many of the refugees were co-religionists His final, clinching plea, is that the Jews of German extraction, his audience, might help to counteract anti-Jewish prejudice by giving generously to this fund for non-Jews, and that they would thereby demonstrate as much devotion to the cause of liberalism as did their fellow-Jews who fought behind the barricades in the Fatherland. The fact that Lilienthal did not appeal to his listeners to assist their own brethren ought to be conclusive evidence that the number of Jewish refugees was so small as to be deemed unworthy of notice. [10]

Now to the authentic Jewish "Forty-Eighters." Most of them were, of course, not prominent Revolutionaries, but obscure young men who had followed the leadership of older men. They were as young and inexperienced with life and unheralded by fame as most other immigrants. It was in America that they lived the major portion of their lives and earned whatever success

5

they came to achieve. There were two exceptions, however, two men whose names were familiar to those who had followed the course of the Revolutions: Abraham Jacobi and Joseph Goldmark. Goldmark had been a member of the student cabal which directed the course of the rebellion in Vienna. With the fall of the city in October of 1848 he had to flee to Switzerland to avoid trial and execution for treason.[11] Jacobi had been an intimate of Carl Schurz and the other leaders in Baden. He was arrested in 1849 and suffered imprisonment for two years before a friendly warden permitted his escape to America.[12]

Jacobi and Goldmark found a warm welcome awaiting them among the intellectual elite of the German-American community. They were regarded as heroes who had sacrificed all for the sake of liberty. Even the Jewish press greeted Goldmark. The *Asmonean* called its readers' attention to his arrival in a lead editorial which concluded with the hope "that his condition in this country may compensate him for what he has lost in the battles and struggles of the fatherland."[13] Jacobi, on the other hand, was ignored by the Jewish editors until 1862, when Leeser of the *Occident* wrote to him inquiring if he knew any of his relatives who had been implicated in the Revolution![14] Most of the others found no welcome whatever, and had to join the hosts of other immigrants in adjusting to the life of their new home. Coming to the United States with family groups or friends, they scattered abroad throughout the country. Only a few stayed in New York. The others found their way to Philadelphia, Richmond, St. Louis, Watertown (Wisc.), Indianapolis, and Hartford. Five, August Helbing, Moritz Meyer, William Langerman, and two men named Wasserman and Mosheimer about whom we know nothing but their last names, arrived just in time to join the gold-attracted throngs who were making the arduous trip to California.[15] Bertha Levy, the grandmother of

Mrs. Arthur Hays Sulzberger, a student at Heidelberg who was exiled because of her Revolutionary participation, was sent by her family to Natchez, Miss., to live with her uncle.[16] Some, like Julius Stein of Baden and I. Brill of Berlin, known to have come to America, simply lost contact with their European family and friends, and disappeared from sight.[17]

Settled in new homes, they turned to the challenge of earning a living and carving a place for themselves in American society. The physicians and journalists, naturally, had less difficulty than their non-professional counterparts. American medicine was in sore need of trained recruits from Europe and the growing German-American population created many opportunities for publicists.

Abraham Jacobi's subsequent medical career in America completely overshadowed his revolutionary activities in Europe. Regarded by medical historians as "the father of pediatrics in America," his contribution to American medicine was inestimable. The respect and affection in which he was held by his colleagues was demonstrated by the number of honors which they showered upon him. He was elected to the presidency of many medical societies, including the American Medical Association, and received honorary degrees from Michigan, Harvard, Yale, and Columbia Universities. During his lifetime he occupied chairs in pediatrics at the College of Surgeons and Physicians of N. Y., New York Medical College, Columbia University, and the City College of New York.[18]

Another medical "Forty-Eighter" to achieve prominence in America was Ernst Krackowitzer, who had been a lesser known member of the Viennese student council which directed various phases of the Revolution. In New York he became an outstanding surgeon, president of the Pathological Society, a contributor to the pioneer American medical journals and a leading staff

7

member of many New York hospitals. Jacobi, who idolized Krackowitzer and named his son after him, called him "the most eminent American physician of European birth." [19]

Joseph Lewi had been an intimate co-worker of the Austrian intellectuals who had inspired the Revolution, but emigrated even before the fall of Vienna because he was convinced that the revolt could not succeed. He settled in Albany and became one of the most popular physicians of that city, serving terms as President of the Albany County Medical Society and senior member of the Board of Censors of the New York State Medical Society. During the Civil War he was attached to the Albany board of medical examiners. [20]

Yet another medical "Forty-Eighter" was Moritz Eisler of Freustadtl who was both editor of a radical Hungarian newspaper and surgeon of a Honved regiment. From Hungary he fled to Leipzig where he busied himself with journalistic activities, including the collection of a volume of revolutionary songs. In 1851 he left Germany for Paris, and two years later came to New York, where he established himself as a physician. [21]

Both a physician and a journalist was Edward Morwitz, who had been a revolutionary propagandist in Konitz. He settled in Philadelphia and practiced both professions, establishing the German Dispensary in that city and serving as publisher-editor of the German-language *Demokrat*. After the Civil War he was instrumental in the creation of the German Press Association of Pennsylvania, and eventually owned a controlling interest in a large number of German-American newspapers and magazines. [22]

Charles Bernays became associate editor of a St. Louis German paper; [23] David Blumenfeld was a partner in the firm which published the first Watertown German paper, *Der Anzeiger*, which Carl Schurz edited in 1857; [24] Michael Heilprin ultimately became one of the editors of Appleton's *New American Cyclopedia* and a foreign affairs writer for the old *Nation;* [25] Max Connheim, who had penned the *Republikanischer Katechismus* in Berlin, became editor of the *New York Humorist* and is reputed to have been the first successful German-American playwright. [26]

Isidor Busch, who had published and edited several of the Revolutionary newspapers in Vienna, founded a German-Jewish weekly in New York a short time after his arrival in 1849, but had to abandon the venture after a very few issues. He moved on to St. Louis and decided to go into business. He was, at various times, a banker, storekeeper and politician, as well as the first Missouri viniculturist. [27]

Another professional was Isaac Hartman, who had edited the republican *Observer of Eastern Franconia* after a few years as head of a Jewish school in Kissingen, Bavaria. Imprisoned in Würzburg after the fall of the revolutionary party, he was fortunate enough to have friends who arranged for his escape — first to England, then on to America. Arrived in New York, he supported himself by teaching languages at various private schools, until advanced tuberculosis sent him into the newly-created Jews' Hospital of New York, where he died on August 13, 1855. [28]

Sigismund Kaufmann, trained for a business career in Frankfurt, had to leave his home because of his implication in Turner affairs, and arrived penniless in New York, where he first earned a living by working in a pocketbook factory and by giving lessons in French and German. He studied law in New York and established a notable practice, serving a German-American clientele in the main. [29]

The non-professional "Forty-Eighters" entered a variety of trades. Meyer Thalmessinger, who had taken part in the Parisian Revolution, eventually headed a prosperous printing and lithographing firm and was elected president of a New York bank. [30] Joseph Goldmark gave up the practice of medicine and established a percussion-cap factory in New York.[31] Tobias Kohn brought with him the latest European techniques in silk-manufacturing and opened a plant in Hartford.[32] Helbing and Langerman opened stores in San Francisco. Julius Blach, a young Bavarian teacher, traveled through the South seeking business opportunities until he finally became a partner in a commercial venture in Concord, N. Car. Ill health sent him North, however, and eventually he became a storekeeper in Vevay, Ind.[33] Julius Bien became one of the outstanding lithographers in America. For many years, it is said, "scarcely a major geographical or geological publication [was] issued by the federal government for which the maps were not engraved and printed by Bien." He received many medals for his work and served as president of the National Lithographers' Association for thirteen years.[34]

Nathan Grossmayer, an Austrian who had been wounded in the street fighting in Paris, was one of the unluckiest of the "Forty-Eighters." On first coming to the United States he peddled his way through the South until he had enough money to open a store in Macon, Ga. Before his death in 1891, he had been in business in New York City, Hoboken, Baltimore, Washington, Houston and Galveston, Indianola (Tex.), Titusville (Pa.), and Denver. His successes were many — at one time he possessed a chain of five stores in various Texas localities, and at another time he owned a sizeable interest in some Pennsylvania oil fields — but some misfortune or other always defeated his enterprise and forced him to move on.[35]

August Bondi was too smitten with a love of adventure to settle down for a long time after he came to the United States in 1848. He had been one of the youngest members of the students' corps in Vienna — fourteen years old! His family settled in St. Louis and he shifted from one unsatisfactory job to another, meanwhile looking for excitement. During a trip to Texas he attempted to enlist in the Lopez-Crittenden expedition to Cuba, and failing in that tried to obtain a berth in the Perry mission to Japan. Back in St. Louis, he finally decided to go to the Kansas frontier where there was adventure enough for a young boy. It was not long before he joined up with John Brown's men, taking part in every major engagement of the bloody border warfare. As Bondi was to write in his autobiography, "To use President Roosevelt's mode of expression, I was most anxious for a strenuous life. I was tired of the hum-drum life of a clerk. Any struggle, any hard work would be welcome to me. I thirsted for it, for adventure . . ."[36] Small wonder that setting type, waiting on store, keeping books, or teaching in a backwoods school, all of which he tried during his first years, couldn't hold him down for very long.

It was not only the thirst for adventure, however, that stirred this young man, for August Bondi was indeed an inflamed liberal. He wrote of his Viennese days: "I became imbued with hatred of spiritual and governmental tyranny . . . [and with] devotion to humanity. We boys were fairly fanaticized with sympathy for the downtrodden of the globe."[37] He fought with John Brown because he was convinced that the spread of slavery was a danger to the welfare of the western frontier, and, when the Civil War broke out, his liberal spirit again sent him into the military fray. He served for three years through many a difficult campaign.

Most of the Jewish "Forty-Eighters," like Bondi, maintained their devotion to liberal principles in America. Some became outspoken adherents of abolitionism almost as soon as they reached America. Michael Heilprin, who had been one of the propagandists for the Kossuth Hungarian Revolution, was almost mobbed at a Frémont meeting in Philadelphia when he delivered a fiery speech against the defenders of slavery. In 1861, he was the first to denounce Rabbi Morris J. Raphall for his attempt to prove that slavery had the sanction of the Jewish Bible. [38] Isidor Busch, in St. Louis, was elected to the Missouri legislature for three terms during the Civil War, and, throughout the sessions, was one of the most extreme abolitionists in office. [39]

Even if abolitionism did not draw them to its banners, most of the Jewish "Forty-Eighters" became ardent supporters of the Republican party. Joseph Goldmark was one of the organizers of the King's County Republican Club [40] and Joseph Lewi was a founder of the Albany Union League. Sigismund Kaufmann was a Republican Presidential Elector in 1860 and wielded, it is said, much influence in the distribution of federal patronage throughout New York state. In 1869 he was a candidate on the Republican ticket for a seat in the State Senate, and in 1870 he was chosen as his party's candidate for the office of Lieutenant-Governor. [41] Meyer Thalmessinger was a devoted Republican who, in 1861, published Einhorn's scathing abolitionist retort to Rabbi Raphall's pro-Southern "Bible View of Slavery." [42] August Bondi's diary records the large number of early Republican meetings which he and his non-Jewish German friends attended in St. Louis. Nathan Grossmayer was a passionate devotee of Lincoln during the Civil War years, believing in him so deeply that, according to an early will, he bequeathed his all to the President for charitable purposes in the event that the war should still be raging when Grossmayer died.

What Jacobi wrote of his friend Krackowitzer probably characterized the majority of the Jewish "Forty-Eighters:"

He did not *drift* into politics; he was a born politician, for he lived, soul and heart, with the people, its development, growth, efforts, its happiness and unhappiness . . . . No oppression or injustice found grace before his eys. Thus he was a freesoiler, thus he was an abolitionist; no matter whether the chains to be broken were those of color, or religion, or sex . . . . He supported Frémont, supported Lincoln, supported energetically the war for the Union . . . . [43]

12

The Civil War aroused not only the political passions of the "Forty-Eighters," but also their military bent. A war-time correspondent of the *Jewish Messenger* stated in one of his Washington dispatches that

Some of the Jewish officers and privates told me that they had taken part in the Crimean, Hungarian and Italian wars, and that they followed the profession of arms from inclination, but not liking the dull routine of a soldier's life in times of peace, they eagerly availed themselves of every opportunity to return to their tents and the battlefield. This was the first time I had ever heard of the existence of such a class of military adventurers among our people. [44]

Would that the *Messenger's* correspondent had taken the trouble to write down their names and stories, for we know only two of these "Forty-Eighters" who became soldiers of fortune.

One was Louis Schlessinger, a veteran of the Kossuth campaigns, who stayed in the United States only a short time before joining the Walker filibuster in Nicaragua. He was given the rank of colonel by his chief but must have had a severe dispute with him because after a few battles he was fighting for the legitimists, retaining his high rank, of course. After the conflict ended, Schlessinger moved to Guatemala and lived out his life as the owner of a coffee plantation. [45]

The other was Adolphus Adler who was commissioned a colonel in the Confederate Army at the outbreak of the Civil War. Adler was a brusque, high-spirited adventurer with a nasty temper. When an anti-Jewish editorial appeared in the Richmond *Enquirer* he challenged its editor to a duel. The editor preferred to apologize rather than risk death. A little later, Adler's temper got him into a worse scrape. He became embroiled in a violent argument with a general in command of the Richmond fortifications and was thrown into prison on suspicion of being a Union sympathizer. This was more humiliation than an officer could bear, so he attempted to commit sui-

13

cide, but only ended up in a Richmond hospital. Ashamed to stand trial, he escaped from the hospital and smuggled himself across the lines to the North. We next find him in Cincinnati, again under arrest, this time on the natural assumption that he was a Confederate spy. He convinced the authorities that he had given up the Confederate cause and then faded from sight. The *Israelite* advertised in vain that it had some letters for delivery to him; he was not heard from again. One cannot but regret that there is no record of his further experiences in America. [46]

The highest ranking Jewish officer of the Civil War was also a "Forty-Eighter." Frederick Knefler had served with Kossuth in Hungary at the age of fifteen before moving to Indianapolis with his family. He volunteered for service with the Union Army a few days after Sumter and was commissioned a lieutenant. His superiors recognized his ability and promoted him so rapidly that he was a Colonel by the time of the great Chickamauga campaign in 1863. During that great battle he led two Indiana regiments up the slopes of Missionary Ridge, one of the most famous feats in all military history. His role in that battle earned him the further promotion to the rank of Brigadier General. [47]

Not all of the Jewish "Forty-Eighters" were passionate Republicans, of course. Abraham Jacobi, strangely enough, appears to have taken little interest in the Civil War, although his friendship with Schurz and other German-American leaders continued unabated. In practically every other important question, immigration restriction, Civil Service reform, slum clearance, to name only a few, Jacobi was always to be found on the side of the liberals and reformers. [48] Edward Morwitz had become a Democrat immediately upon his arrival in Philadelphia and maintained his loyalty to that party all through the years of slavery agitation and war. "Weil von Gernsbach," also called "Weil von Bühl," who fought actively in Baden, served in the Democratic Party ranks during the elections of 1856 and 1860, and attempted to gain the German-Jewish support for Buchanan and Douglas. [49] Liberalism did not have the same meaning for all "Forty-Eighters."

It is natural to think of "Forty-Eighters" as leaders in the life of the German-American community. The Jews among them were no exception. They belonged to the German societies and participated actively in their programs and activities. Busch was for twelve years president of the German Immigration Aid Society of St. Louis. Kaufmann was a founder of the N. Y. Turnverein, the first National President of the Turner Bund, and president of the German Society of New York. [50] Krackowitzer was largely responsible for the founding of a German Dispensary in New York, as was Morwitz in Philadelphia. Jacobi was, year after year, a favorite speaker at German meetings and gatherings in New York. The journalists, of course, were even more closely involved in the life of the German community, because their professional work coincided with its activities. Michael Heilprin and Julian Allen were the only Jewish "Forty-Eighters" who were actively involved in Polish-American affairs. Allen wrote an expose of Russian brutalities in Poland, and served as a Commissioner of the Society of the Joint Polish American Committee. During the Civil War, he attempted to recruit a Polish regiment for service in the Union Army. Heilprin organized a Pro-Poland Committee in Washington, D. C., in 1864, and translated appeals by the Polish National Government into Hebrew. [51]

These Jewish "Forty-Eighters" were, like their non-Jewish counterparts, deeply devoted to the culture and civilization which they left behind in Europe. Many of them never lost their ardent German nationalistic spirit, and the fact that certain aspects of American life appeared to be inferior to their European background helped keep them loyal to Germany. Two of them, in fact, returned to Europe soon after coming to America.

15

Rabbi Wolf Schlessinger, co-author of a well-known translation of Joseph Albo's *Sefer ha-Ikkarim*, had been arrested for preaching the Revolutionary doctrine while serving as Rabbi in Sulzbach, Bavaria, but managed to escape to America. He was accorded a hearty welcome by American Jewry, and the *Occident* published a number of his articles. He returned to Sulzbach, however, as soon as conditions permitted. Fülöp Korn, a Pressburg book-seller, came to America by way of Turkey and England, and attempted here to arouse support for the Kossuth cause. He returned to Hungary in 1863, and was eventually converted to Christianity there. These were the only Jewish "Forty-Eighters," however, who were not immediately won over to a loyalty to America which outweighed their nostalgia for the Fatherland. [52] When Goldmark went back to Vienna in 1868–69 to clear his name and reputation, his Austrian friends begged him to remain. But he was firm in his decision to build his future in the United States. Abraham Jacobi, in his later years, was invited to occupy the chair in pediatrics in Berlin, a supreme tribute to his professional achievement, but he would not consider leaving America.

For some of the Jewish "Forty-Eighters" this ambivalent loyalty to German culture on the one hand and American life on the other did not leave much room for Judaism. Partly because they shared the antagonism of the German intellectual towards all religion, partly because they were convinced that all barriers between men should be broken down, some of them abandoned their Jewish background. Jacobi and Knefler lost almost all contact with Jews as Jews, and completed the process by inter-marriage. Like his friend Krackowitzer, Jacobi's only known affiliation with a Jewish institution was his service as an Attending Physician at the New York Jews' Hospital and his continuing relationship to its staff after it became known as Mt. Sinai Hospital, although he was a subscriber to Isaac Leeser's *Occident* for at least a year during the Civil War. [53] Even though his sister was married to one of the rabbinical leaders of American Jewry — Bernhard Felsenthal of Chicago — David Blumenfeld took so little interest in Judaism that he permitted his children to attend services and classes in both Catholic and Protestant churches in Watertown. [54] Charles Bernays, the St. Louis journalist, is the only Jewish "Forty-Eighter" actually known to have been converted to Christianity after coming to America. But, interestingly enough, he became the central figure in a Jewish *cause célèbre* despite his conversion. In 1862 he was appointed American consul at Zurich. The Swiss still maintained discriminatory legislation against Jews, and refused for a time to accept Bernays' credentials. [55] Others, like the Goldmark family, drifted into a kind of vague cosmopolitanism which was frequently a secular "religion" among Jews who had no interest in religion. Thus, Joseph Goldmark's daughters married two Jewish youths who typified the liberalism of 1848, neither of whom was a Jew religiously: Felix Adler, the founder of the Ethical Culture movement, and Louis D. Brandeis, who was empty of any Jewish interest until the Zionist movement fired his spirit just before the first World War. Jacobi expressed his liberal philosophy when, during the heat of the Franco-Prussian War, he spoke on behalf of German physicians in this wise:

These men speak the language of the human mind, they are the leading citizens of the universal world-republic of science to which we all, equal, free, and fraternal, have sworn allegiance. There is no blockade, no fire, no Franco-German War, that will ever disprove our belonging to the same community. The progress of one man, of one country, is at the present day the common property of all men, all countries, and an isolated civilization or science belongs to the past. Let us hope, and every one at his own wheel-work, that the unity of science may be but the precursor of the unity of mankind . . . . [56]

This indifference to Judaism was not typical, by far, of all of the "Forty-Eighters." John Proskauer joined a synagogue as soon as he settled in Richmond — and an orthodox congregation which observed the Spanish-Portuguese rite, at that! Known to have little personal interest in religion, his friends asked for an explanation. He really couldn't say what it was, but in a somewhat mystic manner he spoke of the preservation of ancient values and the maintenance of traditions, whether in accordance with the views of one man or not.[57] Years later his son became President of the congregation in Mobile, Alabama, and a grandson was President of the American Jewish Committee. Isidor Busch was as violent a liberal as any other "Forty-Eighter," and yet Judaism had been supremely important to him in Europe and continued to be so in America. His editorship of the short-lived *Israels Herold* in New York was only the beginning of years of devoted service to Jewish causes. One of his dominant interests was the B'nai B'rith Order, of which he was an active member on both a local and a national scale. An even more important figure in B'nai B'rith sprang from the ranks of the "Forty-Eighters," Julius Bien, during whose thirty-five years as President the brotherhood developed from a handful of lodges to one of the most powerful organizations in American Jewish life. Another active member of the B'nai B'rith was Meyer Thalmessinger, who was also a founder of the Maimonides Library. He published a number of volumes of Jewish significance, including Maurice Mayer's translation of Geiger's *Judaism and Its History.*[58] Sigismund Kaufmann, one of the radical leaders of the Turner Bund tending towards Socialist beliefs, was nevertheless active as a Trustee of Beth Elohim Congregation of Williamsburg. August Helbing was a founder and the first President of the Eureka Benevolent Society of San Francisco, the first Jewish charitable association to be organized in California.[59]

Dr. Joseph Lewi was an active member of the Albany congregation led by his friend, Isaac M. Wise, whom he had known in Radnitz, Bohemia, and, years later, sent his son Isidor to Cincinnati as an apprentice to Wise in the editorship of the *Israelite*. Michael Heilprin was one of the founders of the movement which organized agricultural settlements in America for refugees from the Russian pogroms of the 1880's, although throughout the previous years he had demonstrated only a faint intellectual interest in Judaism. August Bondi, out on the Kansas frontier, longed for the opportunity to attend Jewish services, and was greatly angered, according to his diary, when he discovered that the only two Jews in his Civil War regiment were not willing to acknowledge their background. In his will, he asked his children to perpetuate his name through a memorial at the Hebrew Union College.[60] Edward Morwitz appears to have devoted far more time to general German activities than those of a Jewish nature, but in addition to his participation in Philadelphia Jewry's philanthropies, there is the record of his publication (at a heavy loss) of the *Jewish Record* for a period of eleven years, as evidence of his Jewish sympathies.[61]

Among Jews, at least, the conception of "Forty-Eighters" as atheists and anti-religionists, therefore, requires some revision, especially in the light of the fact that there were seven rabbis among our group of forty: Isidor Kalisch,[62] Henry Hochheimer,[63] Benjamin Szold,[64] Adolph Huebsch,[65] Maurice Mayer,[66] Bernard Illowy[67] and Wolf Schlessinger. Kalisch and Hochheimer had already entered the rabbinate before 1848, but left their pulpits to participate in the Revolutions, Kalisch as a journalist and Hochheimer as a soldier; Mayer, a young lawyer, who had served in the Ministry of Justice before the Revolution in Bavaria failed, entered the rabbinate after his arrival in the United States; Illowy and Schlessinger became embroiled in the Revolutionary fervor and were subsequently driven from their pulpits through the intervention of reactionary officials; Szold and Huebsch were students who, like thousands of others, dropped their books to join the hosts of Kossuth. All seven became leaders among their colleagues in America, with the exception of Schlessinger who soon returned to Europe. Kalisch was a partner with Isaac Mayer Wise in the summoning of the first American rabbinical conference at Cleveland, in 1855, and a co-author of the first American Reform prayerbook, the *Minhag America*. Three of the others, by coincidence, also participated in the issuance of versions of the prayerbook. Szold and Hoch-heimer were collaborators in the editing of the only nineteenth century revision of the ritual which is still in use today, *Abodath Yisrael*, and Huebsch edited and published a special prayerbook for his New York congregation (1872). Illowy was probably the outstanding Hebraist and rabbinic authority of the period, out-stripping his colleagues by far in depth of learning. Mayer was one of the national leaders of the Independent Order of B'nai B'rith at the time of his early death in 1862, although he had by then returned to the practice of law after occupying pulpits in Charleston and Albany. It is perhaps most important to note that none of these rabbis was an extreme radical theologically. All of them were moderate Reformers or Conservatives in America. Even in Europe their political views were more radical than their religious concepts, and no one of them appears to have taken an active political role in the United States. They were not political radicals because their personalities made them such, but because conditions in Europe had demanded it. America satisfied them; there was no need to be radical here.

*   *   *

These, then, were the forty Jewish "Forty-Eighters" whom we have been able to identify. [68] Undoubtedly, many more came to America, but have been lost in obscurity, those who achieved no fame or notoriety and whose names are not recorded in available source materials. But, the very fact that so small a number has survived in the documents and periodicals upon which we have based our study is an indication that the Jewish "Forty-Eighters" had no concerted, significant influence upon the life of the American-Jewish community or the German-American community. Never a homogeneous group — most of them not even acquainted with one another — scattered throughout the far reaches of the country — what influence could they have as a group?

Their personal, individual achievements and influence, on the other hand, were extremely important, for they were an exceptional group of men. They brought techniques and education, talents and ambitions, which served America in good stead. Some, like Jacobi and Bien, made contributions to America which will remain for generations to come. Others, like the rabbis and journalists, spent their talents in the service of their immediate generation. Still others contributed the talents and achievements of their children and grandchildren: Rabbi Szold's daughter, Henrietta, founded the women's Zionist organization, Hadassah; Blumenfeld's son, Ralph, became the editor of the London *Express;* Rabbi Huebsch's son, Benjamin, heads the publishing firm, Viking Press; Goldmark's daughters were the helpmeets of two of America's leading spirits, Brandeis and Felix Adler. Perhaps the exceedingly high level of their personal and familial achievement can be explained only in psychological terms: in Europe they had the vigor and fearlessness to join the fight against autocracy; in America their strength and creativity, their broad humanity and their faith in progress, found expression in terms other than revolt and battle. The Revolutions of 1848 had, as it were, chosen them from the masses as men of promise. That promise was fulfilled in America.

It is undoubtedly true that there was a larger proportion of intellectuals and men in the professions among the "Forty-Eighters" than among their compatriots who came to America in other years. Nevertheless, the "Forty-Eighters" were not different in the quality of their living and in the nature of their aspirations from the thousands of other German Jews who flocked to America during that age. The talents, imagination, and vigor which the "Forty-Eighters" brought to the United States were matched by the talents, imagination, and vigor of other German Jews who came in that period, and whose names have become part of the legend of America: August Belmont, banker and art connoisseur; Simon Bamberger, mine owner, railroad builder, first non-Mormon governor of Utah; Morris Flexner, Louisville merchant and father of Abraham and Simon; Adam Gimbel, peddler, merchant, and founder of a department store dynasty; Meyer Guggenheim, merchant and mining magnate; Albert Michelson, physicist and Nobel Prize Winner; Adolph Lewisohn, copper mine magnate and philanthropist; the elder Henry Morgenthau, lawyer, financier and diplomat; Samuel Rosenwald, merchant and father of that Julius who established a great humanitarian foundation; the Seligman brothers, seven strong, who established a great name in commerce, banking, civic leadership and philanthropy . . . .

The American Jewish population grew from about 15,000 in 1825 to about a quarter of a million in 1875. All of those immigrants, like the "Forty-Eighters," came to America in search of personal opportunity, political justice, and economic freedom — here they struck their roots, found the country and its life to be good — and they, in turn, enriched America and enhanced its life with the fruit of labors which Europe had been too bigoted to accept.

NOTES

[1] Marcus L. Hansen, *The Atlantic Migration: 1607–1860*, Cambridge, 1940, p. 274.

[2] A. E. Zucker, "Biographical Dictionary of the Forty-Eighters," *The Forty-Eighters, Political Refugees of the German Revolution of 1848*, New York, 1950, p. 269.

[3] Carl Wittke, *Refugees of Revolution, The German Forty-Eighters in America*, Philadelphia, 1952, p. 3.

[4] Guido Kisch, "The Revolution of 1848 and the Jewish 'On to America' Movement," *PAJHS*, No. XXXVIII, Pt. 3 (March, 1949), pp. 185–234.

[5] *ASM*, II, No. 10, p. 76, June 23, 1850. Mr. Andrew Forest Muir of Houston has graciously supplied this identification for the "L. A. L." signature appended to the published letter. Levy, who first appears in the Deed Records of Harris County, Texas, in 1842, had purchased a fifteen acre lot on December 20, 1847. (Mss. Deed Records in County Clerk's Office, Houston.)

[6] Letter from Mr. Herbert Lehman to the writer, August 22, 1948.

[7] Manuscript Memoirs of Isidor Straus, Library of the American Jewish Historical Society.

[8] Josephine Goldmark, *Pilgrims of '48*, New Haven, 1930, pp. 175–6.

[9] *DAB*, XVIII, pp. 223–4.

[10] *ASM*, II, No. 13, p. 100, July 19, 1850; No. 16, p. 122, Aug. 9, 1850. Lilienthal actually refers only to one Jew who came to him; Isaac M. Wise, in his *Reminiscences*, Cincinnati, 1901, pp. 104–6, describes a number of genuine and pseudo-"Forty-Eighters," without giving their names, who sought his assistance.

[11] Goldmark, *op. cit.*, pp. 168–70.

[12] *Medical Life*, XXXV, Nos. 6–7 (May, June 1928), pp. 214–15, 225.

[13] *ASM*, II, No. 20, p. 156, Sept. 6, 1850.

[14] Letter, Jacobi to Leeser, April 6, 1862, Leeser Collection, Dropsie College Library. But, news of Jacobi's arrest and trial was printed in *ASM*, I, No. 10, p. 75, Dec. 28, 1849.

[15] For Helbing and Meyer, Israel T. Naamani, "Gold Rush Days," *Commentary*, Sept. 1948, pp. 260–1; for Langerman, *UJE*, VI, p. 532; for Wasserman, *New Yorker Staatszeitung*, Oct. 17, 1855, and *New Yorker Criminal Zeitung*, Aug. 6, 1858; for Mosheimer, letter from Dr. Dora Edinger to the writer, July 7, 1949.

[16] Adolf Kober, "Jewish Emigration from Württemberg to the United States of America (1848–1855)," *PAJHS*, XLI, No. 3 (March, 1952), p. 232.

[17] *Ibid.*, p. 233.

[18] *Medical Life*, *op. cit.*, pp. 214–258.

[19] Abraham Jacobi, "The Most Eminent Physician of European Birth," *American Medicine*, IX, No. 18, pp. 740–743, May 6, 1905.

[20] Undated obituary clippings loaned to the writer by Miss Alice Lewi, Albany. Lewi died Dec. 19, 1897.

[21] Letter, Dr. Paul J. Diamant to the writer, Dec. 1, 1949.

[22] *DAB*, XIII, pp. 271–2; Henry S. Morais, *The Jews of Philadelphia*, Philadelphia, 1894, pp. 340–2.

[23] *The Reminiscences of Carl Schurz*, New York, 1908, II, p. 40.

[24] Ralph D. Blumenfeld, *Home Town*, London, 1944, p. 14.

[25] Gustav Pollak, *Michael Heilprin and His Sons*, N. Y., 1912.

[26] Letter from Dr. Dora Edinger to the writer, July 7, 1949; Kober, *op. cit.*, p. 233.

[27] *The Reformer and Jewish Times*, X, No. 51, p. 3, Feb. 14, 1879.

[28] *ASM*, XII, No. 10, p. 148, Aug. 24, 1855.

[29] Morris U. Schappes, *A Documentary History of the Jews in the United States, 1654–1875*, New York, 1950, p. 725.

[30] *UJE*, X, p. 259.

[31] Goldmark, *op. cit.*, p. 259.

[32] *UJE*, VI, pp. 434–5.

[33] Blach Mss. Reminiscences, American Jewish Archives.

[34] *UJE*, II, pp. 350–1.

[35] Information and documents provided by his son, Max Grossmayer. Deposited in American Jewish Archives.

[36] *Autobiography of August Bondi*, Galesburg (Ill.), 1910, p. 33.

[37] *Ibid.*, p. 27.

[38] Pollak, *op. cit.*, pp. 169–70; E. M. F. Mielziner, *Moses Mielziner 1828–1903*, New York, 1931, pp. 224–234, for complete text of Heilprin's answer.

[39] James A. Wax, "Isidor Bush, American Patriot and Abolitionist," *Historia Judaica*, V, No. 2, pp. 183–203, Oct. 1943.

[40] Goldmark, *op. cit.*, p. 283.

[41] Isaac Markens, "Lincoln and the Jews," *PAJHS*, No. XVII (1909), pp. 137–8; Schappes, *op. cit.*, pp. 724–5.

[42] *Ibid.*, p. 685; Korn, *AJCW*, pp. 16–21.

[43] Jacobi, *op. cit.*, p. 743.

[44] *MESS*, XI, No. 5, p. 41, Feb. 7, 1862.

[45] *UJE*, IX, p. 410.

[46] Ella Lonn, *Foreigners in the Confederacy*, Chapel Hill, 1940, pp. 177–8; Frank Moore (ed.) *Rebellion Record*, N. Y., 1862, III, p. 51; *ISR*, IX, No. 24, p. 188, Dec. 19, 1862; X, No. 8, p. 59, Aug. 21, 1863.

[47] Information provided by Rabbi Morris Feuerlicht, Indianapolis; G. M. Cohen, "Indiana's Great Jewish Civil War General," *Jewish Post*, New Year's Edition, (Oct.) 1941, pp. 4–5, 60–61.

[48] *Medical Life, op. cit.*, p. 246; Oswald Garrison Villard, "Abraham Jacobi — The Last of the Forty-Eighters," *The Nation*, July 19, 1919, pp. 74–5.

[49] Letter from Dr. Dora Edinger to the writer, July 29, 1949; *New Yorker Staatszeitung*, Sept. 23, 1856.

[50] *Historical Journal, A Souvenir of the Centennial Celebration of the New York Turn Verein*, New York, 1950, pp. 12–3.

[51] Abraham G. Duker, "Polish Political Emigrés in the United States and the Jews, 1833–1865," *PAJHS*, No. XXXIX, Part 2 (Dec., 1949), pp. 152–3, 158. *Wächter am Erie*, April 13, 1870, (cited in Wittke, *op. cit.*, pp. 88, 90) refers to Ernest Christian Friedrich Blume as a German-Jewish tanner who worked for Polish liberation both in Europe and in America, but it is difficult to conceive of an unbaptized Jew's adopting the name "Christian."

[52] *OCC*, VII, No. 9, pp. 473–4, Dec., 1849; No. 10, p. 513, Jan., 1850; No. 11, pp. 529–42, Feb., 1850; VIII, No. 1, pp. 29–30, April, 1850; No. 6, pp. 297–306, 315–6, Sept., 1850; No. 7, pp. 348–54; Oct., 1850; No. 9, pp. 459–64, Dec., 1850; No. 10, pp. 514–9, Jan., 1851; *Allgemeine Zeitung des Judenthums*, XIII (1849), p. 524; XIV (1850), p. 607; XXII (1858), p. 474. *UJE*, VI, p. 455.

[53] *The Story of the First Fifty Years of The Mount Sinai Hospital, 1852–1902*, New York, 1944, pp. 29–31; *OCC*, XXVI, No. 3, p. 141, June, 1868; letter, Jacobi to Leeser, April 6, 1862, Leeser Collection, Dropsie College Library. A Dr. Jacobi (possibly this one) lectured to the Maimonides Library Association of New York in 1855, on the subject, "A Solution of the Slavery Question," Hyman B. Grinstein, *The Rise of the Jewish Community of New York, 1654–1860*, Phila., 1945, p. 204.

[54] Blumenfeld, *op. cit.*, p. 12; data provided by Rabbi Joseph L. Baron of Milwaukee.

[55] Sol M. Strook, "Switzerland and American Jews," *PAJHS*, No. XI (1903), p. 50.

[56] *Medical Life, op. cit.*, p. 258.

[57] Data provided by John Proskauer's daughter, Miss Jenny Proskauer of St. Louis.

[58] *Hebrew Leader*, IX, No. 4, p. 5, Nov. 2, 1866.

[59] Jacob Vorsanger, *The Chronicles of Emanu-El*, San Francisco, 1900, p. 17.

[60] *Autobiography of August Bondi*, pp. 87–8, 133.

[61] *Jewish Encyclopedia*, New York, 1905, IX, p. 38.

[62] Samuel Kalisch (ed.) *Studies in Ancient and Modern Judaism ... Selected Writings of Rabbi Isidor Kalisch*, New York, 1928, p. 5.

[63] *UJE*, V, 404; Adolph Guttmacher, *History of Baltimore Hebrew Congregation*, Baltimore, 1905, p. 67.

[64] Marvin Lowenthal, *Henrietta Szold, Life and Letters*, New York, 1942, p. 2; Isidor Blum, *The Jews of Baltimore*, Baltimore, 1910, p. 15.

[65] *Rev. Dr. Adolph Huebsch, Late Rabbi of the Ahawath Chesed Congregation, New York, A Memorial*, New York, 1885, p. IV.

[66] *MESS*, XXII, No. 10, p. 5, Sept. 6, 1867; No. 12, p. 5, Sept. 20; *Hebrew Leader*, X, No. 25, p. 4, Sept. 27, 1867.

[67] Henry Illoway, *Sefer Milchamos Elohim, Being the Controversial Letters and the Casuistic Decisions of the late Rabbi Bernard Illowy Ph.D. with a Short History of His Life and Activities*, Berlin, 1914, p. 14.

[68] When this study was first published in 1949, only twenty-nine had been uncovered. The additional personalities in this version have been brought to the author's attention through the kindness of many scholars and readers. It is hoped that further persons who should be included in this group will be brought forward by other readers.

II

American Jewish Life in 1849[*]

AMERICAN Jewish history interpreted as the settlement of Jews in the colonies which were to become member states of the American Republic begins in 1654, when those twenty-three bedraggled, poverty-stricken refugees from Dutch Brazil appeared in New Amsterdam, much to the dismay and discomfort of Peg-Leg Peter Stuyvesant. The history of Judaism in America begins at almost the same time, whenever the first religious services were conducted in New Amsterdam — or perhaps not technically until about 1690 when the Shearith Israel Congregation built its first synagogue. Judaism and the Jews have a long history in America.

But when we focus our attention upon the emergence of the American Jewish community — that amorphous, indefinable, multitongued, undisciplined community which today almost defies description — we must perforce set our sights much later than 1654. Almost from the beginning, it is true, there were cordial relations between individual Jewish families living in various localities, and even some few points of contact between the existing congregations. [1] But, generally speaking, the small proportion of Jews to the total population of the country, the isolation which resulted from geographic distance and poor communications, the more pressing problems of earning a living

* Read at the annual convention of the Central Conference of American Rabbis, June 27, 1949, at Bretton Woods, N. H., originally published in *Yearbook*, *The Central Conference of American Rabbis*, Vol. LIX, 1949, pp. 273–304, and reprinted, without notes, in the *Jewish Exponent* (Phila.), Sept. 23, 1949, Section 4, pp. 1, 12–16; Sept. 30, pp. 26, 32; Oct. 7, pp. 20, 23.

and achieving a position in society, and the rawness and experimental character of American life as a whole — all of these factors seemed to preclude the growth of even an unconsciously unified American Jewish community until the great quarter century of gestation and creation — 1843–1868 — when the shape and direction of our contemporary American Jewish scene began to emerge from chaos.

Eighteen Hundred and Forty-Nine may be regarded as a typical year in that fascinating period when American Jewry was attempting to grow up, experimenting with new ideas, trying to create new patterns for a new life. It was an age when the American Jewish community was poised mid-way between the simplicity of a very limited Jewish experience and the bewildering complexities of our own time.

There were, in 1849, approximately fifty thousand Jews in the United States. Thirteen or fourteen thousand lived in New York City alone, already the leading Jewish community in the country. Large communities were also to be found in Philadelphia, Cincinnati, Baltimore and Louisville. About 45 congregations had been organized since the Revolution, thirteen of them in New York, with the others spread far and wide across the country. [2] This population growth was colorfully demonstrated by statistics which were published at Passover time in Cincinnati. In 1824, the year the Bene Israel Congregation was organized, 100 pounds of *Matzos* had met the needs of the few Jews in the Ohio valley. Now, in 1849, twenty-five years later, 20,000 pounds had been manufactured and it was feared that this quantity would be insufficient to supply the demand. [3] Scattered statistics would indicate that during 1849 alone, at least nine new congregations were organized and seven new synagogues built. [4]

One of the new congregations was Sherith Israel in San Francisco, where Jews, like other Americans, had journeyed — attracted by the gold-fever. In one week alone, a Jewish editor counted twenty-eight Jews who sailed from New York for the new Eldorado.[5] The next week a report from New Orleans conveyed the news that:

A vast number of Israelites are leaving this city and section of the South, for [San Francisco]. Not a vessel quits our harbour but carries a large proportion of the enterprising sons of Israel. The majority of these emigrants are possessed of some means, and having extensive facilities amongst our merchants, will build up a new trade for this city; a vast quantity of old style manufactured goods of every description has been paid for in *Cash* . . .[6]

As the High Holy Days of 1849 approached, a group of Jews advertised services in the San Francisco newspapers and urged their co-religionists to join with them. Facilities in the new Mecca were so primitive that the only edifice which could be obtained for use as a synagogue was a tent. Estimates of those in attendance varied from thirty to fifty.[7] But a beginning had been made, and within a year a cemetery plot was purchased (towards which one prospector who had struck it rich contributed $500 — *in gold dust!*), a Hebrew Benevolent Society was organized, and there was already talk of building a synagogue.[8]

No other budding Jewish community had the spectacular quality of the one in San Francisco, but up and down the land, as soon as enough Jews appeared in a locality, they purchased cemetery lots, organized mutual-aid benevolent societies, and worshipped in private homes until there was enough money to rent a few rooms for a synagogue. Jewish life was still centered in the synagogue, although extra-congregational charities had been organized in the larger communities and the B'nai B'rith had been in existence for six years. In 1849 a second fraternal order, the Free Sons of Israel, was founded, apparently foreshadowing the gradual secularization of American Jewry.

Most of the Jews who settled in the newer communities were recent immigrants from Central Europe, Jews who fled the political and social disabilities of their birthplaces and sought their hope for tomorrow in America. What kind of national Jewish life did these immigrants find in America? A small scattered, divided community just beginning to grope for a foot-hold in the future — a community of slightly older immigrants struggling to establish themselves, seeking personal security — struggling among themselves, too, to articulate their needs and create new voices and find new paths — four small Reform congregations seeking recognition for their ideas — a few untrained leaders horrified by the chaos and indifference, building new structures — a community of fifty thousand persons of varied backgrounds, without a sense of unity or direction or common purpose.

I

The development of lines of communication is always an index to the effectiveness of a society. American Jewry — beset with problems and cares — had, previous to 1849, created only one periodical, *The Occident and American Jewish Advocate*, edited by the Rev. Isaac Leeser of Philadelphia. Since its founding, in 1843, *The Occident* had been a lone voice crying in the wilderness of American Jewish life, the sole means of communication between the far-flung Jewish communities and the only indication of the barely discernible impulse towards national community consciousness. Leeser, thinking always in national rather than local terms, sought through his magazine to reach even the most isolated Jew with news of events at home and abroad, and to advance the cause of Torah by printing sermons and articles on learned Jewish matters. In a day when there were practically no books in English on the most elementary Jewish subjects, when each congregation had to fight its own battles against ignorance and indifference, the *Occident* was a superlatively constructive effort. Isaac Leeser must be remembered for many creative advances — but the *Occident* heads the list.

It had many disadvantages, however, which were to militate against complete effectiveness. Despite his German birth, Leeser was the *Hazan* of a Sephardic congregation, pledged to forms and attitudes which were unfamiliar to the majority of the Ashkenazic immigrants. His magazine appeared only twelve times a year, and it could have, at best, only a modest influence on Jews who were literally starving for information and inspiration. Finally, the *Occident* was published in Philadelphia, a large Jewish community it is true, but one which was completely overshadowed by New York's fifteen thousand strong, who needed their own voice.

The year 1849 saw the establishment of two more Jewish periodicals, both weeklies and both published in New York, as if in answer to that need. The first of these, which, unfortunately, survived for only three months, was the *Israels Herold*, which began publication in German on March 30, 1849, under the editorship of Isidor Busch. [9] Busch was, as we have already seen, a Viennese liberal who had taken an active role in the Republican Revolution the previous year. As one of the editors of the *Oesterreichisches Central-Organ*, he had thrown the weight of his intimate connection with the leading German-Jewish thinkers squarely behind the Revolutionary forces. When the liberals were forced to capitulate, however, he had to flee for his life. Arrived in New York, he opened a book-store and within a few months concluded that the New York Jewish community could well use his journalistic training and his knowledge of the currents of Jewish thought in Europe.

Busch was a typical European Jewish intellectual. He believed that nothing was more important than the elucidation of theoretical and theological issues. From the first, therefore, he de-

31

clared his intention of bringing out into the open the conflict between the Reformers and the Traditionalists which was simmering beneath the surface of American Jewish life. He had no fears of the outcome: "Only permit the various opinions and convictions to be expressed, and the truth will and must emerge from the struggle of the contending parties, purified, just as gold is separated from baser metals when in the fire." [10] Busch was convinced that harmony and unity could be attained even though theological differences remained unreconciled.

This high philosophical tone was, in the long run, responsible for Busch's failure to gain an audience for his weekly journal. It was all well and good to hope for theological harmony among the rabbis — but articles debating the merits of Pantheism had little to offer the rank and file of German-Jewish immigrants, whose needs were much less sophisticated. The leaders of the Orthodox party *did* oppose the paper, vociferously, but opposition was not responsible for the *Herold's* demise; indifference was. Busch himself eventually came to realize that the *Herold* was too high-flown, too literary and philosophical to have any popular appeal: "A Jewish literary periodical," he said, "is a complete impossibility here. There are hardly ten people who . . . have any interest in it." [11] We need not dwell at length on what this means for the legendary notion of the German-Jewish immigrant as a philosophical intellectual! Busch, at least, would not have agreed with that tradition. He gave up his venture and moved to St. Louis.

The second Jewish weekly to be undertaken during 1849 was *The Asmonean*, edited by Robert Lyon, a New Yorker of English birth. When Leeser heard of the plans for the publication of *The Asmonean*, he warned with these pessimistic forebodings:

We hope that the enterprise will meet with due encouragement; at the same time, we do not hesitate in saying that it is more likely to result in a heavy pecuniary loss to the proprietors. Our own experience in

publishing for our people is something like a long series of disappointments; and had it not been that we needed not the smallest portion
of the proceeds for our personal support, we should long since have
relinquished the editorial chair. We are always sorry to see an inexperienced person expose himself to the disappointments which are sure
to await him; we know what it is to battle with a public who do not
care to hear from one, no matter what he has to say, and we therefore
had hoped that for the present no more candidates for disappointment
would have presented themselves. We dissuaded Mr. Bush from commencing "Israel's Herald;" he nevertheless went on, printed twelve
numbers, and then stopped, having found that we had advised him
correctly. We wish Mr. Lyons [*sic*] a better success, though we fear
the contrary . . . [12]

Despite Leeser's gloomy prediction, *The Asmonean* received a
warm welcome and survived as long as its editor lived. We know
very little about Lyon as a person, but if we may judge his
character from his newspaper, he had more foresight and genuine journalistic ability than any of his fellow-publishers. Even
before the first issue of the paper had appeared, he had sought
and obtained "the patronage and support of the ministers and
presiding officers" of nine New York congregations, ranging
from the far left of the Reform Temple Emanu-El to the far
right of the Sephardic Shearith Israel Congregation. Listed in a
box on the first page of the first number, these congregational
imprimatures no doubt served to gain for *The Asmonean* the good
will of all affiliated Jews. Such unlikely bed-fellows as Max
Lilienthal the Reformer and Samuel M. Isaacs the arch-Tradi-
tionalist had consented to receive subscriptions for the paper,
thereby lending the support of their personal prestige to its publisher. An effort was made, from the very beginning, to reach
the hinterland: agents were appointed to represent the paper in
the South and Mid-West. Lyon was obviously a better business
man than Leeser or Busch. He had laid his plans carefully. [13]

But beyond the organizational phases of *The Asmonean*, when
one compares it with *The Occident* or the *Herold*, he readily per-

33

ceives that Lyon knew his potential public far better than Leeser or Busch. Its purposes were the same: to disseminate Jewish news, to foster "unity of action" among American congregations, to raise the level of Jewish knowledge. But to achieve those purposes, he first needed readers, and Lyon knew how to attract them. Because most of his fellow-Jews were peddlers or store-keepers or artisans, he endeavored to publish the most recent stockmarket quotations, news of impending ship arrivals and departures, and reports on the latest prices of various merchandise. He even used secular jokes and anecdotes and curiosities as "filler." But, more important, he printed long columns of advertisements for boarding houses, theatres, wholesale houses and jobbers, dentists and school teachers, all of immediate interest to his potential readers. Leeser would not deign to print advertisements in the *Occident;* they would apparently have contaminated its sacred articles and sermons. Lyon knew that most of his readers were busy trying to establish themselves in business, and that the advertisements would attract them as much as, if not more than, the text. Even the news columns were more interesting, chattier and more informative than *The Occident's.* Names appeared in the *Asmonean* with studied frequency — Lyon knew human foibles extremely well. Significantly enough, all of the later newspapers, Wise's *Israelite*, Isaacs' *Messenger*, Eckman's Pacific Coast *Gleaner* and Cohen's *Record*, copied these aspects of the *Asmonean's* format and contents with flattering exactness.

His popular touch did not deter Lyon from attacking all of the serious problems of American Jewish life, however. He was as much a crusader as the others, and his editorial pages are full of vigorous proposals for the strengthening of the synagogue, for more efficient organization of the charities, for the raising of standards in education and in the ministry. In terms of an effective periodical, Lyon certainly accomplished as much as Leeser; and in terms of influence, he outranked Leeser by setting the pace for his journalistic successors.

II

One of the projects to which both Busch and Lyon dedicated their efforts was the establishment of an effective organizational union of American Jewish congregations. The year 1849 was not the first in which this dream was expressed. In 1841 Leeser and a Philadelphia colleague had gained enough support for the idea for their congregations to issue a national appeal for a conference in Philadelphia. Ignored by most synagogues, however, and opposed by a few others, this attempt was marked by an eminent lack of success. [14]

In December 1848, Isaac Mayer Wise, who had been brooding in Albany for two years over the anarchy and chaos of American Jewish religious life, could contain himself no longer. Addressing himself to the only organized Jewish audience in America, the readers of the *Occident*, through an article, and, by circular, to the rabbis and presidents of all of the synagogues, he pleaded for a national conference on the important issues of Jewish life:

. . . [I]n order to fulfil our sacred mission, to send our important message to mankind, it behooves us to be united as one man; to be linked together by the ties of equal views concerning religious questions — by uniformity in our sacred customs, in our form of worship, and religious education. We ought to have a uniform system for our schools, synagogues, benevolent societies — for all our religious institutions . . .
. . . The majority of our congregations in this country have been established but a few years back; they are generally composed of the most negative elements from all the different parts of Europe and elsewhere; they have been founded and are now governed for the greater part by men of no considerable knowledge of our religion, and generally

35

of no particular zeal for our common cause. The consequence of all this is, that many congregations have no solid basis, no particular stimulus to urge on the youth to a religious life, and no nourishment for the spiritual Israelite. This naturally produces an enormous amount of indifference; and each congregation pursues its own way, has its own customs and mode of worship, its own way of thinking about religious questions, from which cause it then results that one Jew is a stranger in the Synagogue of the other Jew. It is a pity to observe that any man who is so happy as to have a license (קבלה) to kill from some unknown person, can become the minister of a congregation, and the teacher of the youth, without any proof of his knowledge of religion, and in the absence of any evidence of his conduct as a Jew . . .

. . . It is lamentable, but true, that if we do not unite ourselves betimes to devise a practicable system for the ministry and religious education at large, — if we do not take care that better educated men fill the pulpit and the schoolmaster's chair, — if we do not stimulate all the congregations to establish good schools, and to institute a reform in their synagogues on modern Jewish principles, — the house of the Lord will be desolate, or nearly so, in less than ten years.

. . . I call upon all my honoured friends, both ministers and laymen, and all who have an interest in the promulgation of God's law — come, let us be assembled in order to be united! Exercise all your influence on your friends and acquaintances, to bring together all men of zeal and piety, of wisdom and knowledge, to consider what should be done for the union, welfare, and progress of Israel. Let the place of assembly be *Philadelphia*, it being nearly the centre of the Jews living in North America; and let the time of meeting be the second day of the Rosh Hodesh Iyar, 5609 . . . [15]

A comparison of the response to Wise's proposal in 1848–9 with the silence which greeted Leeser's effort in 1841 is an indication of the progress which American Jewry had made in the short space of seven years. Now at least there was a national organ in which the debate could be conducted. Leeser gave whole-hearted editorial support to Wise's call and urged a full and complete discussion. For seven succeeding issues, the *Occident* was full of articles and letters debating the idea. Leeser and Wise had announced that a minimum of twenty congregations would be required to appoint delegates before the conference could actually be held. When, in April, despite all the talk, only eight congregations had approved the project and only five had actually designated their delegates, Leeser and Wise decided to postpone the meeting indefinitely. The eight congregations were: Mikveh Israel of Philadelphia; B'nai Jeshurun of Cincinnati; Beth El of Albany; Shaarai Chesed and Nefutzot Yehudah of New Orleans; Shaarai Shomayim of Mobile; Shaaray Tefila of New York; and Beth Shalome of Richmond.[16] At least these eight congregations were supporters of Wise's proposal, and their geographical distribution would indicate that recognition of the need for congregational union had spread all over the country. It is also significant that two of the old Sephardic congregations, representing the more established element, were willing to support the newcomer Wise.

But despite the more vigorous campaigning and the endorsement of a larger number of congregations and rabbis, the effort was actually as much a failure as that of 1841. Why?

For one thing, there was a tremendous difference of opinion over the objectives of the conference. Some thought it should only consider non-religious problems, and others wished to have the agenda limited to religious affairs. Wise (among others) hoped that it would become a force for Reform; others would only consider joining if it were pledged to oppose Reform. One writer even suggested that the real objective of the meeting should be to organize a Chief Rabbinate which could be supported by the income from a strictly regulated national system of *Shechitah*.[17]

Undoubtedly, the struggle between liberalism and traditionalism, still in its infancy in America, played a large part in keeping many groups from joining the movement. When Wise went to New York City to speak in behalf of the union proposal to a group who called themselves the "Friends of Light," he alienated large numbers of the Orthodox who proceeded to identify the

37

union scheme with the radical religious beliefs of the "Friends of Light."[18] Lilienthal, on the other hand, although not ministering to any congregation at the time, appears to have been afraid that the numerically superior traditionalist groups would outvote the Reformers and outlaw modernization.[19] Further light on the matter comes from the argument of one opponent of the idea who insisted that no conference was necessary for the sincerely orthodox; the only conferences in Jewish life of which he knew were those meetings organized in Germany by the Reformers for the announcement of their radical beliefs, and he would have nothing to do with such schemes here in America.[20]

Disagreement and opposition there were aplenty, but there was even more indifference and apathy than opposition. Wise was quite right, theoretically, in his belief that a congregational union was necessary for the strengthening of American Jewish life; but he was altogether wrong in his prediction that, without a union, Jewish religious life in America would be "desolate" within ten years. The apathy and indifference were natural and necessary; time would help rather than harm. Wise was so wrapped up in his zeal for activity that he overlooked some very important aspects of the life of his constituency. More than two thirds of the Jews to whom he was appealing were comparatively recent immigrants; they had hardly been able to establish themselves in a livelihood, had hardly learned the language of their new home or adjusted themselves to the mores and customs of democratic living. They had a world of new ideas to assimilate, a myriad of challenges and disadvantages to overcome. Life in America was literally a struggle from early in the morning 'til late at night. They had no time or leisure to worry about the more theoretical aspects of American Jewish life; enough that they scraped together enough money to put up a synagogue and pay a *Shochet*. Wise and Leeser were expecting too much from them too soon. Not until another generation had passed would the union be created, the Union of American Hebrew Congregations, founded at Wise's behest in 1873. For the present, in the year 1849, Wise could be grateful that some Jews had given careful consideration to his ideas and that he himself had learned something from this fledgeling adventure in the arena of American Jewish politics.

III

American Jewry actually needed trained leadership on the local level more desperately than a union on the national level. Wise, Leeser, Merzbacher of Emanu-El in New York, and Isaacs of Shaaray Tefila, were the leading "rabbis" of the time, although probably only one of them had really been ordained. The other congregations were ministered to by a variety of functionaries, most of whom were completely incompetent as religious leaders and preachers. Innumerable *Shochtim* and *Hazanim* floated from one city to another, frequently acting as rabbis, sometimes going into business. Dissatisfaction with religious leadership was the order of the day: congregations were always advertising for rabbis, and the nondescript functionaries were always seeking new positions. A typical notice of the time proclaimed: "חזן —Wanted, a situation as שוחט, חזן, & Teacher, and if necessary to act as Lecturer in the German language, being duly qualified for any of the above offices. . . ."[21]

Most congregations could not expect to be served by a better trained "rabbi" than this *Shochet* who would preach, "if necessary." Without explaining why he wished to leave a position where he had achieved such success, another "rabbi" who styled himself "A Theologian, educated at an eminent German University" advertised that he was "open to an engagement." "He has occupied for several years, the responsible office of Minister and Teacher, in a large congregation, with much success," he said modestly, and then continued to outline his qualifications. "He is competent to give lessons in English, French, and Spanish languages; also Book-keeping by the Italian method of double entry, &c . . ." Who knows what the "&c." included?[22]

The paucity of trustworthy leadership was revealed in striking fashion in the welcome which New York Jewry accorded to Rabbi Morris J. Raphall when he arrived in late October, 1849. Raphall, a native of Sweden, had been rabbi of Birmingham, England, where he had achieved an amazing reputation as an orator. When he left Birmingham he was given a princely round of farewell parties and testimonials. The local newspapers and the London *Jewish Chronicle* filled columns with the texts of speeches lauding his magnificent leadership. During one of these meetings, a delegation of Christians led by the mayor of the city presented him with a purse of one hundred guineas.[23]

Coming to America at the request of B'nai Jeshurun Congregation of New York, Raphall was received like a conquering hero. The *Asmonean* and *Occident* alike devoted pages to his achievements. After his first Sabbath morning sermon, the *Asmonean's* reporter said:

> . . . Accustomed as we have been to hear many of the great religious and political orators of all parties in both hemisphere[s], we could not divest ourselves of the feeling that we were in the hands of a master of elocution, and the ability of scrutinizing the argument was momentarily lost to us by the facility with which the Rev. Dr. carried us with him by the artistic management of his finely modulated voice, indeed the fact that the sermon was delivered without reference to notes, and poured forth in a continuous flow of most appropriate language, created a vivid impression on all present, and at the conclusion the Rev. and learned lecturer was nearly overwhelmed by the congratulations of the congregation . . .[24]

This sermon, almost an hour in length, insured Raphall's election as the congregation's rabbi at the munificent salary of $2000, the highest remuneration then offered to an American rabbi.[25]

40

His colleagues' salaries ranged from a high of $1700 (Congregation Mikveh Israel of Philadelphia advertised this for a married man, $1300 if he were single) [26] to a low of about $500; [27] one rabbi who received $1200 a year had to pay the salary of his assistant school teacher out of his own wages! [28]

Raphall's election to the B'nai Jeshurun pulpit was hailed as the beginning of a new era in American Jewish life. And, in a way, it was. He appears to have been the first glamour-rabbi in American Jewish history. Throngs of Christians and unaffiliated Jews came to hear him preach at his regular services. He was the first American rabbi to deliver series of lectures for the public — and Christians and Jews alike paid admission to hear him declaim about "The Poetry of the Hebrews" and similar subjects. Only a few months after his arrival in New York, he set out on a national lecture tour which took him as far as Charleston, S. C., where he debated the merits of Reform with Isaac M. Wise, then trying out for the pulpit in that city. Everywhere he went, overflowing praise was accorded to him. [29] After he spoke to a capacity audience at the University of Pennsylvania, in Philadelphia, a number of socially prominent Christians in the audience passed a series of resolutions of appreciation. The chairman, Joseph R. Ingersoll, said,

All of us will cheerfully acknowledge that we are indebted to the lecturer for a series of spirited and successful efforts of learning and eloquence, and for the eminent discretion and enlarged liberality by which his discourses have been distinguished. He has touched with a delicate yet forceful hand, the strings of the golden lyre of sacred song. He has at the same time touched the responsive chords of many a feeling heart . . . [30]

These words of praise were typical of the tribute which Raphall received everywhere he spoke.

For a long time to come, America's ablest rabbis, like Raphall, would be importations from abroad, men who received their training and achieved their reputations in Europe: Einhorn, Adler, Hirsch, Gottheil, Mielziner, Huebsch. Raphall's success added one more requirement to the list of rabbinical qualifications: oratorical mastery.

IV

A more prosaic, but more basic responsibility of the rabbi was the education of the children. Here, if anywhere, knowledge, understanding, patience and imagination were called for. But the *Shochtim* who would preach "if necessary" were sorely pressed to fulfil this duty. It was not merely a matter of Sunday Schools. Although the movement towards the establishment of public schools was gaining ground, at least in the North, most congregations still supported all-day parochial schools, in which the curriculum combined Jewish and secular subjects. In 1849 alone, such schools were organized in Philadelphia, Richmond, Cleveland, and Cincinnati.[31] There were, in addition, private Jewish schools in the great metropolitan areas.[32] In New York City, depressed by an unsuccessful attempt to act as rabbi of three German congregations, Max Lilienthal was conducting "Rev. Dr. Lilienthal's Hebrew, Commercial and Classical Boarding School," in which his pupils were given instruction in "Hebrew, German, English, French, Latin, Greek, mathematics, bookkeeping, drawing and dancing."[33] Parents were deeply concerned that their children should receive some instruction in Judaism. Gentiles or Jews could always be found who were proficient in secular subjects; but if the "rabbi" was himself untutored, and if, in addition, there were no text-books worthy of the name — the fate of the children could well be imagined.

The usual Jewish phase of the curriculum consisted of Hebrew and catechism. More often than not, the pupils were not taught to translate the Hebrew. When the members of the School Committee of B'nai Jeshurun of New York recommended the reorganization of their school, they had this to say:

... Permit us to expose to your view, in plain terms, the evils of the present manner of training our children. The child is taught to read Hebrew; after accomplishing that, his religious education is considered finished. Now, we ask, is it possible for any person to utter a prayer with devotion unless he understands it? . . . Is it right for the descendants of Moses, David, Solomon, Isaiah and Jeremiah not to be able to appreciate, nay not even to understand the sublime, matchless and unrivalled compositions of their own ancestry? . . . [34]

Biblical history was taught in conjunction with Bible; the pupils were generally not informed that there was any Jewish life between 70 A. D. and 1849. The catechisms then in use were, in the main, translations of the books used in Germany, although several had already been published in America. Isaac Leeser's catechism comprised ten chapters and two appendices — 376 choice questions and answers on Judaism, its concepts and ideals, in language which would be certain to break the teeth of any youngster under College age. [35] Within a few years, fortunately, more learned rabbis were attempting to compose text-books in history, ethics, theology and literature, for the pupils of their religious schools, but most, like Leeser, failed to remember that they were writing for childish minds.

Some of the older, more established congregations had Sunday schools directed by men and women who were blessed with a good secular education, but were without a very profound knowledge of Jewish sources. Sentiment generally was expected to substitute for learning. Here is the description of the annual public examination of the Columbia, S. C., Hebrew Sunday School, conducted on May 6, 1849:

The exercises commenced at 10 o'clock, with a prayer by the Directress, Miss Julia Mordecai, whose untiring perseverance in behalf of our holy religion and the dissemination of its principles, fully entitle her to the high respect entertained by our community. This was followed with

43

English hymns by the various classes . . . Next followed the examination of the classes from the lowest to the highest in Bible questions and Sacred History, the repetition of the creeds, commandments, &c., in all of which they displayed unusual proficiency. The promptness and accuracy of their answers to the most difficult questions relative to our doctrines proved conclusively that those doctrines had not only been *instilled*, but deeply impressed on the mind . . . Next in order were recitations by several of the pupils, appropriately commencing with that of the "Holy Bible," by Master Edward Nathans, poetically explaining its objects, describing its attributes, and enumerating its benefits. The pieces were all carefully selected by the directress, in reference to Scriptural History, and in vindication of our faith, subjects entitled to the full justice they received at the hands of the youthful orators . . . Among such may be mentioned, "Miriam," by Miss Louisa Lyons, a child but six years old; "The Destruction of Jerusalem," by Master Theodore Polock; "Hagar in the Wilderness," by Miss Frances J. Levin; "Come Forth Sweet Sister," a dialogue in reference to Purim by the Misses Carolina and Olivia Polock, and "Absalom" by Miss Rachel Lyons . . . The recitations were succeeded by Yigdal, sung by the Hebrew class, now under the tuition of Mr. Philip Jacobs, and Ayn Kaylohenu, by the choir . . . [36]

Sincerity could not take the place of rich Jewish knowledge. Everywhere the complaint was: what of the next generation? The familiar pattern of untrained and incompetent teachers and nondescript text-books was to repeat itself in monotonous fashion throughout the decades. The parochial school was to pass from the scene in the 1860's — destined to return again in our own time under vastly different circumstances; the Sunday School survived, the butt of almost every educational critic who had a theory.

One enheartening step was taken in 1849, however, towards the establishment of a theological seminary, which demonstrated the seriousness with which Isaac Leeser and his supporters regarded the need for a training school for rabbis. Among other things, the charter of the Hebrew Education Society of Philadelphia which was granted that year by the Pennsylvania legislature provided that:

44

It shall also be lawful for said corporation to establish, whenever their funds will permit the same to be done, a superior seminary of learning within the limits of this commonwealth, the faculty of which seminary shall have power to furnish its graduates and others the usual degrees of bachelor of arts, master of arts, and doctor of law and divinity, as the same is exercised by other colleges established in this common-wealth. [37]

Leeser pleaded for the implementation of this provision:

It will be seen that by section *three* we are empowered to establish a college, in the full sense of the word, for the instruction of Hebrew literature in connexion with the sciences, within the limits of the Commonwealth, not confining us even to this city. Of course, the provision was introduced only for the future . . . [but] it is left to the Israelites of America to say whether it shall be merely a legislative grant, or be employed for the advancement of our religious interests . . . The ministers we . . . require, prospectively, if not at the present day, must be those educated in this land, in the midst of us, known to us from their youth for probity of character and an elevated moral standing. All we require to accomplish this are ample means . . . [38]

Not only was there a genuine scarcity of Jewish text-books during our period, but of any kind of Jewish literature. The fate of Isidor Busch's *Israels Herold* was one indication of the lack of support which Jewish cultural ventures might expect. Another such indication was the demise of the first American Jewish Publication Society during 1849. Organized in 1845, the Society was yet another of the creative institutions initiated by that remarkable Philadelphia *Hazan*, Isaac Leeser. Its goal was 1500 members at a subscription rate of $1. a year. The Society planned, eventually, to issue books on every subject of Jewish interest. Its first undertaking, however, was a periodical an-thology, called *The Jewish Miscellany*, composed of essays and chapters extracted and translated from German books on various phases of Jewish life, literature and history. In four years, thirteen numbers of the *Miscellany* were published; but only 450 members had been secured for the Society. [39] Leeser, who rarely curbed his optimism during a long and fruitful career, was chagrined at the lack of support:

That our anticipations have not been realized is not our fault; that the rich have not stepped forward to endow our treasury with the requisite funds, in the absence of subscribers, is no cause of blame to us. But if we Jews had among us a tithe of the zeal of the Christians, who spend their thousands in tracts, prayerbooks and Bibles, for gratuitous distribution all over the land, we should not have been compelled to wait the slow incoming of the individual subscriptions. Still it is time that our men and women whom the Lord has richly endowed with worldly goods, should think it their duty to do something for their religion and its advancement. They live in fine houses, eat dainty food, drive along in easy carriages . . .[40]

Lest we think ourselves so superior to the derelict Jews of Leeser's day whose indifference to Jewish literature forced him to discontinue *The Jewish Miscellany*, it is important to note that the 8,000 persons who today subscribe to our Jewish Publication Society represent less than one-third of the proportion of members who belonged to the 1849 Society to the total Jewish population of the United States.

V

If American Jewry was slow to develop an active educational and cultural program, the same cannot be said of philanthropy. In the area of human need, Jews seemed to be more sensitive than in any other. Particularly during the 1840's, with a steadily increasing flow of central European immigrants, many of whom brought nothing but the clothing on their backs to the dream-goal of America, charitable societies were created by the hundreds. It goes without saying that all of the congregations, large and small, in the metropolitan areas and in small towns, had their own ladies' aid societies and men's benevolent associations, organized to meet the needs of their members and of the clientele

46

which gravitated towards them. In addition, in the larger cities, where more than one congregation existed, secular or rather non-congregational societies were formed, appealing for membership to synagogued and unaffiliated alike. Actually the need was so great that numberless groups could be kept busy, although it must be admitted that the additional number of prestige positions of leadership had an undoubted part in multiplying the number of agencies. The women organized societies for the sewing of garments for the poor, for the care of the sick and orphaned, and for the education of poor children; the men specialized in supplying fuel, housing, bedding, food, *Matzos* for Passover, burial services, and the like. Funds were raised through dues, benefit parties, dances, celebrations, annual banquets, operatic recitals, and what not. One frequently has the feeling, reinforced by hints from the more mordant commentators of the time, that the charities would not have been so successful if they did not also provide an answer to the entertainment-starvation and gregarious instincts of the more well-to-do members of the Jewish community. Here are extracts, for instance, from the *Asmonean's* description of a benefit party given by the New York Young Men's Hebrew Benevolent Association at the Broadway Theatre on January 22, 1850:

... undoubtedly the most spirited and complete affair we have witnessed for some time, and we are somewhat at a loss as to which deserves to hold first rank in our notice. The attractions on the stage or the attractions off the stage ... [the latter] were such as are not ordinarily witnessed in the walls of a Theatre, the young and the beautiful were there in great strength. *The Herald* in a lengthened notice, chronicles the fact that it was 'a most dazzling concentration of beauty,' in which 'the fair daughters of Israel were in the ascendant.'. ... [T]he most fastidious critic could there have found types of his love of beauty. The house was literally one perfect cram ... and the sum of $120 [was] returned at the door to parties who were unable to obtain seats. The performances were of a sterling good character. The Comedy being Sheridan's School for Scandal, got up with a very able cast ...

The talented Orchestra of the Italian Opera, led by its spirited director, Max Maretzek, Esq., who was loudly cheered on entering to wield [*sic*] the baton, played the favorite overture to *William Tell*, and the *Tip-top Polka*, in a style which elicited the most rapturous applause . . . Signorina [Borghese] sang the Rondeau from 'Don Pasquale' with exquisite taste, and Signor Forti gave the Cavatina from Otello, with his usual brilliancy . . . The Committee feel themselves highly indebted to Signorina Borghese, not only for the very graceful manner in which she gratuitously conceded her very valuable assistance as an artiste, but from the lively feeling she evinced to promote the objects of the projectors of the *soiree*. Such conduct invariably meets its recompense, and in the present instance, we know the gallantry of the Hebrew young men too well to permit a doubt to arise about the course they will pursue . . . The whole affording [together with donations from the Governor, Mayor, and other distinguished non-Jews] a surplus in aid of the Charity funds of nearly $800 . . . [41]

The Asmonean's was one of the few voices in New York which was raised in behalf of federated philanthropy. It was still much too early for the general public to recognize the saving in time and money and effort which could be realized through united charities, but, in one instance, 1849 was a notable year. For the first time in a decade of feuding and competition, the two largest New York philanthropies united for their annual dinners. The Hebrew Benevolent Society, composed of Sephardim, English Jews and the earlier German immigrants, and the German Hebrew Benevolent Society, which drew its membership from among the more recent central European immigrants, fore-shadowed their eventual union ten years later with a joint anniversary dinner on November 13, 1849. [42] After a very satisfactory banquet, the toasts began: to the anniversary, to benevolence, to America, to the Jewish community in Palestine, and then to Charity. During the last-named toast, the Rev. Samuel M. Isaacs tugged at the heart strings of his hearers by reminding them of the Europe from which most of them had fled; flattered them by paying tribute to their remarkable progress in making their way in America; humored them with jokes: "You are invited here to consider the cause of the poor man who not only needs your applause but your purse;" and finally promised them a secure place in Eternity for their contributions. To reach those who did not understand English, Max Lilienthal was requested to deliver an appeal in German. Then the collectors scattered through the audience and in a short time announced the results: $4000. Then came further toasts, to the President, the Mayor, education, "the fifty-thousand Jewish soldiers who fought for the liberty of Hungary," agriculture, literature and the arts, and "the fair daughters of Israel." At this juncture Major Noah, the perennial toastmaster of New York Jewry, arose and read letters from Senators Daniel Webster and William Seward, which must have warmed the hearts of those in attendance as much as they do ours today:

Boston, Nov. 9, 1849

My dear Sir: I am afraid it will not be in my power to attend the anniversary of the "Hebrew Benevolent Society" and the "German Hebrew Benevolent Society" on the 13th of the present month. I am however, grateful for having been remembered on this occasion, and desire to present my acknowledgments and thanks to the committee.

I feel, and have ever felt, respect and sympathy for all that remain of that extraordinary people, who preserved, through the darkness and idolatry of so many centuries, the knowledge of one supreme spiritual Being, the Maker of Heaven and Earth, and the Creator of Man in his own image; and whose canonical writings comprise such productions as the books of Moses and the Decalogue, the prophecies of Isaiah, the Psalms of David, the Book of Job, and Solomon's prayer at the dedication of the temple. The Hebrew Scriptures I regard as the fountain from which we draw all we know of the world around us, and of our own character and destiny, as intelligent moral and responsible beings.

I wish, my dear Sir, for the associated societies, who have honored me with their invitation, a gratifying anniversary, and am, with respect your obedient servant.

DANIEL WEBSTER

M. M. Noah, Esq. New York

*   *   *

49

Auburn, Nov. 6, 1849

My dear Sir:

The letter of the managers, inviting me to the anniversary festival of the Hebrew Benevolent Society and the German Hebrew Benevolent Society, has been received together with your note, so kindly urging me to accept the invitation.

The day appointed for these festivities falls within the very brief period I have assigned for the preparation indispensable for an absence from home for a long season. I deeply regret that I am therefore obliged to deny myself the pleasure of becoming personally acquainted, under propitious circumstances with so large and respectable a portion of the Hebrew nation dwelling among us.

Under any circumstances it would afford a rare pleasure to a person of generous sentiments to enjoy the conversation of representatives of that extraordinary people who alone, of all the nations of antiquity, have retained among the vicissitudes of human affairs, their God and their religion: that only ancient people whose doctrines have commanded our unqualified belief through so many ages, whose songs constitute the devotional melody of their most relentless enemies, and whose very prophecies, after the lapse of thousands of years, are still regarded as the infallible oracles of the fate of empires, states and men. But the gathering of the Hebrews, now contemplated, derives additional attractions from its design to welcome to our shores their brethren driven from Europe by fresh persecutions and by new and disastrous revolutions.

I pray you to tender to the societies assurances of my sincere respect, and of my cordial sympathy in their benevolent purposes, with my grateful acknowledgments for their kind remembrance of me, while I remain with great respect and esteem, your friend and humble servant.

WILLIAM H. SEEWARD

M. M. Noah, Esq.

Judging by the newspaper reports, this banquet was typical of hundreds upon hundreds of similar affairs held during the middle years of the nineteenth century. Despite the plethora of organizations and benefits, however, some individual cases were invariably overlooked. Not unlike the sensation-seeking newspapers of our own day, the Jewish editors were prompt to announce such cases to the public and committees sprang forth instantaneously, determined to rescue the individuals from privation and want. In December 1849, just a month after the huge dinner just described, the *Asmonean* printed the following notice;

DESTITUTION — We have been requested to make an appeal to the humane and charitable in behalf of a case of deep affliction accompanied with great distress. A respectable woman, residing at No. 6 Christie Street, confined by childbirth about 14 days since, buried her husband on Sunday last, and is at present with several very young children, suffering great privation. We are credibly informed that the poor woman is highly deserving of the sympathy of our readers. Donations of any description will be thankfully received by M. S. Cohen, 69 Duane St., near Broadway; Samuel Phillips, Division Street; and S. Blankenstein, Division Street. [43]

One of the most interesting cases of the year was an appeal which came to the Rev. Isaacs of New York from the Sisters of Charity who conducted the St. Vincents Hospital of Detroit. The Sisters had nursed a Jewish traveler during a lengthy illness and had notified the Rev. Isaacs of his passing so that arrangements might be made for the body to be returned to New York for Jewish burial. Now, said the letter,

we have since had another of your nation, who, from existing circumstances, excited even a greater interest in our feelings than the lamented Mr. Josephs, it was a Miss Siggel, from New York, en route for St. Louis, became too sick to proceed, was brought to our Hospital and died of congestion of the lungs. A dark mystery hangs over her fate, should any of her friends Rev. Sir, come under your notice, you can state that she died here after receiving every kindness and attention. Poor girl! Now we have a request to present which it is hoped will not displease but rather meet with a fervent reception from every Israelite around you to whom it is addressed, it is to make a little collection for us, to aid us in being enabled to afford a larger share of comfort to the sick stranger . . . [44]

There were then so few Jews in Detroit that a congregation had not yet been organized; therefore this appeal to New York. Whether from a feeling of pride or obligation or gratitude we cannot say, but enough Jews contributed to the fund for Isaacs to send a check for $150. to the Detroit Catholic hospital — certainly an early example, if not the very first, of a public Jewish effort in behalf of a Christian sectarian charity. [45]

It was not unusual for traveling Jews to die in sectarian hospitals. There was not yet a single Jewish hospital in the entire country. Despite the prodding of physicians like Sigismond Waterman, [46] New York Jewry was to spend another five years arguing the matter; Cincinnati took less time. Before 1850 was out, the first Jewish hospital in the United States had been organized in the Queen City. [47]

VI

The third toast at the anniversary dinner of the two Benevolent Societies of New York had been to "Our brethren in the Holy Land; the sentinels of the ramparts; may the hour soon arrive when the banner of Judah will again float on Mount Zion." It must not be presumed that this interest was a purely theological one. Palestinian *M'shulachim* had been coming to the United States in the interest of *Halukah* ever since 1759 when Moses Malki suddenly appeared in America to seek contributions from Shearith Israel Congregation of New York and Jeshuat Israel of Newport, R. I. After the Revolution, they came with increasing frequency — to such an extent that, in 1832, in an effort to dissuade messengers from making the expensive trip and eating up the proceeds of their collections, the three existing New York congregations created a branch of the London *Hebrah Terumat ha-Kodesh* for centralized collections. But the itinerant rabbis were not to be discouraged. [48]

In 1849 at least two of them were at large in the United States: Jechiel Cohen, [49] who was collecting funds for the rebuilding of a synagogue in Jerusalem, and Aaron Selig Ashkenazi who fittingly enough represented the Ashkenazic interests of the Holy Land. [50] The officials of many congregations throughout the country were furious at what they considered to be a veritable "invasion." Shearith Israel refused to contribute to the messengers and determined to send $25 a year directly to Sir Moses Montefiore for transmission to Jerusalem; [51] the Charleston Sephardic congregation decided to tax each of its members $1 a year, again for direct transmission to England and Palestine; [52] Mobile's Shaarai Shomayim passed a resolution to "pay annually twenty dollars towards the support of the poor of Jerusalem and . . . hereafter recognize no messenger or agent from Jerusalem." [53] These actions were repeated all over the country. All of these communities were whole-heartedly interested in the welfare of the Jewish community of Palestine, of course. Their action was motivated by friendship, not hostility. Only in Temple Emanu-El of New York City was there a sign of opposition to *all* collections for Palestine.

Two leading Palestinophiles, Isaacs and Noah of New York, went so far as to publish an appeal to congregations everywhere to ignore the messengers and centralize American collections by dealing directly with Moses Montefiore. [54] Even they relented, however, as did others, when Selig confronted them in person His account book, preserved in the library of the Hebrew University, demonstrates that he was an effective agent and that few could resist his tales of suffering in Palestine. [55] His trip, which lasted into 1850, took him to Baltimore, Cincinnati, Louisville, New Orleans, Mobile, Montgomery, Charleston, Richmond, New Haven, Hartford, Boston and Albany. Whoever advised him in scheduling his itinerary knew a good deal about American Jewish population statistics; he stopped off only in cities with sizable communities. Isaac Mayer Wise, incidentally, showed none of his later indifference to Palestine in the entry which he wrote in Selig's account book:

Our worthy Brother Rabbi Aaron Selig Ashkenasi, messenger of our poor brethren in the holy city of Jerusalem, which the Lord may restore, has come to us to solicit our aid for the poor of our people; but since many of our members are absent from the City, nothing could be done in his favor until פסח next. I will try to constitute בעז"ה a society to aid the poor of Jerusalem. It is a lamentable feature of the total absence of national love among our brethren the remnents [sic] of Israel, that even the rich whom God has blessed with abundance, withdraw their hands from the needy and poor watchmen, that God's mercy allowed to remain in the sacred vineyard חרפה שברה לבי ואנושה. I hope that other congregations and individuals will do more for the house of Israel. [56]

The result of Selig's trip was a tremendous resistance to the extremely costly collection methods of the past, and a popular outcry for a national fund-raising effort. Both the North American Relief Society, organized by Sampson Simson and a number of other Jewish leaders in 1853, and the Board of Delegates of American Israelites, founded in 1859, were an attempted answer to this need. Neither succeeded in winning popular support, however; conflicts about the administration of funds for Palestine seem to be a perennial feature of American Jewish life!

VII

This survey of Jewish life in America in 1849 ends where it began: with the growing impulse towards national organization. The two great leaders of the time, Wise and Leeser, both believed that the future of American Jewry depended upon its ability to fashion the instruments and institutions of Jewish survival: better educated and more effective rabbis; a rabbinical seminary; a union of congregations; a rabbinical conference; federated philanthropies on a local and national scale; books for children and adults alike; newspapers and magazines for communication, creative expression and scholarship. During the intervening years almost every one of these tangible objectives has been reached. American Jewry has been eminently successful in achieving the practical goals outlined for it by its leading spokesmen of the past.

And yet, despite all the panoply of organizations and institutions, we are still plagued by the basic problems which confronted Wise and Leeser in 1849: the eradication of Jewish ignorance, the integration of the individual Jew into his millennial inheritance, the feeding of spiritual hunger, the enhancement and deepening of Judaism. It can truly be said that American Jewish life in 1849 was a wilderness. That wilderness has been conquered. But are we not in danger of transforming it into a ghost city, filled only with pretentious office buildings and sanctuaries, depopulated?

Our challenge is graver than that of a century ago, for we can no longer divert ourselves with neat, practical aims — we can no longer pin our hopes for the attainment of spiritual and religious objectives upon the outcome of conferences and meetings and assemblages of delegates, as Wise and Leeser could. *We* face the responsibility — and may we be blessed in carrying it out — of giving American Jewry a soul and a light and a passion.

NOTES

[1] See, for instance, the letter (dated March 21, 1759) from the Newport congregation to Shearith Israel of New York, requesting financial assistance for the building of a synagogue, *PAJHS*, No. XXVII, (1920), pp. 177–8.

[2] These statistics are derived, for the most part, from the compilations made by Rabbi Allan Tarshish for his unpublished doctoral dissertation, *The Rise of American Judaism* (copy in the Hebrew Union College Library). The New York congregational figures are taken from Hyman Grinstein, *Rise of the Jewish Community of New York 1654–1860*, Phila., 1945, pp. 472–3. The Lyons-De Sola *Jewish Calendar for Fifty Years*, Montreal, 1854, pp. 148–73, contains a useful but incomplete listing of congregations and Jewish organizations throughout America during this period. All such statistics and listings are, without question, estimates. An example of the

divergence of contemporary opinion on the subject of population figures is found in *OCC*, VI, No. 8, pp. 409–10, Nov., 1848, where J. L. Moss claims that there are 15,000 Jews in all of Pennsylvania, about 10,000 residing in Philadelphia alone, and Leeser argues that the statistics are all wrong; at most, he says, there are 3,000 in Philadelphia and perhaps another 1,200 in other localities throughout the state.

3 *OCC*, VII, No. 1, p. 59, April, 1849.

4 The new congregations were organized in Boston, Wheeling, Hartford, Fort Wayne, Lancaster, Danville (Pa.), Buffalo, Montgomery, and San Francisco, the new synagogues were dedicated in New Orleans, New Haven, Philadelphia, Louisville, St. Louis, Wilkes-Barre, and Pittsburgh, according to news reports to *The Occident* during 1849.

5 *ASM*, I, No. 14, p. 109. Jan. 25, 1850.

6 *ASM*, I, No. 15, p. 117, Feb. 1, 1850.

7 *ASM*, I, No. 6, p. 45, Nov. 30, 1849; *OCC*, VII, No. 9, p. 480, Dec., 1849.

8 *ASM*, I, No. 25, p. 196, Apr. 12, 1850; II, No. 25, p. 196, Oct. 11.

9 The only extant copy of *Israels Herold* has disappeared. The writer therefore has had to rely upon Prof. Guido Kisch's description of it in *Historia Judaica*, II (1940), No. 2, pp. 65–84.

10 Kisch, *op. cit.*, p. 72.

11 *Ibid.*, p. 80.

12 *OCC*, VII, No. 7, p. 379, Oct., 1849.

13 *ASM*, I, No. 1, p. 1, Oct. 26, 1849.

14 Joseph Buchler, "The Struggle for Unity, Attempts at Union in American Jewish Life: 1654–1868," *American Jewish Archives*, II, No. 1 (June 1949), pp. 21–46.

15 *OCC*, VI, No. 9, pp. 431–5, December, 1848.

16 *OCC*, VII, No. 2, pp. 61–72, May, 1849.

17 S. Bruel in *OCC*, VI, No. 12, pp. 613–4, March, 1849.

18 *OCC*, VII, No. 3, pp. 139–43, June, 1849; Wise, *op. cit.*, pp. 85–92.

19 *OCC*, VII, No. 3, p. 146.

20 *Ibid.*, pp. 143–6.

21 *ASM*, I, No. 25, p. 196, April 12, 1850.

22 *ASM*, II, No. 10, p. 76, June 28, 1850.

23 *ASM*, I, No. 2, pp. 11, 13, Nov. 2, 1849, *et seq.; OCC*, VII, No. 8, pp. 429–30, Nov., 1849, *et seq.*

24 *ASM*, I, No. 3, p. 21, Nov. 9, 1849.

25 *ASM*, I, No. 10, pp. 76–7, Dec. 28, 1849.

26 *ASM*, II, No. 25, p. 196, Oct. 11, 1850.

27 Grinstein, *op. cit.*, p. 90.

28 *OCC*, VII, No. 8, pp. 424-5, Nov., 1849.

29 *ASM*, I, No. 7, p. 53, Dec. 7, 1849; No. 14, p. 109, Jan. 25, 1850.

30 *ASM*, I, No. 15, p. 117, Feb. 1, 1850.

31 *OCC*, VII, No. 1, pp. 53-5, April, 1849, *et seq.*

32 Grinstein, *op. cit.*, p. 245.

33 *ASM*, I, No. 8, p. 8, Oct. 26, 1849.

34 *ASM*, I, No. 17, p. 135, Feb. 15, 1850.

35 Isaac Leeser, *Catechism for Younger Children*, Phila., 1839.

36 *OCC*, VII, No. 3, pp. 175-7, June, 1849.

37 *OCC*, VII, No. 2, p. 105, May, 1849.

38 *Ibid.*, p. 102.

39 *OCC*, VI, No. 8, p. 411, Nov., 1848.

40 *Ibid.;* see also VI, No. 11, pp. 574-6, Feb. 1849; VII, No. 9, p. 474, Dec., 1849.

41 *ASM*, I, No. 14, p. 109, Jan. 25, 1850.

42 *ASM*, I, No. 4, pp. 29-30, Nov. 16, 1849.

43 *ASM*, I, No. 10, p. 77, Dec. 28, 1849.

44 *ASM*, I, No. 16, p. 125, Feb. 8, 1850.

45 *ASM*, I, No. 21, p. 164, March 15, 1850.

46 Kisch, *op. cit.*, p. 82.

47 *OCC*, VIII, No. 5, pp. 259-61, Aug., 1850.

48 Grinstein, *op. cit.*, pp. 440 ff.

49 *OCC*, VI, No. 10, pp. 523-5, Jan., 1849.

50 *OCC*, VII, No. 4, p. 22, July, 1849 *et seq.*

51 *OCC*, VII, No. 6, p. 330, Sept., 1849.

52 *OCC*, VII, No. 9, p. 477, Dec., 1849.

53 *OCC*, VIII, No. 2, p. 57, April, 1850.

54 *ASM*, I, No. 8, p. 62, Dec. 14, 1849.

55 See pp. 116-141 of Salo W. and Jeanette M. Baron's extremely interesting and useful article, "Palestinian Messengers in America, 1849-79, A Record of Four Journeys," in *Jewish Social Studies*, V, Nos. 2 & 3 (1943), for material based on Selig's ledger.

56 *Ibid.*, p. 133.

III

The Know-Nothing Movement
and the Jews

N O MINOR political party in American history has ever
achieved so rapid a success as did the American or Know-Nothing
Party. Founded in 1849 as a secret patriotic order, it experienced
a period of phenomenal growth from 1852 to 1856, filling the
vacuum created by the gradual disintegration of the old Whig
Party, and attracting many of those who could not or would not
support the Democratic Party. The appeal of the newer Republican Party, however, to those who regarded the spread of slavery
as the paramount political problem of the day, and the split
within its own ranks over the question of slavery, so thoroughly
weakened the Know-Nothing Party that it had virtually disappeared as an effective political power by 1858.

Aside from its mystical appeal, its abracadabra of pass-words,
secret meetings, oaths and ceremonies, the Know-Nothing movement owed its remarkable rise to prominence to its appeal to
prejudice. It capitalized on the traditional Protestant fear and
suspicion of the Roman Catholic Church, and on the widespread
anxiety of native Americans that they would be overwhelmed
by the rising tide of Irish and German immigrants into the
United States. The adherents of the American Party were
pledged to vote only for the native-born, to campaign for a longer
period of probation before the naturalization of immigrants, and
to stand guard against the encroachments of "Popery." [1]

What of the Jews? They were another minority, though far less
numerous at any time and far less harassed than the Catholics in

58

earlier periods of American history. And, indeed, during the 1850's, probably seventy-five percent of the Jews in the United States were recent immigrants. What was the attitude of the Know-Nothing Movement towards the Jews, and what was their reaction to this American Party's brand of Protestant nativism?

I

On the national scene, the Jews were apparently ignored by the leading spokesmen of the movement. Nowhere in their speeches or writings, or in the national literature which they published, is there any indication of anti-Jewish prejudice.

In local situations, likewise, there was no area where anti-Semitism assumed major proportions in the Party's campaigns. When Jews were mentioned, the reference was likely to be incidental, an afterthought, a foot-note.

In Sacramento, California, for instance, Speaker of the House Stowe spoke disparagingly of the Jews when discussion arose on the subject of Jews' doing business on Sunday. Stowe said that Jews did not make good citizens and that he saw therefore no reason for legislating special favors for them; they did not intend to stay in California; their only reason for coming to the state was to make money quickly and then leave. [2] But this was by no means a major pronouncement, and there is no record of further vilification of the Jews by the California politician.

That narrow-minded and dogmatic Protestant clergymen who raved and ranted at Know-Nothing meetings against the Roman Catholic Church should also have been prejudiced against the Jews ought to be no occasion for surprise. According to the *Atlanta Examiner*, a Rev. Dr. H. V. M. Miller mixed some anti-Semitism with his anti-Catholicism at an American Party rally in Cassville, Ga. The reporter said:

.. After exhausting the calendar of abuse and calumny against Catholics and Foreigners, he (Dr. Miller) *un*-wittingly betrayed some of the *secrets* of the Order, unknown to the uninitiated, and perhaps to the supernumary mass of *initiated*. He condemned the course of the President, in having appointed Soule and Belmont, who not alone are Foreigners but foreign circumcised not-shaving and rag-trading Jews. He therefore not only thought them as Foreigners unworthy to hold office, but proscribed them also for being *Jews* . . . [3]

An itinerant missionary to the Jews, one Rev. Bonhomme, traveled through Ohio and Kentucky and "joyously hailed the Know-Nothings as additional living evidence of the truths set forth in the prophesies contained in the Bible," according to the Paducah *Democrat*, before proceeding to his real business of extracting money from Christian purses for the conversion of "the poor, ignorant Jews . . ." [4] Parson William G. Brownlow of eastern Tennessee was another Know-Nothing Protestant clergyman who inveighed against the *"Murderers of Christ"* as well as against the "Whore of Rome." [5]

In a few isolated instances, newspapers with Know-Nothing affiliations found occasion to level their attacks against the Jews. The *Item*, of Fort Adams, Miss., for instance, accused the Jews of attempting to gain control of Louisiana by dishonest business methods; it said that the Democrats, instead of fighting the "avaricious Shylocks," were coddling the Jews by nominating E. W. Moise for Attorney General. [6] The Tuskeegee *Republican* and the St. Louis *Weekly News* also recorded their antipathy towards the Jews in the midst of their Know-Nothing fulminations. [7]

Some Massachusetts Jews thought that Know-Nothing infiltration into Masonic circles had made it difficult for them to gain satisfaction or honor in the secret fraternity, [8] and a St. Louis Jew expressed the opinion that nativism had been responsible for the failure of many Jews to take part in political affairs, [9] but the only public warning of coming anti-Semitism which we have been able to discover appeared in the New York *Express*. The editor of that paper was annoyed at the anti-nativist policy of the *Asmonean* of New York. Jews are free in the United States, the *Express* stated, but the editor of the Jewish journal was arousing antagonism against his people by continuing his denunciations of the American Party. "What an absurdity then for a Jewish journal to be thus creating a prejudice that exists not now, against the Jews of the United States of America."[10]

One remarkable episode, which revealed the existence of both tolerance and intolerance occurred when the Party in Nashville permitted a Jew to be elected Vice-President of the Fillmore and Donelson Club during the 1856 Presidential election. A nativist newspaper thought it extremely unbecoming and inconsistent that this be so:

AMERICANS TO RULE AMERICA

At the Know Nothing meeting on Saturday night, those who went into the Order on account of the influence of the foreign population were a great deal astonished, when they heard the name of Mr. Sultzbacher called out as one of the Vice Presidents of the Fillmore and Donelson Club. Mr. Sultzbacher is a Jew of this city, dealing in ready made clothing, and, for ought we know, may preside at the meetings of the Know Nothing Club with a good deal of dignity. He may be very capable of keeping order when the dark lanterns assemble in the garrets and cellars of the city; but nevertheless the elevation of Mr. Sultzbacher to the high station surprised a good many who honestly thought that 'none but natives were to be put on guard.'[11]

Of course, this was an example of the fact that the Party, in many sections of the country, soft-pedalled its anti-Catholic or anti-foreign keynotes.[12] But it was undoubtedly significant that an immigrant Jew should be accepted into the councils of the Party to the extent of being elected to office.

II

Lest it be thought that these few expressions of anti-Jewish prejudice on the part of Know-Nothing supporters were typical only of the American Party, it is important to balance them by the citation of similar sentiments among supporters of the Democratic Party.

During the 1854 New York state gubernatorial campaign, a bizarre development took place. The Know-Nothings nominated Daniel Ullman, a former Whig lawyer who had been playing with politics for years, as their candidate. But the anti-nativist Democrats went the Know-Nothings one better by circulating various rumors about Ullman's ancestry and birth-place. One story had it that he was born in Germany,[13] another in India,[14] yet another in China.[15] The Albany *Journal* asserted that it had conclusive evidence in the fact that he had signed a hotel register as "Daniel Ullmann, Calcutta, India,"[16] and the New York *Daily Tribune* recalled that "when Mr. Ullman was a candidate for Attorney-General on the Whig ticket in 1850, his friends were very careful to have his name spelt with a double *n* at the end, and to state at the same time in the journals that this mode of spelling came from the German origin of the candidate . . ."[17] Most of these varying reports were agreed on one point: Ullman's family background was Jewish. So the Democrats sneeringly talked of the "turban-headed Jewish oriental" and dubbed the Know-Nothings "Hindoos."[18] In vain did poor Ullman protest the legitimacy of his nativity and religion, producing affidavits certifying to his birth of Protestant parents in Wilmington, Delaware.[19] The stories continued to make the rounds, and undoubtedly contributed to Ullman's failure to win more than one-third of the votes cast in the election. But the Democrats indicated that they were not averse to some underhanded and dishonest connivance at nativism when it helped their cause, for there was no truth whatever to the allegation that Ullman was of foreign and Jewish origin.

Of similar cloth was the 1856 effort of a Philadelphia German language newspaper to discredit the Republican nominee for the Presidency, John Charles Fremont, with the charge that he was born of Jewish parents and reared in Judaism. Much more frequent, however, were the charges that he was of Catholic birth. [20]

In Philadelphia, in 1855, the Democratic Party divested itself with great haste of one Sickels who was about to be nominated for the office of County Treasurer when he admitted belonging to a society "directed to preventing the Jews from holding those positions, and enjoying such rights as they may claim to occupy and enjoy under the Constitution." [21] Sickles, apparently, was of the opinion that his fellow Democrats would be quite willing to support a person with his kind of feelings towards the Jews.

In the South Carolina election campaign of 1854, serious anti-Jewish leanings were evidenced by the opponents of M. C. Mordecai, who was running for the office of State Senator. A campaign ticket was published with the heading "Hear, O Israel," listing Mordecai as the Jewish candidate for the Senate and sixteen other Jews as candidates for the office of Representative, which they were not! Most interesting, however, was the fact that Mordecai's opponents tried to smear him by circulating the rumor that he was a member of the Know-Nothing Party and that he agreed with its policy of "persecution of the Roman Catholic Religion and disfranchisement of naturalized citizens." Evidently there was no possibility of anyone's thinking that the Know-Nothings in South Carolina or Charleston were anti-Jewish. [22]

In New York City, a politician who spoke at a party rally in behalf of Fernando Wood, the Democratic candidate for Mayor, attacked the U. S. District Attorney for "appointing a

Jew," Philip J. Joachimsen, as an assistant in his office. Wood denied any knowledge of the speech, but Joachimsen, a Republican, thought it was convincing proof that the Democratic leaders had absorbed some of the Know-Nothing principles.[23]

It would make just as much sense, in other words, to say that the Democratic Party was anti-Jewish as to label the Know-Nothings as being intolerant towards the Jews. The truth of the matter is that evidences of such prejudice in the records of both parties are isolated and sporadic, by no means characteristic of national party policy.

III

It is clear, then, that the Know-Nothing Party was not anti-Jewish. How did Jews react to its appeal to prejudice, suspicion and fear?

Mr. Sultzbacher of Nashville was not the only Jew to be attracted to the Know-Nothing Movement. The *Asmonean* was bitterly sarcastic time and again about "our German friends" who were in favor of the anti-Catholic point of view — probably because they shared the anti-clerical sentiments of many European refugees. Isaac M. Wise asserted that he was attacked for his opposition to the Know-Nothings by "a number of Jews," presumably Cincinnatians, as well as by a favorite correspondent who, Wise felt, leaned towards nativism in order to be "like other American aristocrats."[24] Wise had several times to decline printing lengthy propagandistic articles in favor of Know-Nothing ideas which were sent to him by Jewish correspondents; they were too long, he said, or their reaction to his own stand was too vituperative.[25]

Why did these, and other Jews favor the American Party? For many reasons, some of which had no relationship to their being Jewish, we may be certain. Some Jews were honestly convinced that Roman Catholics could not be loyal Americans so long as they owed a "temporal" allegiance to the Pope; some were sincerely afraid that the millions of German and Irish immigrants would hold a balance of power in political affairs before they were well oriented to the American scene. But there were other Jews who felt that this was an admirable opportunity to take revenge on the Church which had been "Israel's persecutor," and to forestall any future opportunity the Church might have to become the majority religion in America and then begin to treat the Jews as they had been treated in some Catholic countries in Europe. These Jews gloried in the chance to ally themselves with the dominant Protestant forces in a movement which implied they were better Americans than the Catholics. This would seem to be the train of thought which led some Jews into active sympathy with the Know-Nothing Movement. [26]

It is, therefore, somewhat surprising that the great majority of recorded Jewish opinion on the merits of the Know-Nothing program was strongly in the negative. With the single exception of Lewis C. Levin of Philadelphia, who had been a leading Native American Party journalist and Member of Congress from 1845 to 1850, and who took only a minor role in the activities of the Know-Nothing Movement, [27] Jewish political figures seem to have been unconditionally opposed to its intolerant principles.

Although he had toyed with nativist ideas in 1844, by 1855 Judah P. Benjamin had altogether rejected the Know-Nothing philosophy. He said, in an interview published in the New Orleans *Daily Delta*, that he could not agree with the American Party

... because they are anti-republican in refusing equal political rights to all American citizens; because they violate the spirit, if not the very letter on the Constitution, by the proscription of citizens on the grounds of their religious belief; because they are a [tendency] towards a union of church and state ...; because the present issues are addressed to the passions and prejudices of the people ... [28]

65

Another Jewish Southerner, Congressman Philip Phillips of Mobile, Alabama, registered his opposition to the Know-Nothing agitation in no uncertain terms. He was scornful of its logic and bitter over its pretense of patriotism. Its leaders were doing the very thing they accused the Catholics of doing: dragging religion into politics. He began a lengthy epistle on the subject, which was published in the Mobile *Register* and republished in several Jewish journals, with a glowing tribute to the doctrine of separation of church and state:

... There is nothing clearer than that in the formation of the constitution it was intended emphatically to exclude all connection with any religious faith whatever. Separation of Church and State, eternal divorce between civil and ecclesiastical jurisdiction, were cardinal principles with the sages and patriots to whom not only we, but all mankind, are indebted for this model of a republican government ... They distinctly saw the evil fruits which the conjunction of political and religious power had everywhere traduced, and in the discharge of the high duty intrusted to them — the highest that man could be charged with — they determined to profit by the example, and inaugurate a "political system," whose dominion should be exclusively confined to the political relations of its constituents, acknowledging in the eye of the law the perfect equality of all sects and faiths, and leaving the whole subject of religion, and its requirements, to the dominion of that Higher Tribunal which alone can search the hearts and judge the motives of men ...

This American tradition clearly outlawed any such activities as were now being pursued by the Know-Nothing adherents. Moreover, said Phillips, what sense did their charges against the Catholics make, other than a sense compounded of hatred and prejudice:

... If a Catholic citizen, however capable and honest, be appointed to political position, a howl is heard throughout the land, and denunciation follows the appointment. What is the meaning of all this? I cannot be deceived by any "set phrase of speech." I tear off the flimsy disguise of words, and I behold the naked and hideous truth: Religious Intolerance! Party assemblies have met ere this; declarations of political principles have been common in our practice; new parties have been formed; old ones have been modified; but when before in our history has it been considered necessary to anathematize "the aggressive policy and corrupting tendencies of the Roman Catholic church?" When before has it been found proper to introduce religion into our political organization? When before was the fitness for political office tested not by the honesty or capability of the candidate, but by the religious faith he professed? Times have, indeed, changed, and we have changed with them. When the venerable Carroll took up the pen to affix his name to the immortal "Declaration," no man cried "Hold! you are a Catholic." If a new necessity has sprung up justifying a new law, then, I ask, where does it exist, and in what form does it appear? Surely Protestantism has not become so weak as to require protection from the arm of a political party . . . [29]

Phillips' analysis of the evils of the Know-Nothing Movement was theoretical and philosophical. Of a similar frame of reference was the declaration of opposition to the American Party formulated by the proponents of a fledgling political group in San Francisco in 1855 who styled themselves only as a group "opposed to Know-Nothingism;" one of the nine signatories calling for support in the battle against intolerance was A. C. Labatt, one of the founders and officers of Congregation Emanu-El of San Francisco. [30]

On the other hand, when M. C. Mordecai of Charleston spoke out gainst the Know-Nothings, his reasoning was personal and his reference to his own religion was obvious. He was astonished that he should be charged with membership in that party:

. . . It will, I hope, surprise most of you, my fellow citizens, to know that one of my race and creed is gravely charged or chargeable, at this day in the history of the world, with religious intolerance or national proscription. Such a charge is utterly untrue, and I respectfully suggest, that one moment's reflection will satisfy every one of you. I am not and would not be a member of any society that does not hold up the Constitution as the paramount law of the land, which guarantees civil and religious liberty to all. I should have no safety for my own rights of

67

conscience if I were to conspire to destroy them in others. I am utterly and unalterably opposed to any intermingling of sectarian religion with political affairs and contests . . .[31]

Mordecai's was the only forthright declaration of a Jew, as a Jew, who was in active political opposition to the Know-Nothing Movement.

But other Jews, who were not engaged in politics, believed that *as Jews* it was to their advantage to defeat the Know-Nothing bid for power. Said one who signed himself "L" in a letter to the *Asmonean*:

. . . The Israelites should *proscribe proscription;* and if all others are willing to connive at this stab on the Constitution of the United States, they, the sufferers for age after age, in almost every land, should to a man, stand firm . . . Let precedent be established, and you will find out, that Jews will have no better claim, than other unpopular minorities . . .[32]

Said another, one who used the name "Schwarzenski" in a letter to the *Israelite*:

. . . *We*, poor children of persecution, exiles for centuries, the oppressed of ages, we have felt too keenly the pangs, the humiliations, the untold and untelling miseries, which religious *intolerance* can inflict. Shall *we* assist bigots, in subjecting a church or sect, to all those horrors, which we have borne in the dark and blood-stained ages of the past? This surely should teach us *tolerance*, should teach us *liberty of conscience;* if our hearts be closed to *this* unresisting plea, *self-preservation* should prompt us to battle in the cause of *pure* religion, by opposing the invaders of both the *constitution* and the *Bible;* should these be unavailing incentives, to enlist our sympathies in the case of religion and republicanism. Can we as *Israelites*, disobey the very spirit and letter of our religion, which teaches "*To love thy neighbor as thyself.*". . .[33]

Isaac Mayer Wise, editor of *The Israelite* and a Democrat almost from the time of his arrival in America, followed a consistently anti-Know-Nothing policy in his editorials and news notes, although he frequently tried to call a halt to extended political discussions. Wise was convinced that the policies of the

American Party were bound to be injurious to the Jews, even though, according to the Cincinnati *Commercial*, "the Hebrew vote" of the city was, in 1854, "thrown almost unanimously in favor of the Know-Nothing candidates; and . . . the Know-Nothing leaders entertain strong hopes that they have attached the Hebrews permanently to their party." [34]

Firstly, as Jews, he thought, his co-religionists had a right to be suspicious of Know-Nothing intentions. Even though some Jews were admitted into the lodges, it was likely, Wise believed, that the leaders of the movement were prejudiced against the Jews as a group. The few examples of anti-Jewish propaganda on the part of the nativists which had been brought to his attention were enough to convince him that there was more here than met the eye. In addition, Jews had best beware, since so many of them were foreigners, and it was the avowed intention of the Party to curtail their rights. [35]

Furthermore, felt Wise, Jews ought to oppose the nativists out of patriotic concern for the integrity of America:

. . . [E]ven if there was actually anything to fear from the Romish Church, we would still abhor the very idea of religious intolerance. Is our republic so weak, so unsatisfactory, that we must fear its downfall by those, who enjoy its benefits, then it is high time, that the politicians repair those deficiencies, instead of persecuting those who are dissatisfied. If the idea of Romanism is dangerous to the republic, are the Catholics not a small minority? have we not a free press, liberty of speech? are these powerful instruments not strong enough to guard our republican institutions? where is your host of hired missionaries and book-peddlers? We beg you, in the name of common sense, do not so badly slander and outrage republicanism, as to tell us the lowest and most despicable passions of man, religious fanaticism and intolerance are necessary to guard republicanism. Do not, in the face of all history, past and present, endeavor to make us belief, [sic] Protestant fanaticism is any better than Roman fanaticism, or that a republic with exceptional laws, with a system of proscription for religious opinions is any thing like a republic . . . [36]

69

Wise rejected the arguments of those who felt that Jews would receive more decent treatment at the hands of a Protestant majority than they would in a society dominated by Catholics. "We cannot coincide," he said, "with Catholics or Protestants in politics; we want our constitution, but not their religion, nor their tolerance or intolerance." [37]

Although Wise was a Democrat, he did not urge his readers to vote the Democratic ticket in elections where Know-Nothing candidates were involved; nor did he urge a united front against the nativists. This was, however, the editorial urging of *The Asmonean*. Robert Lyon, its editor, seems to have been opposed to the Know-Nothing program not only for ideological reasons, but also on political grounds.

True, he wrote passionately against the "wretched croakings of the 'night raven of Jesuitism,' the present Know-Nothing Secret party." [38] "We abhor the thing," he said, "and our hatred is shown, not in the utterance of loud speeches, but in an unceasing activity to be effective at the ballot box." [39] He printed many letters and news reports with an anti-Know-Nothing cast, and was bitter about the Jews who "went, like sheep to the shambles, and voted the native ticket." [40]

But the *Asmonean* was also pro-Democratic. A box on the editorial page during the fall campaign of 1856 featured, week after week, the names of Buchanan, Breckenridge and Wood; it did not look like the paid advertisements which Tammany Hall inserted on other pages. [41] One long editorial calculated the chances of the Democratic Party, state by state, in a canvass which the editor felt frankly was a contest "between the friends of progress — of an unsectional government, and the advocates of sectionalism, abolition and intolerance;" Lyon felt assured the Democrats would win, as indeed they did. [42]

Lyon's advice to his fellow-Jews was clear: ". . . [W]hat

Hebrew can consistently support the standard of *Fillmore*, the nominee of the bitter Know-Nothings; or of *Fremont*, whose chief aid will be from the bigoted and persecuting New-England States?" [43] All Jews should join in supporting the Democratic Party:

... The Israelites are Democrats of old ... The policy of the Buchanan party is that of progression; the Israelites are progressionists — haters of papacy and priestcraft, opponents of proscription for religion sake, they, if not devoid of sense, cannot vote for a candidate who is mixed up with the advocacy of doctrines so fatal to republican freedom ... [44]

This was exactly the kind of policy which Isaac Leeser deplored, in his monthly *Occident*. He was not altogether convinced that the Know-Nothings were anti-Jewish. But even if they were, he felt that it was impractical for Jews to unite against them, because the Jews were so small a minority. What could they accomplish if religious lines were drawn taut?

... [W]e must say, that the Jews, as such, have no concern whatever in the question, while the new party has not displayed, as a portion of its doctrine, any marked hostility to our religion; and even then, it is very questionable whether any open combination would have the desired result, of permanently injuring a body which evidently can recruit on the very principle of anti-Judaism, if it be made its interest, from the vast amount of those differing from us, to a far greater extent than all the votes we could count on among ourselves to counteract its deeds and opinions ...

Leeser was not, of course, in favor of the Know-Nothing Party. He reprinted, at length, Phillips' eloquent appeal to reason and against bigotry. His own inclination was to avoid any admixture of religion and politics. He was convinced that

... in sober truth we have nothing to expect, no mercy to look to, if either the Protestant or Catholic party were to obtain the sole dominancy; they would soon put Judaism under the ban of proscription by legal and illegal means ...

The best counsel he could give his readers was this: "In the Synagogue and congregational meetings we want Jews; in public matters, only American citizens." [45]

Not so wary of committing themselves publicly, as Jews, were three rabbis who registered their opinion that the intolerance and bigotry aroused by the Know-Nothing Party were un-American. They were Bernhard Felsenthal of Lawrenceburg, Ind., David Einhorn of Baltimore, and Solomon Deutsch of Syracuse. [46] There was no doubt in their minds but that it was their duty as Jews and as Americans to oppose the spread of a movement which threatened the very foundations of civil and religious liberty.

IV

That the majority of Jews, most of whom were recent immigrants to the United States from countries where they themselves had suffered disability and discrimination, if they had any opinion at all, should have been among those who rejected the Know-Nothing philosophy, because of their own experience and the experience of their co-religionists, would seem altogether reasonable.

But why should the Party itself have all but ignored Jews, and, affirmatively, even accepted them into membership? For one thing, there were not enough Jews in the United States for any party to be able to create a case against them. What possible danger, on a national level, could there be to America from the approximately one hundred thousand Jews who were in the United States by 1855? If there had to be an enemy, the Catholics and the Irish and German immigrants (many of whom were Catholics) were at least numerous enough to be frightening to those who hated the Roman Church and were worried about the influx of immigrants. Jews were highly visible, but not in comparison with the others. That there was latent anti-Jewish prejudice was evidenced by a few bigots in all parties and by the sharp rise in propaganda against the Jews during the Civil War — but all this was on an individual and local level, never in an organized, national fashion. For another thing, the true objective of the Know-Nothing leaders was political power; one may question the sincerity or depth of their adherence to bigotry without doubting its danger. They were not interested principally in creating a multiplication of scape-goats; so other minorities, the Mormons for instance, against whom there was great prejudice, were not singled out any more than were the Jews. The omission of the Jews was not necessarily an indication that they were well regarded; rather was it an indication that they were not an indispensible victim of the Know-Nothings' drive for power.

The low incidence of anti-Jewish prejudice during a period of strong religious and ethnic tension and antagonism had a significant influence on the emotional attitudes of Rabbis Leeser and Wise. They were probably relieved that so little anti-Semitic propaganda was expressed in the midst of severe strain between Catholics and Protestants. This experience of 1850's was undoubted proof, to their way of thinking, that America would never be the scene of widespread prejudice against the Jews. Imagine their dismay and astonishment when, during the Civil War, as anti-Catholic propaganda gradually decreased, they sensed a growing antipathy towards the Jews. From our point of view, judging by the experience of Ku-Kluxers and Christian Fronters, the anti-Semitism of the Civil War period was of minor significance; but from Wise's and Leeser's point of view, judging by their own experience during the Know-Nothing period, the attacks and accusations of the 1860's *were* a rising tide which, by comparison, was cause for great concern and alarm.

73

V

An interesting aftermath to the relationship between the Jews and the Know-Nothing Movement occurred in late 1858, when Jews throughout the world were protesting the forcible abduction by Papal guards of young Edgar Mortara, the child of a Bologna Jewish family who had been secretly baptized a few years before at the behest of his Roman Catholic nurse. Protest meetings were held in Jewish communities throughout the United States, representative groups of Jews unsuccessfully urged President Buchanan to intervene, and petitions were circulated among Christians as well as among Jews.

The *cause célèbre* was ready-made for the Know-Nothings who had not yet given up hope of recouping their political losses. They joyfully participated in the protest activities, seeking to turn the Mortara case and the shocked feelings of American Jews to their own uses. In Albany, the Know-Nothing lodge passed a severe resolution against the Roman Catholic Church for refusing to yield up Edgar Mortara, joined with the Jewish community in a mass protest meeting, and then proceeded to hold another meeting of their own in which some Jews took part.[47] The Congressman who offered a resolution on the case in the national House of Representatives on January 10, 1859, was a Baltimore Know-Nothing leader, James M. Harris.[48] A Philadelphia Know-Nothing lawyer, Thomas Latimer, spoke at the large public meeting in that city and urged united action by Jews and Protestants; he said he had come to the meeting because he, "in common with many other Protestant Christians, felt the same as Israelites do in the outrage which had brought us together; that we should not be satisfied with merely passing a few resolutions and then dropping the subject, but we ought to agitate without ceasing in conjunction with Protestant Christians at large, so as to effect a security hereafter . . ."[49]

74

Undoubtedly there were other cases in which Know-Nothing sympathizers took an active role in the Mortara effort. Equally important, however, were the Republican politicians who hoped to draw Know-Nothing as well as Jewish voters to their standard by means of the Mortara hook and bait. Representative Schuyler Colfax was not reluctant to announce his opposition to the Democratic Party's refusal to register America's strong feelings in the case.[50] Philip J. Joachimsen, the New York Jewish Republican, took great pains to have a letter of protest which he wrote to Secretary of State Lewis Cass reprinted throughout the Jewish and general press.[51] Abraham Jonas of Quincy, Illinois, Lincoln's closest Jewish friend and an old Whig political figure who became one of the founders of the Republican Party in Illinois, wrote a frank and revealing letter on this subject to his friend Senator Lyman Trumbull, dated 26, 1858:

... By the Bye — a little honest *Bunguno* for you, preparatory to the fight of 1860, will do no harm — here in Illinois — we have no chance in the world for the Catholic vote. The Jewish abduction case at Rome is making considerable stir, among the Israelites here and among the liberal & free thinking Germans and also among our *Know-Nothings* — Could you not introduce some Resolution into the Senate on the subject — and get the Republican vote for it — Cass' answer to the Jewish Rabbi [refusing, as Secretary of State, to protest to the Pope] has offended *all my church* — and if you can consistently offer some resolution — *anti-Cass in sentiment* — it will make in this county a change of 100 votes — and unite the Jewish all over the Union — in the free states there are 50,000 Jewish votes — two thirds of whom vote the Democratic ticket — it would be an object to get them all on our side — *this is confidential*, but think of it — I conversed on yesterday with an intelligent German Jew from Cin[n] who is a Democrat — he is satisfied that 1000 votes in that city would be brought over to the Republican side, if the course suggested by me could be adopted ...[52]

Between Jewish, liberal German and Know-Nothing voters, Jonas hoped the Republicans would be able to profit from the Mortara episode. Trumbull's answer to Jonas cannot be located;

but the Illinois Senator never did introduce the suggested resolution.

With all this agitation and discussion, however, most of the Jewish protests, petitions and meetings concerning the Mortara Case were not tinged with Know-Nothing adherents or sentiments. Once again the Jewish community of the United States preserved its integrity from too close an identification with any political party or platform.

NOTES

[1] *Dictionary of American History*, New York, 1946, I, p. 64; Ray. A. Billington, *The Protestant Crusade*, New York, 1938; Gustavus Myers, *History of Bigotry in the United States*, New York, 1943, pp. 185–210.

[2] *ASM*, XII, No. 3, p. 21, May 4, 1855.

[3] *ISR*, II, No. 11, p. 86, Sept. 21, 1855. Soule was, of course, not a Jew; see *AJCW*, p. 287, for Belmont's lack of interest in Jewish affairs.

[4] *ISR*, I, No. 34, pp. 268–9, March 2, 1855.

[5] See below, pp. 104–5.

[6] W. Darrell Overdyke, *The Know-Nothing Party in the South*, Baton Rouge, 1950, p. 238.

[7] *Ibid.*, pp. 278, 282.

[8] *ISR*, II, No. 3, p. 20, July 22, 1855; No. 7, p. 52, Aug. 17; No. 12, p. 96, Sept. 28; No. 13, p. 101, Oct. 5; No. 15, p. 115, Oct. 19.

[9] Isidor Bush, "Historical Sketches of the Jews of St. Louis," *The Jewish Tribune*, Dec. 21, 1883, cited in Schappes, *op. cit.*, pp. 631–2.

[10] *ASM*, XII, No. 12, p. 92, July 6, 1855.

[11] *ISR*, III, No. 8, p. 62, Aug. 29, 1856.

[12] In Florida, for instance, the Know-Nothing Party proclaimed itself completely loyal to the principle of religious liberty; although it attacked David Levy Yulee, no mention was made of his religious origins; Arthur W. Thompson, "Political Nativism in Florida, 1848–1860," *Journal of Southern History*, XV (1949), No. 1, pp. 52–3, 56.

[13] *New York Times*, Oct. 17, 1854, p. 4.

[14] *New York Daily Tribune*, Oct. 13, 1854, p. 4.

[15] *New York Times*, Oct. 17, 1854, p. 4.

[16] *Ibid.*

[17] Oct. 13, 1854, p. 4.

[18] Harry J. Carman and Richard H. Luthin, "Some Aspects of the Know-Nothing Movement Reconsidered," *The South Atlantic Quarterly*, XXXIX (1940), No. 2, pp. 218–9; Louis Dow Scisco, *Political Nativism in New York State*, New York, 1901, pp. 121–5.

[19] *New York Times*, Oct. 19, 1854, p. 4; *New York Daily Tribune*, Oct. 25, 1854, p. 5.

[20] Myers, *op. cit.*, p. 208; Allan Nevins, *Frémont, The West's Greatest Adventurer*, New York, 1928, pp. 499–501.

[21] *ASM*, XII, No. 4, p. 28, May 11, 1855. Nothing further is known of this purported organization.

[22] *ASM*, XI, No. 1, p. 6, Oct. 20, 1854.

[23] *ASM*, XV, No. 4, p. 29, Nov. 7, 1856.

[24] *ASM*, XII, No. 9, p. 69, June 15, 1855; Wise, *Reminiscences*, pp. 310–2.

[25] *ISR*, I, No. 28, p. 224, Jan. 19, 1855; No. 38, p. 303, March 30.

[26] *ISR*, II, No. 2, p. 12, July 20, 1855; No. 13, p. 102, Oct. 5; *ASM*, XII, No. 2, p. 12, April 27, 1855.

[27] *DAB*, XI, pp. 200–1; Schappes, *op. cit.*, pp. 630–1.

[28] Louis Gruss, "Judah P. Benjamin," *Louisiana Historical Quarterly*, XIX (1936), No. 4, p. 34; Meade, *Judah P. Benjamin*, pp. 103, 119, 296; Overdyke, *op. cit.*, p. 9.

[29] *OCC*, XIII, No. 6, pp. 274–81, Sept., 1855; *ASM*, XII, No. 15, p. 116, July 27, 1855.

[30] *ASM*, XII, No. 9, p. 68, June 15, 1855. *ASM* prints the initials as "A. J." but this was undoubtedly an error. See Jacob Vorsanger, *The Chronicles of Emanu-El*, San Francisco, 1900, pp. 26 ff., for data about his activity in the congregation. On the other hand, it might have been Henry C. Labatt, author of a lengthy attack on Speaker Stowe which was originally printed in several northern California newspapers and reprinted April 7, 1855, in the Los Angeles *Star*, (copy provided to the writer by Rabbi Max Vorspan). Another signatory was Charles D. Judah. It has been impossible to identify him. Most members of that wide-spread family, however, had been Christians for several generations as, for instance, Theodore D. Judah, also of San Francisco, who was a Know-Nothing nominee for the office of Surveyor-General in 1855; Peyton Hunt, "The Rise and Fall of the 'Know-Nothings' in California," *Quarterly of the California Historical Society*, IX (1930), No. 1, p. 42.

[31] *ASM*, XI, No. 1, p. 6, Oct. 20, 1854.

[32] *ASM*, XII, No. 15, p. 116, July 27, 1855.

[33] *ISR*, II, No. 11, pp. 86–7, Sept. 21, 1855.

77

[34] *ASM*, XII, No. 2, p. 12, April 27, 1855.

[35] *ISR*, II, No. 13, p. 102, Oct. 5, 1855.

[36] *ISR*, II, No. 2, p. 12, July 20, 1855.

[37] *Ibid.*

[38] *ASM*, XII, No. 9, p. 71, June 15, 1855.

[39] *ASM*, XII, No. 10, p. 76, June 22, 1855.

[40] *ASM*, XIV, No. 18, p. 140, Aug. 15, 1856; see also XI, No. 26, p. 204, April 13, 1855.

[41] *ASM*, XV, No. 1, p. 4, Oct. 17, 1856, and preceding issues.

[42] *ASM*, XV, No. 3, p. 20, Oct. 31, 1856.

[43] *ASM*, XIV, No. 17, p. 132, Aug. 8, 1856.

[44] *ASM*, XIV, No. 18, p. 140, Aug. 15, 1856.

[45] *OCC*, XII, No. 11, pp. 557–63, Feb., 1855.

[46] Emma Felsenthal, *Bernhard Felsenthal, Teacher In Israel*, New York, 1924, p. 283; *PAJHS*, No. XVII (1908), p. 220; *AJCW*, pp. 21, 118. It is interesting to note that Felsenthal and Einhorn both became strong supporters of the Republican Party, and were the only two pronounced abolitionists in the American rabbinate.

[47] Schappes, *op. cit.*, p. 675.

[48] *Sinai*, IV (1859), p. 6.

[49] *OCC*, XVI, No. 9, pp. 450–3, Dec., 1859.

[50] See below, pp. 110–11.

[51] *New York Herald*, March 9, 1859, p. 1.

[52] Trumbull Collection, Library of Congress. For Jonas, see *AJCW*, pp. 189–94. This is Jonas' only opinion on a Jewish matter which the writer has located. But later, when Jonas feared that Lincoln might be smeared as a Know-Nothing sympathizer, he wrote in haste to Lincoln, who promptly urged Jonas to scotch the rumor. *AJCW*, p. 227.

IV

Judah P. Benjamin as a Jew*

THREE AUTHORS of recent books about Judah P. Benjamin, the brilliant Louisiana Senator, Confederate statesman and British barrister, have attempted to investigate the question of his interest in Judaism, and two of the three have chosen to accept, quite uncritically, some of the traditions which link him with Jewish religious worship. [1] It appears possible for the first time, however, to trace these stories to their origins, to determine their relative reliability, and to decide, somewhat more realistically, what kind of Jew Judah P. Benjamin actually was.

I

The first of these traditions which we shall examine is that one which asserts that when Benjamin was in San Francisco in the fall of 1860, participating in one of the leading mining suits of the day, *United States* v. *Castillero*, he revealed his religious loyalty by preaching a Yom Kippur sermon in one of the San Francisco synagogues. Herbert T. Ezekiel, the historian of Richmond Jewry, was the first to tell this story. [2] He quoted Rabbi Isaac Mayer Wise as his oral authority for the statement. Wise, of course, had not been in San Francisco in 1860; he made trips that year, as usual, but none to the West Coast. Where, then, did he get the idea that Benjamin had preached in a California synagogue?

* Published originally in *Publications of the American Jewish Historical Society*, No. XXXVIII, Pt. 3 (March, 1949), pp. 153–171.

Wise was a zealous reader of all of the Jewish papers which were published in the United States. He quoted news items from them many times in his *Israelite*; frequently his citations were only the prelude to objections to their proposals and opinions. In 1860, so far as we know, only one Anglo-Jewish paper was published in San Francisco, *The Weekly Gleaner*, edited by the Rev. Julius Eckman, a fire-brand immigrant who had traveled the length and breadth of America, occupying pulpits in Richmond, Charleston and Mobile before reaching the Pacific Coast. He created trouble (personal and ideological) wherever he appeared, and the *Gleaner* was even more a personal organ than the other Jewish periodicals of the time. Wise obtained practically all of his California news from its columns. Upon examination, however, the *Gleaner* proves to have published nothing about Benjamin's appearing for worship in one of the San Francisco synagogues, let alone preaching a sermon, on Yom Kippur, September 26, 1860.

On October 20, 1860, A. Englander, a San Francisco Jew, wrote the Rev. Isaac Leeser a full report of Jewish religious occurrences in the city, including digests of the sermons preached on the High Holy Days. He did not mention any sermon delivered by Benjamin. Indeed, his only comment about the famous lawyer and political figure was that he was in town: ". . . Senator Benjamin of Louisiana [is here] attending the celebrated New Almaden case." [3]

So much for that. Benjamin could not have preached in one of the synagogues on Yom Kippur or on any other occasion without its being noted in the *Gleaner* or in Englander's report to Leeser. The Jews of San Francisco would have wanted their coreligionists all over the country to know about so extraordinary an event, if it had actually taken place.

But Wise must have had some basis for the episode which he related to Ezekiel. And he actually did, although it became so confused as he remembered it in later years that it bore no resemblance to the facts. He had undoubtedly read, in the *Gleaner* of November 9, 1860, Eckman's report of an address which Benjamin had delivered two days previously:

Lecture. — Hon. J. P. Benjamin delivered a lecture on Wednesday evening last, at Tucker's Academy, which was indeed the gem of the season. The subject, although so dry and threadbare that every politician is familiar with it, has been handled by Mr. Benjamin, in a manner which elicited the admiration of both ladies and gentlemen.

We were agreeably disappointed [*sic!*] to hear such a masterly display of logic and erudition on the subject of Politics and Government; the lecturer used chaste and flowerly language — passed some fine encomias upon the immortal Washington, the States of California and Louisiana. *He next referred in a very happy manner to the injustice in the distribution of offices and asked why the citizens of his religious tenets were not favored by those who have it in their power to bestow offices of emolument and trust. In a very pathetic manner he asked, "Would the great Washington have excluded a citizen from holding a federal appointment because of his religion?"* Mr. Benjamin gave very excellent expositions of the machinations of the government; compared its workings under the guidance of the framers of the Constitution with those of the present day.

We have, for the first time in our life listened to an orator of the Roman School and are happy to claim such a man as our co-religionist. The Hall was crowded, not merely filled; and to such a degree that there was scarce standing room left for any one person. The great statesman and lawyer was repeatedly cheered during his discourse, which lasted an hour and a half, and he sat down amidst the prolonged applause of the audience whom he had delighted and edified. [4]

This, then, must have been the source of Wise's misinformation. All he remembered from Eckman's report was that Benjamin had spoken in San Francisco and referred to a Jewish problem. What more natural than that through the many intervening years Benjamin's reference to Jews in a public address should become embellished into a religious sermon? But Wise would probably have been more accurate in his transmission of the episode to Herbert Ezekiel if Eckman had not omitted one essential fact from his report in the *Gleaner*. The address had been delivered under the auspices of an Episcopal Church! Young Mr. McAllister, Pastor of the Church of the Advent of San Francisco, was the son of the judge who was presiding over the New Almaden trial; he had little difficulty, we may assume, in persuading the noted orator to deliver a lecture for the benefit of the church. [5] An unidentified San Franciscan, incidentally, believed that this event was a tribute to Benjamin's breadth of good-will; he wrote Attorney-General Jeremiah S. Black that "when you consider that Benjamin is a Jew, his labors in behalf of a Christian Church display a spirit of toleration pretty nearly unexampled." [6] Is it not ironic that the only instance in which Benjamin was supposed to have spoken in a synagogue turns out to be one of the many occasions when he spoke in, or for the benefit of a church?

Nevertheless, even if it was not a Yom Kippur sermon, the *Gleaner* had reported that Benjamin had made public reference to his Jewish origin and identified himself with his coreligionists by noting the prejudice against Jews which had, he said, made some headway in political circles. This report was, however, quite inaccurate. Eckman was either drowsy that evening and did not hear Benjamin aright, or he was so eager to identify Benjamin as an affirmative Jew that he misinterpreted what the Louisiana Senator did say. According to the printed version of the address, Benjamin was referring to the spoils system and political prejudice, not religious prejudice:

. . . I cannot, for my life, distinguish between the injustice of excluding entire masses of citizens from all offices of trust, honor or profit, and excluding them from all share in any other of the common advantages and benefits intended by the Constitution to be shared equally by all; and *when we find in the express language of our fundamental charter of government a prohibition against requiring any religious test as a qualification for office, can any rational man pretend that a partisan test would become the established, rigorous and exclusive rule in dispensing Executive patronage?* . . . I do reiterate a deliberate conviction that any indiscriminate removal of all subordinate encumbents from offices which they discharge with ability and fidelity, for the sole purpose of bestowing them as rewards on political adherents for partisan services, is to the last degree subversive of political morality; is a system . . . which the upright nature of Washington would have regarded as a contamination of his official integrity . . . [7]

This attack on the practices of the rival political parties had great merit; but it bore no relation to Benjamin's being Jewish. Indeed, this is quite in keeping with what we know of Benjamin's reluctance to speak of his own personal affairs, and with the absence of Jewish references in his published addresses. Mrs. Jefferson Davis said of him that "no more reticent man ever lived where it was possible to be silent." [8] It would have been completely out of character for Benjamin to have made public reference to the misfortunes of his people.

It is necessary, then, for us to expunge from our evidence concerning Benjamin's attitude towards Judaism, this unreliable story which is based on Wise's faulty recollection of Eckman's erroneous news report.

II

Isaac Mayer Wise is also the authority for another oft-quoted story about Benjamin's religious interests. He wrote in his *Reminiscences*, originally published in *Die Deborah* in 1874–75, of a visit to Washington in the fall of 1850, and of two discussions on religious subjects which he held with Daniel Webster, then Secretary of State, Lieutenant Matthew F. Maury, the famous oceanographer and scientist, and Judah P. Benjamin. When he called to pay his respects to the famous Massachusetts statesman, whom he had met on a previous visit to Washington, Wise was introduced to Maury and Benjamin. Then the conversation began:

"Mr. Senator," said Webster to Benjamin, "my friend is of your race. I would have said coreligionist, but I do not know how much or how little you believe; and in truth we four are all coreligionists, since we are all Unitarians." Maury objected to this, since he had never belonged to any Church organization, and had never made any confession of faith; and Benjamin protested likewise, since in his opinion Judaism and Christianity were entirely different . . .[9]

According to Wise, Benjamin was so interested in the discussions that he suggested a continuation of it during supper that evening. The other three accepted his invitation . . .

We assembled for dinner in a private apartment at Willard's Hotel. Webster began the interrupted conversation at once, and wanted to know my opinions. I referred to Theodore Parker's conception of Unitarianism, and set over against this my conception of Judaism. This forced me to the conclusion that there was no essential difference in the matter of doctrine, but in historical development which, however, did not enter into the question of doctrine. "It is well," said Webster, extending his hand to me; "you are indeed my coreligionist." Maury made the droll confession that he believed something of the same kind, but he had never had time to give it a definite form. Benjamin alone was not satisfied. He had a confused notion of orthodox Portuguese Judaism; and although he rarely heard anything about it, and was never guided by it, he yet insisted that he had no coreligionists beside the Jews. The conversation was most interesting to me; only I felt very sorry that Benjamin could not cite one Jewish source, while Webster was thoroughly versed in the Bible, and had a full knowledge of history . . .[10]

Wise's report of these conversations has generally been accepted by those who were in search of some evidence concerning Benjamin's religious concepts, even though his actions at all times belied these supposed sentiments. How square the opinion that Jews were isolated religiously from their fellow men with his lecture in behalf of the California church and with dozens of indications that he felt very much at home in Christian church services?[11]

No one, apparently, has sought to verify Wise's chronology. He nowhere states the exact day and month of his visit to

Washington; it apparently took place sometime in the fall or early winter of 1850–51, immediately after the formation of his new congregation in Albany. But Benjamin did not take office as Senator from Louisiana until March 4, 1853, the day on which Pierce was inaugurated! Webster, who became Secretary of State on July 22, 1850, had died on October 24, 1852! At no time, therefore, could Webster have addressed Benjamin as "Mr. Senator." Even more decisive is the fact that, so far as we know, Benjamin was nowhere near Washington during the time of Wise's visit, the fall of winter of 1850–51! The only time he traveled up to the north during 1851 was in *July*, when he conferred with President Fillmore about the Tehuantepec Isthmus railroad project. Webster was not then in Washington and Benjamin found it necessary to make the additional trip to Marshfield to consult the Secretary of State.[12]

The conversation, obviously, could not have taken place at the time and place and under the circumstances which Wise detailed. Perhaps Wise confused Benjamin with some other participant in the discussion. If Wise ever met Benjamin, on the other hand, it could not have been in Webster's office and presence.

That the entire episode is suspicious is documented by further evidence. On January 5, 1861, the *Boston Transcript* published, under title of "The Children of Israel," an editorial which asserted that the actions of Benjamin, Senator David (Levy) Yulee of Florida, and Mr. Benjamin Mordecai of Charleston, who had contributed $10,000 to the Confederate cause at the outbreak of the secession crisis, demonstrated the disloyal proclivities of American Jewry as a whole. Wise wrote a bitter reply to this editorial, arguing that the Jews were bound together only by their religion and that they were as divided in political affiliation as all other Americans, adducing as proof the Republican politics of thousands of Jews in the North. In commenting on the three men whom the *Transcript* had selected as typical Jews, Wise said, "we have had the pleasure of a personal acquaintance *only* with Mr. Mordecai, of Charleston, and know him as a man of distinguished intelligence and integrity . . ."[13] This obviously implied that he had met neither Benjamin nor Yulee. Was this not the time, if any, to record his meeting with the Louisiana Senator? On many other occasions, including his obituary sketch of Benjamin in the *Israelite*,[14] Wise had an ample opportunity to recall the alleged episode. He did not do so. One must conclude, therefore, that his memory was playing him false when he sat down to write his *Reminiscences*.

Unless further supporting evidence be located, the authenticity of this anecdote must of necessity be subject to question.

<h1 style="text-align:center">III</h1>

Herbert Ezekiel was one of those who made an effort to "prove" Benjamin's interest in Judaism. In his *History of the Jews of Richmond* he wrote:

> . . . it has been positively stated by the late Ellis Bottigheimer that he had seen Benjamin "called up" to the reading of the Law at Beth Ahabah Synagogue . . .[15]

It is extremely difficult to believe that Benjamin ever attended synagogue services in Richmond, let alone that he recited the Hebrew blessings before and after the reading of the Torah.

He lived in New Orleans for over thirty years and there is no evidence that he ever attended a religious service in that city. Had Benjamin ever indicated an active interest in New Orleans Jewish affairs, the fact would probably have been noted by Gershom Kursheedt, the hard-working leader of the New Orleans Jewish community, in one of the frequent reports which he wrote to his friend Isaac Leeser, many of which have been preserved in the Leeser Collection in the Dropsie College Library. Kursheedt was involved in every Jewish activity in New Orleans and was closely associated with the Jewish benefactions of that well-known New Orleans merchant and philanthropist, Judah Touro.[16] The only reference to Judah P. Benjamin in all of Kursheedt's letters to Leeser is contained in a communication dated March 20, 1848:

... Before I forget it let me state on Friday last Mr. J. P. Benjamin handed me $5.50 for you. I enclose in this a $10. note out of which please pay yourself that out & also a small sum which I owe you for an obituary, the Occident & anything else ...

Why should Benjamin give Kursheedt this sum for transmission to Leeser? When Leeser first began the publication of the *Occident*, he followed the practice of his day and entered subscriptions for certain persons known to be Jewish, without their approval, hoping that they would like the journal well enough to pay for it. If not, they were to notify him. Benjamin was one of a group of persons noted on the original list of subscribers to the *Occident* as "those who have not returned the earlier numbers, wherefore we consider them as subscribers ..."[17] It is not, of course, possible for us to say whether Benjamin ever read a single page of the magazine, but the fact that it was not until five years after the first number of the *Occident* appeared that Benjamin paid for it, and that he did not again give Kursheedt any money to forward to Leeser, would imply that he had not even been interested enough to ask Leeser to stop sending it, and that frequent billings were required before he consented to pay for the magazine he had not ordered. The only facts indicated by the *Occident* episode are, firstly, that Benjamin was identified as a Jew by Leeser, and, secondly, that he was acquainted with Kursheedt, Leeser's agent in New Orleans.

Furthermore, Benjamin's background had been Sephardic; this was a well-known fact — witness Wise's knowledge of this,

87

and his reference to it in his narrative of the Washington conversation. It is suspicious, therefore, that Benjamin should be reported to have attended services at the Germanic-ritual Beth Ahabah Synagogue, rather than at the Portuguese-ritual Beth Shalome Synagogue. The writer has discussed this point with the daughters of the Rev. George Jacobs, who was the rabbi of Beth Shalome Synagogue during the Civil War, and they do not remember that their father ever mentioned Benjamin's attendance at synagogue. Neither does George Jacobs' splendid Civil War scrapbook contain any clippings about Benjamin — strong presumptive evidence that Jacobs was not acquainted with the war-time cabinet member.

Indeed, Benjamin's actions were watched so closely that had he paid a visit to a synagogue, the hostile Richmond newspapers, or Representative Henry Foote of Tennessee, his arch-enemy, [18] or John Beauchamps Jones, the War Department clerk who cherished a venomous hatred for Benjamin and all Jews which he expressed on page after page of his Civil War diary, [19] would surely have made some comment on Secretary Benjamin's fellowship with his coreligionists. Actually, so many reports were current about his favoritism towards Jews that any visit to a synagogue would have been fodder for the propaganda mills which ground out attacks upon him all during the war.

Again, as we know, when prominent Jews wish to identify themselves with Jewish religious life, they tend to express their interest through the regular payment of membership dues rather than through occasional attendance without nominal membership. It is perfectly logical for an indifferent Jew who can afford it to support a synagogue financially; it is illogical for a prominent, wealthy man to attend services even rarely without being willing to be enrolled as a member. Neither the minute books of the Richmond congregations, which Ezekiel consulted, nor the accounts of the Kahl Montgomery congregation, [20] which the writer has studied, reveal any such nominal membership on Benjamin's part.

Definite as was Bottigheimer's statement to Ezekiel, the evidence to the contrary appears to be so weighted that we are unable to accept the account of Benjamin's attending services and being called up to the pulpit to participate in the reading of the Torah.

IV

Another legend relates Benjamin to the Washington Hebrew Congregation. Rabbi Abram Simon in 1905 published a report which he had heard from an old member of his congregation, to the effect that while they were "worshipping at Finkman's Hall (near the Engine House)," the members "rejoiced in the possession of a new Scroll and the distinguished honor of holding it on this special day of celebration fell to the happy lot of the Hon. Judah P. Benjamin."[21]

Judah P. Benjamin was, needless to say, not a member of the Washington Hebrew Congregation, which was not formally organized until 1856. He was not a signatory to the petition for a Congressional charter; he had no comment to make when the petition was presented to the Senate; his name does not appear on the congregation's membership lists. Indeed, had he ever applied for membership, it is questionable whether he could have been accepted; one of the articles of the congregational constitution provided that "any member marrying contrary to our religious laws shall forfeit his or her membership."[22]

Had Benjamin been invited to the celebration, then it would have been as an outsider. The facts of the case, as given in the *Washington Evening Star*, February 25, 1856, are that Benjamin was invited to attend a benefit party at Harmony Hall, on February 24, which the congregation gave *in order to raise funds for the purchase of a new Torah scroll.* Not only was there no new Torah for Benjamin to hold, but he was not even there. The *Star* article gives the conclusive information that "letters were read from the Hon. J. P. Benjamin, of Louisiana, and the Hon. P. A. Phillips, of Alabama, the latter enclosing a check for ten dollars." [23]

Phillips, former Congressman from Mobile, showed enough interest to send a contribution; Benjamin did not even take the opportunity to indicate his concern for Jewish religious life in the nation's capital. The letter which he wrote cannot be located, but in all likelihood it said little other than the usual formalities of "regrets." Had Benjamin made any positive Jewish affirmations in the letter, the congregational officers, with their customary zeal, would have sent copies of it to the Jewish periodicals of the day, to spread it far and wide throughout the country. Here again, a tradition pursued to its source indicates Benjamin's total indifference to his ancestral religious faith.

V

There was at least one occasion which seemed to demand a public affirmation by Benjamin of his Jewish background and familial ties. It was in 1854, a little over a year after he took his seat in the Senate, when Jewish public opinion was aroused over the injustice of the 1850 American commercial treaty with Switzerland. The Swiss cantons which would not allow Jews to take up residence within their borders insisted that each canton be permitted to determine whether non-Christian American citizens should or should not be exempted from such restrictions. There was much debate in the daily press and in the Senate on this question of discrimination against American citizens by a foreign power. [24] Senator (later Secretary of State)

Lewis Cass took a very strong position against the Swiss when he presented a petition from a committee of New York Jews to the Senate on April 19, 1854. He said, in part,

... In their migrations [the Jews] have at length reached a continent unknown to the patriarchs by whose rivers they may sit down without weeping in the language of their psalmist, even when remembering Zion, and where the law secures equal rights to all, be they Jew or Gentile. Exposed as the members of this persuasion yet are in portions of Europe and America, both Protestant and Catholic, to the most illiberal prejudices and to religious disabilities, the position of our citizens abroad who belong to it has peculiar claims to the consideration and interposition of the government. Beside their legal right to equal protection there is no portion of our population whose peaceable and law-abiding conduct better proves than theirs does, that they are well entitled to all the privileges secured to every American by our system of government . . . [25]

Webster, Clay and President Fillmore were among those American statesmen who had, during previous years, announced their opposition to the ratification of a treaty which would permit the Swiss cantons to discriminate against some American citizens. [26]

Benjamin was a Senator during the later period of this lengthy debate. He may even have been present when Cass made his appeal for justice to American Jews. He himself would or might have been excluded from several of the Swiss cantons had he ever visited that country. Was not this the time to stand up and be counted? Was not this, more than any other occasion, the ideal opportunity for him to identify himself with his coreligionists and to use his great influence for a righteous cause? (The treaty, incidentally, was finally passed with the discriminatory clause worded differently, but nevertheless intact.)

We may not even excuse him on the ground that the matter had been referred to a committee and was therefore not open to debate. Benjamin had the chance on May 10, 1854, when

91

he presented a petition on the subject. He had the floor and the opportunity to express his convictions, but, according to the *Congressional Globe*, all that happened was this:

MR. BENJAMIN presented . . . a petition of citizens of the United States, professing the Jewish religion, praying that measures may be taken to secure to American citizens of every religious creed, residing or traveling abroad, their civil and religious rights; which was referred to the Committee on Foreign Relations. [27]

Perhaps his colleagues in the Senate were impressed by the fact that the only Jew then serving in the Senate (Yulee served in 1846–51 and 1855–61) was not interested enough in the Swiss affair to comment upon it from the floor.

In 1860 the Jews of America faced the same problem in reference to the commercial treaties with China and Japan. Provision was made only for the protection of the right of Christians to worship as they chose. [28] Rabbi Max Lilienthal of Cincinnati wrote to Senator Benjamin and urged his support for the Jewish effort to make the guarantee a general one which would apply to all American citizens, whatever their faith. Benjamin's answer was polite and proper:

Washington, March 24, 1860

My dear Sir:

I have received your favor of the 21st inst., and shall be watchful of the China treaty, in order to take care that by no omission shall the Israelites of the United States be debarred the privileges secured by the treaty to their Christian fellow citizens.

Thanking you for your complimentary expression toward myself, I remain,

Yours with great respect,
J. P. BENJAMIN.

Rev. Dr. Lilienthal. [29]

Even though he had no serious intention of taking a public stand in the matter (as he did not) the least that the Senator could have done would have been to indicate that he was a Jew and recognized his own personal stake in this question of equal rights.

The fact that Benjamin did not feel obliged, in either of these cases, to register himself as a Jew would appear to be much more significant than any of the questionable traditions and legends concerning allegedly defiant answers which he is purported to have made to anti-Jewish attacks upon himself. [30]

VI

Altogether, then, it would appear that *Benjamin had no positive or active interest in Jews or in Judaism.* The only known facts are that he was born into a Jewish family, [31] that a Hebrew volume was among his possessions during his student years at Yale University, [32] that he received and paid for the *Occident* for at least one year, and that he never denied being Jewish or sought to escape his background through conversion to the Catholic faith of his wife and daughter. [33]

Nevertheless, he was unquestionably one of the most distinguished Jews in all American history. Unless we are so fast fettered to the abolitionist interpretation of the Civil War and its causes that we cannot admire strength of character and brilliance of administration in a slave-owner and cabinet leader of the "Lost Cause," we must surely rank Benjamin high in the story of America.

But what is his importance for American Jewish history? What role shall we assign him in the story of the American Jewish community, recognizing the fact that he did not participate by word or deed in the affairs of that community.

Benjamin's career has a two-fold significance for the American

Jew. In the first place, he is a symbol of American democratic practice as it functioned in the life of a member of the Jewish religious minority. Without abandoning his faith or denying it, he was elected to high positions of authority and was offered such diverse appointments as the Ambassadorship to Spain and a seat on the Supreme Court of the United States. The most serious responsibilities of the Confederate cause were entrusted to him: he was, successively, Attorney General, Secretary of War, and Secretary of State, serving in the cabinet in one capacity or another during the entire period of the organized Confederacy. Without a question he achieved greater political power than any other Jew in American history. This was an indication that American political life was open to some Jews of outstanding ability.

On the other hand, as the obverse of this fact, the expressions of anti-Jewish prejudice [34] to which his opponents (both North and South) stooped during his years of high office were a clear warning that some Americans would use any weapon, including the appeal to latent bigotry, to attempt to destroy a political opponent in a time of severe social stress. The countless attacks upon Benjamin *as a Jew*, which have been duplicated more recently in the cases of such political figures as Louis D. Brandeis, Felix Frankfurter, David Lilienthal, and the late Sidney Hillman, served to make him important in American Jewish history *as an object of prejudice*. Like every Jew who rises above the average to positions of prestige, affluence, or power, Benjamin had to pay the price of his birth, and the community to which he belonged and yet in whose life he showed no interest had to suffer intolerant and unjustified attacks as a concomitant of his political career.

Here lies Benjamin's role in the story of American Jewry: despite his origin, he rose to a position of commanding importance in the American political system; because of that position, his opponents turned for aid to the ancient political weapon of anti-Jewish prejudice, thereby uncovering the latent hatred-suspicion of Jews which then existed and which, unfortunately, continues to exist today, in the American social fabric.

NOTES

[1] The two volumes are Robert D. Abrahams, *Mr. Benjamin's Sword*, Philadelphia, 1948, a fictionalized tale for young people, (see p. 141), and Martin Rywell, *Judah Benjamin, Unsung Rebel Prince*, Asheville, 1948, an undocumented biography (see pp. 37, 45–46). Robert Douthat Meade's *Judah P. Benjamin, Confederate Statesman*, New York, 1943, is a fine, critical biography. Meade is very cautious in his acceptance of some of the traditions treated in this essay. He has a realistic grasp of Benjamin's relationship to his background (see pp. 49–50, 285). The only questionable interpretation Meade makes is his statement (p. 285) that "[Benjamin] was friendly, but not partial to the Jewish soldiers, of whom over 10,000 served the Confederacy, some with conspicuous bravery." (The statistics, of course, are greatly exaggerated. The figure might be true for *both* Union and Confederacy, but should probably be cut to one-fifth for the South). Meade refers here to an article by one M. Goldsmith (reprinted in Simon Wolf, *The American Jew as Patriot, Soldier and Citizen*, Philadelphia, 1895, pp. 102–4) who says that, when asked by the Rev. Michelbacher of Richmond to intercede with Benjamin for religious furloughs for Confederate Jewish soldiers during the High Holy Days, he assured the rabbi that he could pledge Benjamin's interest, although the whole question was not within the province of the (then) Secretary of State. Meade takes Goldsmith's word for it that, if he had been asked, Benjamin would have been "friendly." There is no supporting evidence for this assertion, as there is none for Goldsmith's highly exaggerated statistics of Confederate Jewish soldiers.

[2] Herbert T. Ezekiel and Gaston Lichtenstein, *The History of the Jews of Richmond from 1769 to 1917*, Richmond, 1917, p. 169; Ezekiel, "The Jews of Richmond During the Civil War," in *ISR*, LXI, No. 51, p. 1, June 17, 1915. See Rywell's rhapsodic description of this supposed episode, *op. cit.*, p. 37.

[3] Letter in Leeser Collection, Dropsie College Library.

[4] *The Weekly Gleaner*, IV, No. 40, p. 5, Nov. 9, 1860. Italics ours.

[5] Meade, *op. cit.*, p. 133.

[6] Letter, Nov. 9, 1860, in National Archives, quoted in Meade, *op. cit.*

[7] *An Address upon the General Changes in the Practical Operation of our Constitution Compared with its Theory, Delivered by Invitation of the Church of the Advent, In San Francisco, November 7th, 1860, by the Hon. J. P. Benjamin, of Louisiana*, San Francisco, 1860, pp. 14–16. Italics ours.

[8] Meade, *op. cit.*, p. 297.

[9] Wise, *op. cit.*, p. 184.

[10] *Ibid.*, pp. 187–88.

[11] See, for instance, Meade, *op. cit.*, pp. 313–14, for the Rev. Dr. Moses Hoge's comments on Benjamin's attendance at Christian prayer services.

[12] *Ibid.*, pp. 74–75, 86.

[13] *ISR*, VII, No. 30, p. 238, Jan. 25, 1861. Italics ours.

[14] *Ibid.*, XXX, No. 46, May 16, 1884, p. 3.

[15] Ezekiel and Lichtenstein, *op. cit.*, p. 170.

[16] In this connection, is it not strange that Benjamin, apparently, ignored Touro's death, so widely heralded in the city in which he lived and the state which he represented in the Senate? The newspapers, civic officials, Christian as well as Jewish organizations, participated in the public mourning and in the funeral exercises. (See Leon Huhner, *The Life of Judah Touro*, Philadelphia, 1946, pp. 102 ff.) There is no record of a statement by Benjamin, although one might have been expected from the Louisiana Senator.

[17] *OCC*, I, No. 4, p. 216, July, 1843.

[18] For Foote's prejudice against Benjamin and the Jews, see, for instance, "Proceedings of the First Confederate Congress, Third Session," *Southern Historical Society Papers*, XLVII, 1930, pp. 121–22, 144; Meade, *op. cit.*, pp. 235, 305; *AJCW*, pp. 178–9, 183–4.

[19] See almost any page of *A Rebel War Clerk's Diary at the Confederate States Capital*, 2 vols., New York, 1936.

[20] In American Jewish Archives. Nor did Benjamin affiliate with a synagogue or any other Jewish institution during his years of residence in London; *The Jewish Chronicle*, May 9, 1884.

[21] Abram Simon, *History of the Washington Hebrew Congregation*, Washington, 1905, p. 19.

[22] Abram Simon, "Notes of Jewish Interest in the District of Columbia," *PAJHS*, No. XXVI (1918), pp. 213–17.

[23] Reprinted in *ISR*, II, No. 35, p. 283, March 7, 1856.

[24] For the fascinating story of this "crusade" see Sol M. Stroock, "Switzerland and American Jews," in *PAJHS*, No. XI, (1903), pp. 7–52.

[25] Quoted in *ibid.*, pp. 20–21.

[26] *Ibid.*, pp. 8–10.

[27] *Congressional Globe*, 33rd Congress, First Session, Vol. XXVIII, Part 2, p. 1144.

[28] Stroock, *op. cit.*, p. 47.

[29] *ISR*, VI, No. 40, p. 317, April 6, 1860.

[30] See Max J. Kohler, "Judah P. Benjamin: Statesman and Jurist," *PAJHS*, No. XII (1904), pp. 83-4, for the various versions of the legend that Benjamin replied in this wise to an anti-Jewish utterance: "It is true that I am a Jew, and when my ancestors were receiving their Ten Commandments from the immediate hand of Deity, amidst the thunderings and lightnings of Mt. Sinai, the ancestors of my opponent were herding swine in the forests of Great Britain." Four different sources are referred to, each detailing a different time, place and opponent; all this in addition to the coincidence that the retort is also credited to Disraeli. Benjamin was reticent to the extent of self-effacement; it is extremely unlikely that he ever made this or any other reply to an anti-Jewish attack. Nor should we expect him to have done so, in the light of his silence during the Swiss affair.

[31] Meade, *op. cit.*, pp. 3 ff.

[32] *Ibid.*, p. 22. As Meade points out, Hebrew was a required subject for all students. It is entirely possible, therefore, that the Psalter he owned was not a personal possession brought from home, but a textbook purchased in New Haven for use in class.

[33] On May 29, 1901, in a letter preserved in the Kohler Collection, Library of the American Jewish Historical Society, E. W. Kruttschnitt, Benjamin's nephew, wrote as follows to Max Kohler:

> ... You refer to a statement in some unauthoritative works that Mr. Benjamin shortly before his death became a convert to Catholicism. I would state that I never believed this statement, although I have frequently heard it. While I was in Europe in 1886 I was the guest of Mrs. Benjamin at her residence in Paris and I there heard some reference to this matter. The conviction which was forced upon me, although I can hardly give you any definite basis for the conviction, was that when Mr. Benjamin was practically dying, and possibly unconscious, his wife and daughter, who were most devout Catholics may have obtained his consent for the call of a priest, and he may even have gone through some form of joining the Catholic Church, and may have received the last rites of that church ... [A]t the time that I was a visitor in Paris, Catholic priests of great intelligence, and of high standing, were constant visitors at the house, and many of them were quite accomplished men of the world. You will therefore see that Mr. Benjamin being surrounded by a Roman Catholic atmosphere for a couple of years before his death, may have become a convert when on his death bed ... My own impressions, for which again I have no positive basis, are that he did not actively affiliate with any church or religious community subsequent to his departure from Orleans to join the Confederate Cabinet in 1861, and I also think that this would apply to his life for a good many years prior thereto, although he certainly, up to a very short time before his death, was an avowed, though probably not a practising Jew ...

[34] See notes 18 and 19 above, Meade, *op. cit.*, pp. 112, 173, 218, 224, 250, 251, 280, 322, and *AJCW* p. 177, for a few examples of this anti-Jewish propaganda.

V

The First Jewish Prayer in Congress*

I

FEBRUARY 1, 1860, marked an important stage in the growth of the Republican Party and, therefore, in the chain of events which culminated in the secession of the Southern states after the election of Abraham Lincoln. For the eight weeks since Congress had been called to order, a mixed multitude of Administration Democrats, anti-Lecompton Democrats, Know-Nothing Americanists, radical and conservative Republicans had been jousting for power. Because no one group had been able to gain control of the House by the election of a Speaker, no business whatever had been transacted. There had only been, day after day, increasingly acrimonious debate on the bitter issues which were dividing the political forces of the nation. Forty-three ballots had already been conducted, each revealing the failure of any group of Representatives to gain enough adherents to form a majority. Finally, on that day, the Republicans switched their support from John Sherman of Ohio, generally regarded as a dangerous radical, to William Pennington of New Jersey, a self-proclaimed moderate, and, on the forty-fourth ballot, succeeded in electing him as the first Republican Speaker of the House of Representatives. This opening gun of the 1860 Presidential election gave dramatic proof of the growing strength of the new Northern party, barely four years old.[1]

By a remarkable coincidence, February 1, 1860, also marked a significant event in the history of American Jewry. For the

* Published originally in *The Hebrew Union College Annual*, XXIII, Part II (1951–2), pp. 95–125.

first time in all the years since sessions of Congress had been opened with prayer by a clergyman, a rabbi performed that religious office. In more than a theoretical sense, therefore, this was the initial recognition by the House of Representatives of the equal status of Judaism, with Christianity, as an American faith. Presidents and other public officials had long since issued statements and written letters which took cognizance of the existence of Judaism, [2] but, except for an implied, unspecified inclusion of Judaism in the general category of "religion," as for instance in the Bill of Rights, Congress had never heretofore given its official sanction to the faith of Israel.

The rabbi was one of the most distinguished leaders of the age: Dr. Morris J. Raphall of Congregation B'nai Jeshurun of New York City, whose reputation as a preacher we have already noted. It was, as we shall see, more accident than design that Rabbi Raphall gave this first Jewish prayer in Congress, but no more representative spokesman could have been selected. [3]

This is the prayer with which Rabbi Raphall opened the session of the House of Representatives at noon on that significant day in 1860, as it was printed (including the transliterated Hebrew!) in the *Congressional Globe,* [4] predecessor of the *Congressional Record* of today:

Almighty and most merciful God, we approach Thy presence this day to thank Thee for Thy past mercies, and humbly to beseech Thee to continue and extend the same to Thy servants, the Representatives of these United States in Congress assembled.

Lord, great and manifold have been Thy bounties to this highly-favored land. Heartfelt and sincere are our thanks. While the vast despotisms of Asia are crumbling into dust, and the effete monarchies of the Old World can only sustain themselves by yielding to the pressure of the spirit of the age, it has been Thy gracious will that in this Western hemisphere there should be established a Commonwealth after the model of that which Thou, Thyself, didst bestow on the tribes of Israel, in their best and purest days. The Constitution and the institutions of this Republic prove to the world that men, created in Thy image and obedient to Thy behests, are not only capable, fully capable, of self-government, but that they know best how to combine civil liberty with ready obedience to the laws, religious liberty with warm zeal for religion, absolute general equality with sincere respect for individual rights. In acquiring and carrying out these most wise institutions, Thy protection, Lord, has been signally manifest. It was Thy right hand that defended the founders of this Commonwealth, during the long and perilous struggle of right against might. It was Thy wisdom that inspired them when they established this Congress, to be what Thy tabernacle, with the urim and thummin — right and equity — were intended to have been for the tribes of Israel — the heart of the entire nation, where the wants, the feelings, and wishes of all might become known, to be respected by all, so that union might create strength, and concord keep pace with prosperity.

Lord, the ordinary life-time of a man has barely elapsed since this Constitution came into force, and under its auspices our country, from being feeble and poor has become wealthy and powerful, ready to take rank with the mightiest, and Thou, O Lord, wilt realize unto it Thy gracious promise unto Thy chosen people: Vehosircha adonai letobeh — the Lord will distinguish thee for that which is good.

Supreme Ruler of the universe, many days and many weeks have gone by since thy servants, our Representatives, first met in this Congress, but not yet have they been able to organize their House. Thou who makest peace in Thy high Heavens, direct their minds this day that with one consent they may agree to choose the man who, without fear and without favor, is to preside over this assembly. To this intent, Father most gracious, do Thou endow them with Thy spirit; the spirit of wisdom and of understanding; the spirit of counsel and of amity; the spirit of knowledge and of fear of the Lord. Grant, Father, that amidst the din of conflicting interests and opinions, Thy grace may direct them so that each one of them and all of them may hold the even tenor of their way — the way of moderation and of equity; that they may speak and act and legislate for Thy glory and the happiness of our country; so that, from the North and from the South, from the East and from the West, one feeling of satisfaction may attend their labors; while the whole people of the land joyfully repeat the words of Thy Psalmist: "How good and how pleasant it is when brethren dwell together in unity."

Lord God of Abraham, of Isaac, and of Jacob, I, Thy servant, beseech Thee bless these Representatives, even as Thou has directed Thy priests to bless Thy people.

Yebarekeka adonai Veyishmireka.

Ya-air adonai panaraleka wy-chaneneka.
Yissa adonai penar aleka veyasem Leka Shalom.
May the Lord bless ye and preserve ye.
May the Lord cause his countenance to shine upon ye and be
gracious unto ye.
May the Lord raise his countenance unto ye and grant ye peace.
May this blessing of the one who liveth and who reigneth forever rest
upon your counsels and yourselves this day, and evermore. — Amen.

According to the *Globe* and other reports, the galleries were
crowded that day when Dr. Raphall gave the invocation. It was
anticipated that the Republican-Democrat deadlock would be
broken, and an enthusiastic and eager assemblage of spectators
was present to witness the final decision. How did the Representatives of the American people and the non-elected political
sight-seers in the galleries react to Rabbi Raphall and his prayer?
Were they conscious of the fact that Congressional tradition had
been ignored, and that a non-Christian was praying for his
country in the Capitol for the first time? Did those who stood
with bowed head understand the drama of the moment?

The prayer itself appears to have been well received. The
Washington representative of the Associated Press wrote that
it "abounded with fervently expressed patriotic and religious
sentiment . . . [and] was listened to with marked attention."
Most newspapers, unable to maintain their own staff in Washington, utilized the services of the Associated Press and, therefore, this comment, together with a brief precis of the prayer
itself, was printed widely throughout the country. [5] The Washington correspondent of the *New York Herald*, however, actually
sensed an air of drama in the House that noon. He telegraphed a
most enthusiastic dispatch to his managing editor: "the beautiful prayer of Dr. Raphall . . . produced a profound impression
upon the minds of the multitudinous and intelligent and liberal
Christian audience that surrounded him, and a profound recognition, too, of the sublime American principle of civil and

religious liberty." [6] A reporter for the Philadelphia *Press* sounded the one sarcastic note: beautiful as the prayer was, he said, it was long enough to be a sermon! [7]

A Southern Jew who happened to be in Washington that day heard that this extraordinary event was to take place, and succeeded in obtaining a seat in the gallery of the House. He made most meticulous notes on the proceedings, [8] recording particularly his own awe-stricken reaction:

... As the minute hand of the large clock opposite the Speaker's chair was approaching the hour of noon, a kind of impatient expectation seemed to prevail in the galleries which was interrupted by a buzzing sound, "There he is," and every eye was turned towards the Speaker's chair. Next to that chair, but one step lower, was seated an old man with a *Tallith* over his shoulders, and a velvet cap on his head. I at once recognized the Rev. Dr. Raphall, whose lectures on the Poetry of the Bible I had attended ten years ago, at Savannah. He appeared fatigued; and, as he looked languidly around him, I asked myself, How would I feel if, young and strong, and business-man as I am, I were about to address two hundred and fifty of the most talented and gifted men in the country, besides the immense crowd in the galleries, whose feelings, I have no reason to expect, are prejudiced in my favor? and, as I did not feel quite sure of my own moral courage, I began to doubt whether that pale old man would have nerve enough for the occasion. . .

This "American Jew," as he proudly signed his letter to the Rev. Isaac Leeser, need have had no fears for the composure of Dr. Raphall, as was readily apparent within a few moments. The Clerk of the House banged his gavel, the assemblage arose, and the rabbi began his invocation:

... He had uttered but few words, when his eye kindled, his pale face became flushed, and, with a voice strong, clear, and filling the entire hall, he offered his orisons to the "Lord God of Abraham, of Isaac, and of Jacob." The effect was wonderful; the members had all risen from their seats. At first their feeling seemed to be that of malicious curiosity; but as his melodious sentences, his correct elocution, and impressive intonation fell upon their ears, the change was most striking both in the hall and in the galleries. Curiosity made room for attention, and that soon became devotion. Startling was the effect when he besought Him "that maketh peace in the high heavens," to direct the minds of the Representatives to elect a man to preside over them "without fear and without favor." . . .

But, above all, our reporter was most entranced with his own emotional response to the spectacle of a religious leader of his own faith praying in the manner of the Fathers in this legislative chamber of the nation. He did not attempt to conceal his enthusiasm:

. . . And when he pronounced the benediction, my heart leapt within me for joy, as I saw the proud Representatives of the United States submissively bow their heads to receive the blessing of "the ONE who liveth and reigneth forever." So proud, so happy, so delighted was I with the impression made by this beautiful prayer, delivered with the fluency and self-possession of a practiced orator, and with the fervent piety of the faithful servant of his God, that I intended to have the words engrossed on vellum, framed, and glazed, as an ornament to my home in the Sunny South.

A son of Israel would naturally be so profoundly moved. What of those who looked at the rabbi with "malicious curiosity?" The *Herald's* reporter jotted down some of the comments he overheard during the prayer and afterwards: [9]

"The old chap in his regalia. Beautiful white embroidered scarf over his shoulders. Velvet cap on his head . . ."

"Going to pray for ten per cent. a month . . ."

"A Jew praying for the American House of Representatives! The next thing we shall have will be a Shaking Quaker dancing a reel . . ."

"Yes, or Brigham Young, surrounded by his harem, threatening to send the administration to hell . . ."

"Or a pawn shop in the basement . . ."

"But he is a Jew . . ."

"Yes, the real genuine original Jacobs — the high priest of the tribe of Levi in New York . . ."

"Well, after that I am ready for a black [radical] republican speaker . . ."

Puns, jokes and witticisms were quite naturally the order of the day. Caricature conceptions of the Jew were already part of the

American folklore. But many of the gibes were good-natured; they were probably stimulated just as much by the self-conscious-ness of Christians who never thought of Judaism in the dignified terms represented by Rabbi Raphall, as by downright hostility to the ancient people whom he symbolized. A writer who sent occasional reports to the *New York Times* began his article with a jocular reference to the eight-week deadlock: "The Rabbi did it today — Christianity, so far as the House is concerned, having proved a failure . . ."[10] The next day, another *Times* reporter, who styled himself "Nobody," was beside himself with merriment:

It is now high noon, and ring-masters Sherman and Keitt crack their whips on the floor and begin to stir up the animals. The Christian religion having failed to produce an organization, resort is now had to a learned Rabbi, who appears in full canonicals, and delivers a very excellent prayer. *Ben Perley Poore*, who sits beside me, suggests that this is the result of the irrepressible conflict — the crush between the North and the South having at length squeezed out the "juice." Some think that the Rabbi has been produced by Secy. *Cobb* to insure favorable discount for certain Treasury Notes, while others give the affair a political signification, and suspect that Mr. Levy, of this city, is laying pipes for a ticket to consist of Senators *Benjamin* and *Yulee*, as the President and Vice-President of a Southern Jerusalem. At any rate the Rabbi makes an excellent prayer — the crumbling despotisms of Asia figuring largely in the foreground of his invocation . . .[11]

One can well understand why every political wit felt he had to add his pun or wise-crack: never before had this phenomenon occurred. The jokes were an indication of the astonishment with which the onlookers reacted to Rabbi Raphall's invocation.

But, for some, jokes were not in order. They regarded this prayer, symbolically, as a serious challenge to Christian hege-mony in America. A Catholic paper, printed in Baltimore, ob-jected in principle to any prayer in Congress which was not addressed to God through Jesus.[12] Down in Knoxville, Ten-nessee, the well-known Parson William G. Brownlow, part-time evangelist and full-time politician, let loose with a typical tirade:

HEBREW RELIGION IN CONGRESS. — We see it stated in one of our exchanges that the House of Representatives at Washington was to have been opened some days back, by religious services, to be performed by the RIGHT REVEREND EMINENT DOCTOR RAPHALL, of the Jewish or Hebrew Denomination, the people who killed Christ! We think this is well enough. In the first place, as a *foreigner*, he will be acceptable to the Democrats; and in the next place we think that a majority of the present Congress are about prepared to sell their interest in *Christ's Atonement!*

Then, utterly ignoring the fact that the Republicans had won the prize of the Speaker's desk before the day was out, Brownlow, in characteristic Know-Nothing fashion, proceeded to nail down the identification of Jews with the Democratic Party which he so despised:

SIGNIFICANT! — It was not until an old *Jewish Rabbi*, Father Raphael, by invitation of the *Democracy*, opened the proceedings of the House with prayer, that they were enabled to organize, by the election of Pennington. Whenever they called into their aid one of the *murderers of Christ*, their hearts and minds were prepared for anything. Had Sherman been the candidate, he could have succeeded. The old Jew's prayer moved upon "the great deep" of the hearts of the anti Le Compton Democrats, and over they went to the strong side! We advise more prayers, provided they are not offered up by *Protestants*. Let *Jews* and *Catholics* pray for Democrats, if you want the prayers to have effect.

This was not the first, nor was it the last time, that Brownlow used his anti-Jewish proclivity as a weapon in political debate.[13]

The editor of *The Churchman*, an unofficial Episcopalian organ published in New York City, limited himself to theological objections, eschewing the political. He interpreted the invitation to the rabbi as a downright rejection of Christianity:

. . . it was with extreme sorrow, and almost disgust, that we read that announcement . . . The nation that could quietly acquiesce in such an act has hardly any principle left to which one can easily appeal . . . [The members of the House] would say, and the great mass of the community would say it with them, that they were merely listening, while a good and sincere and devout man prayed to the common

Father of us all, to give wisdom and guidance to them in their acts. They were doing something very different. They put forward as their official representative and mouth-piece before God — they, a branch of the highest representative body of this land, did it — a minister who denies the Son of God, whose existence and ministry were of themselves the positive assertion that Jesus of Nazareth was *not* the Christ. Their act was no less than the official rejection of Christianity by the Legislature of the country. Either they declare that this nation, in its rotatory patronage of all creeds, chose upon this day of their session to be Jewish, and not Christian, or they declare, (its equivalent), that the difference between Jew and Christian is not in any essential thing . . .

Insisting that Christianity *is* the recognized religion of the United States, *The Churchman* branded the invitation to Raphall a sin and an "evil in the sight of God." Now, it continued, will Congress continue the policy of regarding Christianity as just one of many religions by inviting Mormon elders and Buddhist priests to offer invocations?[14] Another Protestant journal, *The Freeman*, expressed the same conviction that further affront would be offered to Christianity by Mormon prayers, now that the "monstrous" sin of a Jewish prayer had been committed.[15]

Deploring the fact that many would be inclined, like these Christian editors, to criticise the action of the House, because they were still "strongly tinctured with that old leaven of Christian prejudice which, from the crucifixion to this day, has pursued the poor Israelite into every corner of the earth," the *New York Herald* reporter described the event as a great advance in the creation of the American democratic tradition:

A Jewish rabbi opening the proceedings of the House of Representatives of the United States of America with prayer! It has been done. It was done today . . . It was a concession to the great principle of religious liberty, without a parallel in any other country since the destruction of Jerusalem by Titus. We are not aware of any precedent of the kind . . .

He even tried to discover why this development should have taken place at this particular time and surmised that it must have resulted from the wave of indignation which swept through the United States after the publication of the facts of the Mortara case.[16]

Yes, Rabbi Raphall and his prayer were the cause of much discussion. The newspaper comment, friendly and unfriendly, humorous and serious, indicated that something unusual had indeed taken place in Washington that Wednesday in February, 1860. That night, in Willard's Hotel, which Carl Sandburg has fittingly described as "the conversational capital of the United States," the discussion fluctuated back and forth between the two subjects of interest: Pennington's election, and the singular nature of the invocation.[17] While Pennington's merits were being evaluated, one member of Congress jokingly paid tribute to the rabbi's responsibility for the successful outcome of the election: "after every Christian influence had failed during sixty days to make a Speaker, they had to go beyond the pale of Christianity." This comment was answered with a tumultuous shout, "Yes, the Rabbi did it!"

Those gathered at Willard's seemed to agree that Raphall's prayer was beautifully constructed and delivered, but there was some disapproval of his costume. Some criticised his *Tallith;* others thought his wearing the *Yarmulka* was in "bad taste." But one of the Congressmen defended the use of the ritual garb:

... [T]he Rabbi did right in adhering to his costume; he came among us to pray according to his faith. For the moment, the Hall of Congress was his Synagogue. He had to maintain the perfect equality of his persuasion and of its religious practices, with that of any other denomination. Had he departed from the regular practice of the Synagogue, had he yielded to our habits, so far as to come with his head uncovered, and without his vestments which a Jewish Rabbi wears at the time of solemn service, such concession to our views and feelings would also have been renouncing of that perfect equality which it was his duty as a Jew and a minister of religion to uphold ...

So far did a member of Congress go in his logical unfolding of the true significance of the concept of religious equality.

The most wistful comment of all came from England, from Sir Moses Montefiore, grand sage and exemplary champion of Jewish rights everywhere, who would never be able to hear a Jewish prayer spoken in the Parliament of his country:

> ... It gave me extreme gratification to learn ... that the cause of religious toleration has made such progress that it leaves scarcely anything to be wished for, and has led to a triumphant recognition of our faith in the hall of so illustrious an assembly as the Congress ... It would be egotistical on my part were I to withhold such interesting information from the English public; I shall therefore take the liberty of laying [it] before the Board of Deputies of British Jews at their next meeting ...[18]

II

Why had no rabbi previously been invited to deliver the opening prayer for Congress?

Firstly, although Congress represented the nation as a whole, it turned for its prayers to the clergymen of local Washington churches; the Jewish congregation in Washington was of comparatively recent origin. Indeed, it was not until 1852 that any effort was made to assemble the Washington Jewish community for worship even in private homes; prior to that the few Jews resident in the capital had gone to Baltimore for religious services. Congress had not even anticipated the formation of a Jewish congregation: the laws governing the District of Columbia granted property rights only to Christian churches. When the Washington Hebrew Congregation was finally organized in 1855, therefore, application for a charter was made directly to Congress. When finally approved, the charter provided that "all the rights, privileges and immunities hitherto granted by law to the Christian churches in the city of Washington, be, and the same hereby are extended to the Washington Hebrew Congregation of said city ..." Like most newly organized synagogues throughout the country, the congregation was, for its first few years, served by lay readers and unordained men who served as cantors and teachers, but who could not be regarded as, and did not pretend to be, rabbis. [19]

The second reason was a very technical one: by the time the Washington Hebrew Congregation had established its existence as a legal entity, Congress had already adopted the policy of electing a permanent chaplain who alternated between the Senate and the House. So long as this policy prevailed, it could not be expected that a rabbi would be elected to serve as chaplain, even if the Washington congregation had been led by a rabbi, since the Jews were a small minority. This practice was suspended in 1858, however, and during the Thirty-Fifth Congress, the House adopted a resolution requesting that all "the ministers of the Gospel in this city . . . attend and alternately perform this solemn duty." [20] That year, 1858, was the first year, therefore, in which a rabbi could have been invited to pray for Congress.

Finally, these were the years when American Jewry was just becoming self-conscious, beginning to strive for recognition and status. This developing maturity becomes apparent when we compare, for instance, the rather feeble requests for American intervention which were made to the President and State Department by representative Jewish leaders in connection with the Damascus case, in 1840, with the self-assurance and dignity with which similar requests were made in 1859 during the discussion of the Mortara case. [21] Another indication may be found in the matter of Jewish chaplains: during the heat of the Mexican War, when hundreds of young Jewish men volunteered for service, no one appears even to have thought of requesting the appointment of a chaplain of the Jewish faith; the Civil War had hardly begun, however, before the question was immediately projected into the arena of public controversy. [22] The most obvious illustration of this growth to mature self-consciousness was the fact that it was not until 1859 — under the impact of the Mortara case — that American Jewry was able to create its first representative national organization to deal with national and international affairs of importance. [23] Previous to this time, very few Jews would have been concerned enough even to inquire about the religious status of the clergymen who prayed for Congress: the overwhelming majority of them were immigrants, busy integrating their personal lives into the American pattern; anything else had to wait.

The first reference to the subject which it has been possible to discover was, indeed, during the Thirty-Fifth Congress, when for the first time in many years the Congressional invocations were delivered not by one chaplain, but by a number of clergymen who were associated with all of the denominations which were represented in Washington. A Jewish citizen of Evansville, Indiana, had written to his Representative, Schuyler Colfax, later Vice-President during Grant's first term, inquiring into the question, and Colfax' answer was published in the *Evansville Journal*: [24]

HOUSE OF REPRESENTATIVES,
Washington, February 7, 1859.

My Dear Sir: —

I had spoken several times with fellow-members, before the receipt of your letter, of the omission to include Jewish ministers in the list of those who offer prayers in turn at the opening of Congress, and had regreted it, as their rights in this regard are certainly equal to those of any other denominations. But as no member of the House, except the Speaker, has any power in arranging the list of ministers who are invited for the purpose, no motion had been made in regard to it.

On the receipt, however, of your letter to-day, the House was in Committee of the Whole, and the Speaker, consequently, in his room; I called upon him and asked him the reason for the omission — adding, that it had attracted attention as far distant as Indiana. He replied, that he had included in his list ministers of all denominations resident here, whose names had been furnished him, but that he had not been informed of any Jewish Rabbi officiating in this city, and hence had invited none. I told him that there was a Synagogue here, but the name of its minister I had not heard. As the list is now filled up till the 4th of March, and the persons named in it all invited, no change could be effected now, unless some one should surrender his place upon it. But I can assure you that, if this system is continued during the next Congress, I will take special pains to learn who the Rabbi here is, and furnish his name to the Speaker, so that he shall be included.

I notice your allusion to the Mortara case — one of the saddest and most touching I have ever read of lately. I need scarcely say how much I am disappointed that our Administration could not, with a disclaimer of all desire to intervene, have frankly declared that the people of our Republic regard with as much disappointment and regret, the abducting of a Jewish child from its parents on the plea of a surreptitious baptism, as they would the robbing of a Catholic child from *its* parents, if it had, in a similar manner, received the Jewish rite of membership.

> In haste, yours truly,
> SCHUYLER COLFAX.

Colfax' constituent, whose name we do not know, forwarded a clipping from the Evansville newspaper to Isaac Leeser, who promptly reprinted it in his *Occident*. Leeser added his own comments: it seemed to him to be a clear matter of neglect on the part of American Jewry. He knew that S. M. Landsberg (or Landsburgh as the name is spelled elsewhere), the officiating minister of the Washington Hebrew Congregation, was a newly arrived immigrant, and, though a fine scholar in Jewish lore, unable to discourse in English. Leeser therefore recommended that the leading American Jewish congregations send a joint note to the Vice-President, or the next Speaker, volunteering the services of their rabbis for invocations of Congressional sessions, "so that the name of the God of Israel, in his unity, may also be invoked to send his wisdom among the national legislators . . ."

Colfax' letter and Leeser's editorial spurred the Washington Hebrew Congregation to action. The acknowledge leader of the community was Captain Jonas P. Levy, brother of Commodore Uriah P. Levy, and a Naval officer who had distinguished himself during the Mexican War. He it was who had organized the movement to obtain a charter for the congregation from Congress.[25] A few days after the appearance of Leeser's editorial, he wrote to Leeser[26] (and, apparently, to many of the rabbis of existing congregations):

Washington April 11th 1859.

Sir

I have advised with the President of the Washington Hebrew Congregation about the test (?) made to have our Holy Religion represented in the United States Congress, on a par with other Denominations and shall be pleased to confer with you and all other heads of Congregations that may be disposed to aid us in this important Representation.

I suggest that a competent Reader or Hasan, in the English Language shall be selected monthly or otherwise and paid for by Contributions from all Congregations.

Our talented & able Hasan is not sufficiently versed in the English language to perform that duty, and our Society cannot afford an Extra Reader.

You will please lay this before your members, and give it such publication in your Paper — as in your Wisdom may deem best, and confer another obligation to the Children of Israel & your friend & ob[edient] s[ervan]t

JONAS P. LEVY.

Revd Isaac Leeser
Phila

Washington Jewry was happy to be the nation's representative Jewish congregation — at the expense of the other congregations! But the other congregations seem to have declined the honor. And so the matter was dropped.[27]

But Representative Colfax had not forgotten! And so, on Jan. 21, 1860, the Clerk of the House communicated with Jonas Levy and requested that the rabbi be present to deliver the opening prayer the following Tuesday, Jan. 24th. Now that the request had been granted, the congregation was in a quandry. The Rev.

Landsberg still spoke with an accent. Apparently the Baltimore rabbis were unacceptable for the same reason. Levy declined the invitation, but hastened to his desk and wrote Leeser, Raphall, the Rev. S. M. Isaacs of New York City, and possibly others, asking if they would consent to come to Washington. Raphall, probably the first to answer, was chosen to offer the prayer on Feb. 1, the next time the Hebrew Congregation would be called upon to send a rabbi. [28]

The same day Levy also forwarded a formal request for help to the Board of Delegates of American Israelites. He asked the Board to circularize the congregations throughout America for contributions of ten to twenty dollars each, which would be used to augment the meager salary of $400 which the Washington congregation paid its cantor, and which therefore would enable the congregation to obtain the services of a fully qualified rabbi. Although the Board recognized the desirability of the goal, it did not feel able to assume the burden of asking for national support for one local congregation. Levy's ambitions were again thwarted. [29]

There was, of course, every expectation that the Thirty-Sixth Congress would adhere to the procedure established by the previous Congress. But the House resolved to return to the earlier policy of a permanent chaplain and, therefore, Levy's proposal became entirely academic. There would no longer be a rotating system which would call for a rabbi's presence every two weeks. Leeser was inclined to think some members of the House preferred to have a permanent chaplain because that would avoid any future possibility of Jewish prayers. But, "for all practical purposes," he felt, "the appearance of Dr. Raphall was sufficient in principle; and at the first fitting occasion, that is, when no regular chaplain is elected, the Israelites, we are sure, will take care that their claim shall not be overlooked. But a little vigilance will have to be exercised, and this must and should be done . . ."[30] Leeser need not have been concerned; objection was never again raised in the Congress to prayers by a rabbi.[31]

III

Although Raphall's prayer was the first to be delivered by a rabbi at the opening of a session of a federal legislative body, the state of Virginia had given such recognition to Judaism ten years previously.[32] In 1850, the Rev. Julius Eckman, newly arrived in Richmond as the minister of the Beth Shalome Congregation, was invited to open sessions of the House of Delegates during the weeks of Janurary 15–19 and March 18–22.[33] One of his prayers was printed by request in the Richmond *Enquirer* and copied, in turn, by Isaac Leeser's *Occident:*

Before the commencement of the legislative proceedings of this day, I again, in the name of this honourable assembly, lift up my eyes to Thee, our Father who art in heaven, most humbly beseeching Thee to vouchsafe to be with us during the labours of this day; that Thou mayest direct our judgment, enlighten our minds, and incline our hearts, that we may think, speak, and act, according to Thy will and to our good.

May truth be our guide, justice our rule, and the welfare of mankind our only aim; so that this State, upon which Thou hast lavished so many blessings already; whose sons, by Thy grace, have rendered signal services to our Union in particular, and to the cause of liberty in general; that this State may continue to rise, to shine, and flourish.

May tranquillity, order, safety, and prosperity reign within, and no troubles, vexations, or grievances, break in from without.

May it please Thee to crown our endeavours here with success, to the contentment of our hearts; to the satisfaction of those who entrusted us with so important a charge; to the advancement of plenty and ease, of happiness and peace.

May the tree of liberty, which has been planted here so early, and which has now taken root so deeply, be like a tree planted by the rivers of water, that bringing [sic] forth fruit in its season, whose leaves do not wither; but may its branches spread forth more and more, till all mankind may find shelter under its shadow. Amen. [34]

Eckman, whom we have already met as the editor of the San Francisco *Gleaner*, was, therefore, the first Jewish spiritual leader to be invited to invoke God's blessing before a session of a state legislature.

His appearance in the House of Delegates did not, apparently, establish the inclusion of Judaism once and for all. In 1861, the outburst of patriotic sentiment which drove Virginia into the Confederacy prompted the Rev. George Jacobs of Beth Shalome to request permission to give a prayer for the legislature. To his surprise he was informed that each session had the privilege of fixing its own rules in regard to chaplains' prayers, and that the present session (perhaps inadvertently) had specified prayers by Christian ministers. Ex-Governor Wyndham Robertson of Richmond promptly offered a resolution to the effect that "the Speaker be requested to invite the clergy of all religious denominations of the city to open the sessions of this House daily with prayer." [35] Robertson said in support of his motion, after paying homage to Virginia's long record of religious freedom:

I offer [this resolution] at the instance of the Pastor of the Israelites in this city. He earnestly and humbly begs to be permitted to invoke before us, and upon us, the blessings of God in our labors. Is there one here who would deny him? I understand his walk of life is humble, pious and benevolent. The Jew as well as the Gentile is equally part of our political system, and affected by our legislation. He comes to ask equality of religious privileges, and it is fit, at a time when we are standing on our rights of equality in other respects, we should be careful not to refuse lightly the benefit of that principle to others . . .

In conclusion, the Representative clinched his argument with a personal reference:

. . . we have now our equal in all respects, on this floor, in the person of [our] respected colleague (Mr. Myers), a member of the Jewish denomination, and the House, [I am] sure, would not reject the petition, and repel from our desk the pastor of his choice.

The motion was carried, and a few weeks later the Rev. Jacobs offered his prayer. [36]

Meanwhile, shortly after Eckman had been appointed one of the rotating chaplains in Richmond, Isaac Mayer Wise, in Albany, had received a similar appointment. His story of its background is well worth knowing:

On January 2, 1852, a resolution was passed in both Houses of the Legislature of the State of New York to the effect that the clergymen of the city of Albany be asked to hold a meeting to prepare a list of all ministers stationed in the city, and submit it to the Senate, in order that chaplains for both Houses might be elected. The resolution was printed and copy sent to every minister; hence also to me. On the following day I read to my astonishment in the evening paper that a meeting of ministers had taken place. The list that had been prepared by them appended. It was to be submitted to the Senate on the morrow. My name was not on the list.

"Ye miserable hypocrites, I will teach you a lesson," mused I. I went to the clerk of the Senate, and acquainted him with the proceeding. "Very well; write a short protest, and hand it to me." said he. I wrote the protest and gave it to him. The next morning the report of the clergy, accompanied by my protest, was read in the Senate chamber, and was rejected on the ground that it did not comply with the law. The ministers ought to have called a second meeting, and to have invited me to be present. Instead of that, they prepared a protest against the action of the Senate on the ground that I was not one of their number, saying that I was a Jewish rabbi and not a Christian minister. Dr. Wykoff objected, was outvoted, left the meeting, came straight to my house, and informed me of the action. The protest had to be printed; so I went to the different newspaper offices, found the document, read it through, wrote a reply, had it printed at once, and on the following morning the protest and my reply were lying on each desk. This caused no end of merriment. One of the senators said I must be a prophet since I had answered a document point for point even before it had appeared. Upon the opening of the session the clerk announced the receipt of the two documents, but they were not read nor filed since the Senate did not wish to lend official notice to the protest prepared by the clergy. After that was disposed of, my friend, Senator Thayer, arose and moved that I be appointed chaplain of the Senate temporarily until the clergy should have obeyed the law. This motion was carried unanimously without debate. The clergymen made wry faces; but I was chaplain of the Senate until such a time as they would act in accordance with the law and place the name of the terrible rabbi upon the list, a step which they could not make up their minds to take for a long time. Thus I became the first Jewish chaplain of a legislative body . . .[37]

Unfortunately, no corroborating evidence for this "battle of the clergy" has been preserved; the documents mentioned cannot be located, nor do the Albany newspapers mention the problem. Wise did deliver several prayers,[38] although he was, of course, not the first rabbi in America to do so. This is one which was printed in the newspapers:

Lord of hosts! Rock of salvation whose unlimited power, wisdom, and love is revealed in the innumerable millions of creatures that populize the Universe, whose providence, especial care and benignity is reechoed on every page of the history of nations! Hear our supplications, listen graciously to our petitions that we offer up unto Thee on behalf of our beloved country and her faithful legislators, who have assembled again to give us laws and regulations to the promotion of liberty, prosperity, justice and humanity. O Lord! Thou hast inspired and assisted our ancestors, when they rose lion-like against their oppressors, and bought, for the warm blood of their hearts the liberty and independence of these United States. Inspire, Our Father! O inspire our legislators with the same spirit of truth and justice, with the same love of liberty and independence, with the same desire to promote happiness and prosperity among their fellow-citizens; remove prejudices, partiality and factional endeavors from every mind; give unto them the same spirit as the venerable fathers of this republic manifested; let them be firmly united in the discharge of their sacred duty to the country, that she may bloom and prosper before Thee; that she may be an example of liberty, equity, and humanity; that she may be imitated by those nations, that still suffer and sigh under the iron rod of despotism, that her citizens be united before Thee, to do Thy sacred will, to proclaim Thine holy name! Blessed be the name of the Lord from sunrise to sunset, from now to evermore, Amen![39]

That there was no concerted effort, at this same time, to obtain similar recognition in other states, was an indication of the lack of unity among American Jews — but it was also an indication that the rabbis were permitting the natural, normal course of events to bring the subject to their attention and to the attention of the legislators. In some states, like Tennessee, there was excited public controversy before the desired object was achieved;[40] in others, like Wisconsin, it was only necessary for a rabbi to indicate his interest — the invitation was immediately extended.[41] Although during this same period there was strong agitation by certain Protestant denominations to have the Constitution amended so that Christianity would be recognized as the American national faith,[42] nevertheless the recognition of the equal status of Judaism was gradually extended from state to state.

There is now probably no state whose legislature has not been opened with prayer by a rabbi; in some states rabbis have served as permanent chaplains or have been appointed temporary chaplains at regular intervals.[43] The Senate and House of the federal Congress permit their permanent chaplains to invite whatever guests they please; rabbis have frequently been among those who have joined the succession begun by Rabbi Raphall. In this regard, certainly, the American principle of religious equality has been faithfully upheld.

NOTES

[1] John T. Nixon, "The Circumstances Attending the Election of William Pennington of New Jersey, as Speaker of the Thirty-Sixth Congress," *Proceedings of the New Jersey Historical Society*, Second Series, Vol. II (1870–1872), pp. 205–220. Coincidentally, Pennington's Newark home was demolished in 1911 to make room for the construction of the Oheb Shalom Synagogue. His son, William, spoke at the dedication ceremonies — altogether unaware of the relationship between the election of his father as Speaker of the House, and this significant event in the life of American Jewry, *Oheb Shalom Review* (Newark, N. J.), XLVI, No. 31 (April 12, 1950).

[2] See the letters by Washington, Jefferson and Madison, collected in Lewis Abraham, "Correspondence between Washington and Jewish Citizens," *PAJHS*, No. III (1895), pp. 87–96.

[3] Israel Goldstein, *A Century of Judaism in New York*, N. Y., 1930, pp. 110–113 ff.; see pp. 40–1 above.

[4] *Congressional Globe*, 36th Congress, First Session, Part 1, pp. 648–9; reprinted in *OCC*, XVII, No. 46, pp. 275–6, Feb. 9, 1860. The transliteration is that which appears in the *Globe*, all misspellings intact.

[5] The issues of Feb. 2, 1860, of the *New York Times, New York Herald, Cincinnati Gazette, North American and U. S. Gazette* (Phila.), *The Press* (Phila.), *Public Ledger* (Phila.); and the *Daily Dispatch* (Richmond), of Feb. 3.

[6] *New York Herald* as reprinted in *The Jewish Chronicle and Hebrew Observer* (London), March 2, 1860. The original article cannot be located in extant files of the *Herald* nor in any other newspaper.

[7] *The Press* (Phila.), Feb. 2, 1860, column signed "Ezek Richards."

[8] *OCC*, XVII, No. 46, p. 275, Feb. 9, 1860.

[9] See note 6.

[10] *New York Times*, Feb. 3, 1860, column signed "N."

[11] *Ibid.*, Feb. 4, 1860. Cf. *The Press* (Phila.), Feb. 2, 1860: "Rabbi Raphall . . , dressed in full canonicals, characteristic of the priests of the Old Testament . . ." John Sherman has been referred to above; Lawrence M. Keitt was floor leader of the Democrats, an inveterate champion of the most extreme Southern position; Ben Perley Poore was one of the most popular political reporters and commentators of the day; Howell Cobb of Georgia was Secretary of the Treasury; "Mr. Levy" is probably Captain Jonas P. Levy, leader of the Washington Jewish community; Judah P. Benjamin of Louisiana and David (Levy) Yulee of Florida were, of course, the only Jews then serving in the Senate. Several Jews had previously served in the House; none, coincidentally, was serving during this session.

[12] *OCC*, XVII, No. 50, pp. 298–9, March 8, 1860.

[13] Cited in *ISR*, VI, No. 36, p. 283, March 9, 1860. For further material on Brownlow's anti-Jewish prejudices, see *AJCW*, pp. 166–8. Isaac Mayer Wise, after reprinting Brownlow's comments verbatim, called upon his remarkably colorful vocabulary to describe the Parson: ". . . an impious, ungodly man . . . a sinner before the constitution . . . a narrow minded bigot . . . a child of hell, the servant of despotism, arbitrary violence and mean prejudices . . ." It hurt Wise, a lifelong Democrat, to find Brownlow's prejudice leading him to blame the Democrats for calling Raphall, when actually it was a non-political issue altogether. Said Wise, more temperately, "it is strange, that Mr. B. knows not that the *Know Nothings and Republicans* had the majority . . . hence the invitation to the Hebrew Clergyman came from B's own party . . ."

[14] *The Churchman*, Feb. 16, 1860, p. 424, referred to in *ISR, op. cit.* The writer is

indebted to Mr. Niels H. Sonne, Librarian of the General Theological Seminary, New York City, for assistance in locating files of this very elusive periodical.

[15] Referred to in *OCC, op. cit.*, Files of this periodical could not be located.

[16] See note 6. Also cf. *Philadelphia Dispatch*, Oct. 27, 1861, where Raphall's prayer is referred to as evidence of the government's respect for Judaism, in connection with the discussion of the right of rabbis to serve as Army chaplains. For the latter see *AJCW*, pp. 58–62.

[17] The material on the conversations at Willard's is quoted from the letter of "An American Jew," *OCC*, XVII, No. 46, p. 275, Feb. 9, 1860.

[18] Letter from Montefiore to Jonas P. Levy, published in *MESS*, VII, No. 13, p. 93, March 23, 1860. Montefiore was a kind of patron saint of American Jewry and it was conventional to notify him of all important developments in American Jewish life. This was not done in an organized fashion, but was almost instinctive on the part of most American Jewish leaders.

[19] *OCC*, X, No. 6, p. 317, Sept. 1852; Abram Simon, "Notes of Jewish Interest in the District of Columbia," pp. 211–218; Abraham I. Shinedling, art. "Washington," *UJE*, X, p. 465.

[20] J. M. Barclay (comp.), *Digest of the Rules of the House of Representatives, U. S., The Joint Rules of the Two Houses, and of so much of Jefferson's Manual as under the rules governs the House*, Washington, 1861, pp. 442–3. During the years prior, there had been downright electioneering campaigns over the political plum of permanent appointment as chaplain. One Representative urged support for a clergyman friend with the promise that all his prayers would be short; another said in favor of his personal candidate that he was "a regular Hard Shell Ironside Baptist, . . . a very pious man; and though not of eminent ability, he has enough talent to pray for such a crowd as this." *The Military Chaplain*, XX, No. 4, pp. 14–5, April-May 1950.

[21] For the documents and other data concerning the Damascus case, see Jacob Ezekiel, "Persecution of the Jews in 1840," *PAJHS*, No. VIII, (1900), pp. 141–5; Joseph Jacobs, "The Damascus Affair of 1840 and the Jews of America," *PAJHS*, No. X (1902), pp. 119–128; Cyrus Adler and Aaron Margalith, "American Intercession in Behalf of Jews in the Diplomatic Correspondence of the United States 1840–1938," *PAJHS*, No. XXXVI, (1943), pp. 3–5. Unfortunately, an exhaustive treatment of the Mortara case in America has not yet been written. See Grinstein, *The Rise of the Jewish Community of New York 1654–1860*, pp. 430–436, for material on the reaction in New York City, and the pertinent issues of the Jewish periodicals of 1859, for further material.

[22] *AJCW*, pp. 56–97.

[23] See pp. 35–9 above.

[24] Reprinted in *OCC*, XVII, No. 2, pp. 11–12, April 7, 1859.

[25] Henry S. Morais, *The Jews of Philadelphia*, Phila., 1894, p. 471; Abram Simon, *op. cit.*

[26] Letter in Leeser Collection, Dropsie College Library.

[27] There is no exact record of the number of Jews then in Washington, but the fact that the congregation did not possess a synagogue would indicate that the request for outside help was justified. Washington Jewry made frequent appeals for financial assistance to other communities: in connection with campaigns for the building of a synagogue, see Copy of a letter of regret from the Board of Delegates of American Israelites, Aug. 15, 1860, in Library of the American Jewish Historical Society; *OCC*, XXI, No. 7, pp. 273–85, Sept. 1863; *MESS*, XXXI, No. 13, p. 5, March 29, 1872; for appeals during the Civil War in connection with work among Jewish soldiers, see *MESS*, IX, No. 25, p. 196, June 28, 1861; XIII, No. 25, p. 211, June 26, 1863.

[28] *MESS*, VII, No. 5, p. 37, Feb. 3, 1860; *OCC*, XVII, No. 46, p. 275, Feb. 9, 1860; letter, Levy to Leeser, Jan. 23, 1860, Leeser Collection. The fact that at least three rabbis were invited by Levy (not by an official of the House or other politician) ought to be sufficient evidence to set to rest the hunch of Morris U. Schappes, as expressed in a letter to the *Jewish Chronicle* (London), May 5, 1950, that Raphall was invited "not only because he was known in rabbinical and literary circles in New York, but because of his connections with the Democratic Party and its politicians in New York . . ."

[29] Letter, Levy to Henry Hart, President of the Board, Jan. 23, 1860, Library of the American Jewish Historical Society; First Annual Report of the Executive Committee of the Board, *MESS*, VII, No. 24, p. 188, June 22, 1860; Minute Book, Executive Committee, Board of Delegates, pp. 18, 19, 22, Library of the A.J.H.S.

[30] *OCC*, XVII, No. 52, p. 306, March 15, 1860.

[31] It has not been possible to ascertain when the next rabbi appeared in Congress as chaplain. The Rev. Abraham de Sola, Sephardic minister of Shearith Israel Congregation of Montreal, who received that honor on Jan. 9, 1872, and who was the first non-American rabbi to offer a prayer in Congress, said in a letter to *MESS*, XXXI, No. 2, p. 2, Jan. 12, 1872, that Dr. Isaac M. Wise of Cincinnati had previously been invited to the Capitol, but the writer has been unable to locate verification of this statement. Rabbi Marcus M. Jastrow of Congregation Rodeph Shalom, Philadelphia, preceded de Sola by more than six months according to *MESS*, XXIX, No. 22, p. 5, June 9, 1871, which quoted a Hartford, Conn., newspaper's objections to a procedure by which members of the Senate should "stand with bowed heads and reverent mien before one whose mission it is to preach that Christianity is humbug and Christ an arrant imposter," and another Hartford journal's editorial assertion that "the prayer of the Rabbi was doubtless as sincere and as earnest as any offered by a Christian." Interest in the subject of rabbinical prayers in Congress continues today: in early 1950 Rabbi Nachum David Herman was described in the public press as being the first Orthodox rabbi to be invited to Congress; Dr. David de Sola Pool, in a letter to the *New York Times*, March 14, 1950, corrected the impression and recalled Abraham de Sola's prayer in 1872. But Dr. Pool would be the last to impugn the orthodoxy of Raphall or Jastrow; both prided themselves on their adherence to tradition.

De Sola's appearance in Congress, arranged by Adolphus Solomons, then a member of the legislature of the District of Columbia, created almost as much interest and comment as Raphall's. Newspaper reaction to the prayer (printed verbatim in *MESS*, XXXI, No. 4, p. 2, Jan. 26, 1872), as collected in *MESS*, XXXI, No. 3, p. 4, Jan. 19, 1872, was altogether favorable. The *New York Tribune*, for instance, hoped that it would not be long before such events were so commonplace that they would not even be deemed worthy of newspaper comment. The *Herald*, on the other hand, was so impressed that it printed (Jan. 13, 1872) an interview with the rabbi, describing his personal reactions to the experience. The *Christian Union*, quoted in *MESS*, XXI, No. 11, p. 2, March 15, 1872, applauded this further evidence of the " 'breaking down of the wall of partition' between Israel and the Gentiles." The only levity referred to, in contrast to the reaction to Raphall, was noted by a Washington correspondent who said: "Considerable amusement was created this morning by the fact of the House being opened with prayer by a Jewish Rabbi, who kept his hat on while conducting devotions. Several members, who did not understand that he was a Jew, thought he had forgotten to take his hat off." (Clipping, Jan. 9, 1872, from an unidentified newspaper in *Lucien Moss Scrapbook*, Library of the A.J.H.S.).

Rabbi Henry Pereira Mendes of Shearith Israel Congregation of New York was invited to open the Senate with prayer on April 24, 1888, and again the reaction was very favorable, except for a German paper in Baltimore which was quoted as having sentiments similar to some of those expressed in 1860: ". . . perhaps for a change they will next allow even a Buddhist to pray there, for even this religion has its adherents here . . ." (*Jewish Exponent*, May 4, 1888; see also April 27, 1888).

The *New York Herald's* hope was realized. A few weeks after Rabbi Mendes appeared in the Senate, Rabbi Abraham Blum of Galveston, Texas, on his way north to preach in Philadelphia, was invited to pray for the House. Rabbis in Congress were becoming so common an experience that even the Jewish press, with the exception of the Philadelphia *Jewish Exponent* (May 11, 1888), took no notice of the event.

[32] It is even possible that Virginia's history in this regard went back thirty years: According to the recollection of Isaac Leeser (*OCC*, VII, No. 12, p. 615, March 1850; XVIII, No. 47, p. 283, Feb. 14, 1861 — probably the source of similar data in Ezekiel and Lichtenstein, *The History of the Jews of Richmond*, p. 244), the Rev. Abraham Hyam Cohen, minister of Beth Shalome Congregation of Richmond had given such an official prayer in 1829 or 1830. The Virginia State Convention was then meeting to revise the state constitution, and its daily sessions were opened with prayer by the local clergymen. Cohen objected to the failure of the chairman to include him among the others and asked that he be added to the list. His request was granted according to Leeser. Cohen's name is not mentioned, however, in the *Proceedings and Debates of the Virginia State Convention of 1829–30*, Richmond, 1830, and the evidence does not therefore appear to support Leeser's memory. This was just the time, however, that Leeser was about to leave Richmond for Philadelphia to take up his duties as minister of Mikveh Israel Congregation, and it is entirely possible that Cohen was attempting to change the ruling when Leeser left, and that Leeser had not been informed of the rejection of the request.

[33] *ASM*, I, No. 20, p. 158, March 8, 1850.

[34] *OCC*, VII, No. 12, pp. 615–616, March 1850. None of his other prayers can be located either in the *Enquirer* or in the *Journal of the House of Delegates 1849–50*, Richmond, 1850.

[35] Richmond *Daily Dispatch*, Jan. 29, 1861; *OCC*, XVIII, No. 7, p. 283, Feb. 14, 1861. Note how Robertson's carefully worded resolution avoids the implication that Christianity was to be rejected. "Mr. Myers" is Gustavus A. Myers, who represented Richmond in the Virginia General Assembly in the session of 1859–60 and in January-April, 1861; Myers was a member of Beth Shalome Congregation.

[36] Richmond *Daily Dispatch*, Feb. 19, 1861; *OCC*, XVIII, No. 49, p. 298, Feb. 28, 1861. Jacobs prayed more than a few times during the following years. In 1866, his colleague, the Rev. M. J. Michelbacher of the other Richmond congregation, Beth Ahabah, was accorded the same privilege: *Journal of the House of Delegates, 1865–6*, Richmond, 1866, pp. 164, 170, 175. On May 26, 1870, the Rev. Aaron S. Bettelheim, who succeeded Michelbacher, injected a controversial note in a prayer which he delivered before the House of Delegates:

> Almighty God! still we are in want of justice, righteousness, and truth; still we are anxious to see *Virginia governed by Virginians* through virtue and integrity. Justice, truth and peace, were the pillars upon which Virginia has been resting. O Lord! shall these pillars totter in our days? Shall Virginia, the star of the States, be trampled down by *Heartless Strangers* and by *Native Enemies?* . . .

This obvious attack upon the Republican Party brought down upon Bettelheim a stinging rebuke from members of that party, who offered a resolution that "no minister of any denomination is authorized to pray for either the Republican or Democratic parties of the State or nation . . ." Bettelheim promptly printed a rejoinder, nonchalantly disclaiming any such interpretation of his prayer. Interestingly enough, he had not even been in the United States, let alone Virginia, during the Civil War; his Confederate sympathies were undoubtedly stimulated by his Virginia-born wife. Clipping from an unidentified Richmond paper, *George Jacobs Scrapbook*, American Jewish Archives; Rebekah Kohut, *My Portion*, N. Y., 1927, pp. 28–9.

[37] Wise, *Reminiscences*, pp. 217–219. Wise's recollection of the date, at least, was wrong. His prayer printed in *ASM* and referred to below was delivered in June 1851!

[38] *ASM*, VII, No. 26, p. 305, April 15, 1853. A report to the writer from the N. Y. State Library, Dec. 13, 1949, refers to prayers delivered (texts not printed) on April 11 and June 16, 1853. In connection with the entire problem of legislative chaplains in New York State, see the 1832 "Report of the Select Committee of the New York State Assembly on the Several Memorials Against Appointing Chaplains to the Legislature," by David Moulton and Mordecai Myers, reprinted in Joseph L. Blau, *Cornerstones of Religious Freedom in America*, Boston, 1949, pp. 141–156.

[39] *ASM*, IV, No. 12, p. 97, July 11, 1851.

40 *MESS*, XXXIII, No. 4, p. 4, Jan. 24, 1873; *ISR*, XX, No. 3, p. 6, Jan. 17, 1873. The Jews of Nashville published an open letter of protest after noticing that the state Senate had invited Christian ministers to open sessions with prayer. The Senate considered the subject on Jan. 11, 1873. A resolution was offered "inviting the ministers of God, whether Christian or Jewish, to open the morning sessions with prayer." In the ensuing discussion only one objection was offered, by a Mr. Jones, who said that "it seems to me that those members of the Senate, who are believers in the Lord Jesus Christ, would stultify themselves in asking those to come and pray for us who do not believe in Jesus Christ. It would appear to me as a mockery." Supporters of the resolution expressed various ideas. One said that "the purest religion I ever heard fall from the lips of man, fell from the lips of a Jewish Rabbi, of Cincinnati;" another urged good logic: "I am perfectly willing to consent to a broad invitation — as broad as you can make it — as broad as the Declaration of Independence. In the Constitution we know no Religion;" a third did not think that "in standing here while a Rabbi is invoking the Divine blessing, we are risking our faith, or that by so doing, we indorse his . . ." The resolution was adopted.

41 *MESS*, XXVI, No. 9, p. 4, March 4, 1870; *ISR*, XVIII, No. 35, p. 7, Feb. 24, 1871.

42 *MESS*, XXXI, No. 3, p. 4, Jan. 19, 1872.

43 Results of a survey conducted in February, 1950, by the writer, among the alumni of the Hebrew Union College and Jewish Institute of Religion. Such states include: Ala., Calif., Conn., Ga., Ill., N. Y., No. Car., Ohio, Penna., So. Car., Texas and Wisc.

VI

Isaac Mayer Wise on the Civil War*

In 1861 there were nine Jewish periodicals published in the United States; seven were written in English, two in German. Of these, Isaac Mayer Wise's *The Israelite* was the second oldest in continuous existence and the oldest weekly publication; its influence was strongest in the middle west and in the south. Galvanized by Wise's dynamic energies and exciting ideas, *The Israelite* exerted a powerful force in the formation of Jewish public opinion on Jewish and national problems. A study of its editorial policy, especially during the early years of Wise's editorship, when it claimed a great deal of his attention, is interesting and rewarding, because such a study reveals not only the thought and psychology of its editor, but also the ideas and attitudes which were transmitted to American Jewry. This paper will constitute an examination of Wise's editorial policy during and concerning the Civil War.

When the war broke out in April, 1861, Wise published his decision to refrain from comment on the war, in the following editorial:

SILENCE OUR POLICY

The excitement runs high, very high, wherever we turn our eyes. They say civil war is commenced. We are the servant of peace, not of war. Hitherto we sometimes thought fit to say something on public affairs, and it was our ardent hope to assist those who wished to prevent civil war; but we wasted our words. What can we say now? Shall we lament and weep like Jeremiah over a state of things too sad and too threaten-

* Originally published in *The Hebrew Union College Annual*, XX, (1947), pp. 635–658.

ing to be looked upon with indifference? We would only be laughed at in this state of excitement and passionate agitation, or probably abused for discouraging the sentiment. Or should we choose sides with one of the parties? We can not, not only because we abhor the idea of war, but also we have dear friends and near relations, beloved brethren and kinsmen in either section of the country, that our heart bleeds on thinking of their distress, of the misery that might befall them.

Therefore silence must henceforth be our policy, silence on all the questions of the day, until a spirit of conciliation shall move the hearts of the millions to a better understanding of the blessings of peace, freedom, and union. Till then we might stop publishing *The Israelite* if our friends say so, or continue as usual, if we are patronized as heretofore. But we shall be obliged to abstain entirely from all and every commentary on the odd occurrences of the day.

In writing these lines we feel as sorrowful and disheartened as we only once before felt — on leaving our native country. The land of our choice and adoption thus in a destructive commotion is much more than common misery to us. Still the will of God be done.[1]

But Wise was not telling the entire story in this brief editorial. He was not a neutral, a mere spectator, a fence-sitter, as his words might lead one to believe. He was a Peace Democrat,[2] like so many of his fellow-citizens in the border-states, the "border-state eunuchs," as Henry Ward Beecher called them. He was opposed to the ideas of both the extreme abolitionists and of the extreme secessionists. The Republican victory in the fall of '60 was, to his mind, a national calamity. The Republican radicals and the southern radicals would, together, tear the country apart. "Here is the house divided against itself," he said, "the irrepressible conflict." "Either the Republican party must be killed off forever by constitutional guarantees to the South, to make an end forever to this vexing slavery question, or the Union must be dissolved."[3] Peace and Union at any cost were his objectives in the weeks before the outbreak of war, even if the price involved the everlasting legalization of slavery. He published only pro-peace sermons and letters in *The Israelite;*

who can say whether these were the only ones he received, or the only ones he could conscientiously publish? There were sermons by Szold, DeCordova, and Hochheimer, pleading for moderation as Wise did; letters from "Scrib" and "Millotiz" in favor of any compromise on the slavery issue, any revision of the constitution, to effectuate a peaceful solution, matching Wise's editorials; even advertisements by M. Loth favoring "Union Forever" in the place of his usual offerings of merchandise. And Wise was confident, for a while, that the counsel of moderation and compromise would win out, counsel such as his, that "a second sober thought of the people will decide in favor of union at any risk." Once South Carolina seceded, however, to be followed in rapid succession by the other slave states, Wise gave up hope altogether. He believed that every state had the right to secede; and, further, that a resort to arms was illogical: "Force will not hold together this Union; it was cemented by liberty and can stand only by the affections of the people." What, then, could a Peace Democrat do but lapse into a resentful silence when the extremists on both sides achieved their goals? [4]

If Wise, then, was prepared to see slavery established as a permanent American institution, to save the Union, was he proslavery, as he has generally been regarded? [5] The answer is "no" if it must be stated in one word. But it cannot be stated in one word, for the slavery issue itself was such a complex of ethics and politics that only the extremists on both sides could answer in one word. Many of the rabbis declared themselves to be abolitionists or pro-slavery men; Wise did not. In fact, he avoided discussion of the question on a political plane, since it was obvious to him that the political and economic aspects of slavery were paramount in most discussions. [6] As a rabbi, he said, he had no right to use his religious office, or his religious journal, for political purposes; and we shall see that he attacked the abolitionist clergymen for what he thought was their degradation of religion into a political tool. After the war ended, Wise was willing to admit that the abolition of slavery had been a desirable and progressive step; but he never supported it as a reason for going to war with the South.

On an ethical and moral plane, however, Wise was obviously not pro-slavery, although he never reached such heights of moral indignation as the leaders of the abolition movement. Far from approving the stand taken by Rabbi Raphall in his famous "Bible View of Slavery" [7] sermon, as has been charged, Wise refuted several of the Biblical arguments for slavery which were used by Raphall and other pro-slavery divines. "Among all the nonsense imposed on the Bible," he wrote, "the greatest is to suppose the Negroes are the descendants of Ham, and the curse of Noah is applicable to them . . . Canaanites are never mentioned in the Bible as men of color . . . Besides we can not see how the curse of Noah could take effect on the unborn generations of Canaan . . . when the Bible teaches that God visits the iniquity of parents to the third and fourth generation only and [upon] those who hate Him?" [8] When Raphall died in 1868, Dr. Wise, perhaps using hind-sight, wrote that Raphall had given "a divine sanction to an inhuman institution," and "this was a great blunder." Wise even tried to clear the pro-slavery blot off of Raphall's name by recording that "in a subsequent thanksgiving oration he attempted to correct his error, but it was too late, the impression of his first sermon on the subject was firmly seated among friend and foe." [9]

Wise was always horrified at the thought of a reopened slave-trade. He believed that this was the intention of the extreme southerners, and hoped this could be avoided in a compromise settlement before the war. During the war, he broke his political silence once to warn of another possibility of the same thing.

In late '61 he became convinced that the European Confederate agents would be successful in aligning France and Spain against the north, that Spain would invade Mexico and place a Spanish monarch on the throne, and that Mexico would then join hands with the Confederacy. The idea of a European monarchy transplanted to the western hemisphere was a frightening one to him; he wanted America to bring democracy to Europe! His youth in Austria left him with only hatred for monarchy. So he appealed for an immediate drive to crush the rebellion, or, if this was impossible, a compromise peace with the South. But a secondary reason for his fear of a European invasion of Mexico was that "Spain is the only slaveholding power of Europe . . . the only power that has not prohibited the slave trade." If a juncture were effected between Mexico and the Confederacy, then the slave-trade, with all its horrors, would begin anew. The war and the abolition of slavery were unimportant to him, when there was, to his mind, a real danger that the greater evil of the slave traffic would be reinstituted. [10]

Long after the final draft of the Emancipation Proclamation was issued, Wise finally gave an expression of his views on slavery in the Bible. He showed no unwillingness to state his beliefs once slavery had ceased to be a political issue. They are, of course, the ideas of a man opposed to slavery. In a series of articles in late '64, he made a thorough survey of the Biblical laws and concluded that Moses had attempted to abolish slavery "by indirect-direct laws which rendered its existence impossible." "It is evident," he claimed, "that Moses was opposed to slavery from the facts: 1. He prohibited to enslave a Hebrew, male or female, adult or child. 2. He legislated to a people just emerging from bondage and slavery. 3. He legislated for an agricultural community with whom labor was honorable. 4. He legislated not only to humanize the condition of the alien laborers, but to render the acquisition and the retention of bondmen contrary to their will a matter of impossibility." So much for the Biblical view of slavery.

Then he offered a few general comments of his own. "We are not prepared, nobody is, to maintain it is absolutely unjust to purchase savages, or rather their labor, place them under the protection of law, and secure them the benefit of civilized society and their sustenance for their labor. Man in a savage state is not free; the alien servant under the Mosaic law was a free man, excepting only the fruits of his labor. The abstract idea of liberty is more applicable to the alien laborer of the Mosaic system than to the savage, and savages only will sell themselves or their offspring." Wise was still unwilling to come to grips with the evils of southern slavery which so infuriated the north, or with the economic conditions which perpetuated those evils. He even bespoke an idea which had long motivated the program of the American Colonization Society which had, since 1821, colonized freed Negroes in Liberia: "Negro slavery, if it could have been brought under the control of the Mosaic or similar laws, must have tended to the blessing of the negro race by frequent emigration of civilized negroes back to the interior of Africa." [11]

But nowhere in his writings on slavery does he approach the radical and violent anti-slavery position of the abolitionists. Actually he was constitutionally unable to adopt a radical attitude on any issue. Passionate and vehement he was many times, but never radical. In a very revealing editorial on "Radicalism and Reform," published before the war, Wise expressed his utter opposition to radicalism in politics and in religion. "The present state of political affairs should convince every sober-minded and well informed man that radicalism will not do in any province of human activity. There are no leaps in human history . . . Radicalism will not do in politics, because there are historical

rights, inveterate views and habits, thousands of interests connected with the existing state of affairs which will not yield to
theories. It is easy for agitators to excite the passions of the
populace, make friends and arm defenders for any theory; but
it is impossible to revolutionize radically all historical rights." [12]

It was no coincidence that the two leading lights of the American Reform movement were at odds in both religion and politics.
Rabbi David Einhorn the abolitionist, who almost paid for his
political radicalism with his life, was a radical in religion as well.
Wise opposed him in both. After a visit to Baltimore in '60, Wise
wrote that Einhorn's congregation "is half very radical in practice, and entirely so in theory." Much more to Wise's liking was
Rabbi Benjamin Szold, also of Baltimore; Szold shared Wise's
political and religious opinions. Wise sympathized with Szold
because his conservative religious opinions "made hin the aim
of the warfare of both extreme parties" in Baltimore, Einhorn's
radical reform and the extreme orthodoxy of Rabbi Illowy. And
Szold preached a sermon pleading for peace at any price which
Wise printed in *The Israelite* in January, 1861. [13]

Although Wise never attacked Einhorn directly for his abolition
ideas, he wrote with deep acrimony and rancor of abolitionists
in general. He considered them to be "fanatics," "demagogues,"
"red republicans and habitual revolutionaries, who feed on excitement and delight in civil wars, German atheism coupled with
American puritanism who know of no limits to their fanaticism,
visionary philanthropists and wicked preachers who have that
religion which is most suitable to their congregations," and
"demons of hatred and destruction." [14] He saw only war and
bloodshed, chaos and suffering, as the result of their agitation,
and he could not be convinced that this was desirable or advisable under any circumstances, certainly not with slavery as the
crucial issue.

And the most guilty of all the abolitionists, in his eyes, were the Protestant clergymen. No minister should participate in the "vulgar business" of politics, he thought; one who does, "abuses the place and misuses the trust placed in him." But if politics had any place in the pulpit, surely now that the Union was in danger, clergymen should plead for peace and conciliation, save the Union from bloodshed and the horrors of war. Instead, they were, in Wise's opinion, the instigators of the war. "Who in the world could act worse, more extravagant and reckless in this crisis than Protestant priests did. From the very start of the unfortunate difficulties the consequences of which we now suffer so severely, the Protestant priests threw the firebrand of abolitionism into the very heart of this country . . . There was not a Protestant paper in existence that had not weekly an abolitionist tirade. There was scarcely a sermon preached without a touch at least of the 'existing evil.' You know who made Jefferson Davis and the rebellion? The priests did, and their whiners and howlers in the press. The whole host of priests would rather see this country crushed and crippled than discard their fanaticism or give up their political influence." [15]

One characteristic of the abolitionists which, Wise said, aroused his heated resentment was the ethical inconsistency revealed in their lack of concern for other minority groups. In 1859, for instance, the people of Massachusetts, by referendum, adopted an anti-alien law whereby the right to vote and hold office was denied to the foreign-born until they could certify a residence of seven years in the United States, and naturalization as citizens. [16] This curtailment of the rights of white men in a state notorious for its violent abolitionists, convinced Wise that the abolitionists were not humanitarians, but that they, rather, were politicians with a peculiar program for achieving power. "Do you think the Israelites of the South must be your white slaves," he asked, "as you in your naturalization laws treat the foreigner, placing him below the negro?" Bitterly conscious that the Jew still had

132

to fight for the recognition of his rights, even against the pretended defenders of fairness and righteousness, he pointed his finger at them and exclaimed, "Too often . . . those who faint away on hearing of a negro thousands of miles distant having been abused, are always ready to wrong their next neighbor." [17] When abolitionist newspapers and senators selected the southern Jews as their special targets, abused them for supporting their gentile fellow-citizens in the Confederacy, and branded Judah P. Benjamin, with special vehemence, as a member of that "race that stoned prophets and crucified the Redeemer of the world," Wise was almost prepared to become an out-and-out copperhead. He believed that the anti-Semitic character of some abolitionists discredited the entire movement. [18]

Indeed, few of the non-Jewish leaders of the time were interested in defending the Jews against the anti-Semitic attacks so characteristic of the Civil War period. Logically, of course, the abolitionists should have been the first to champion the Jew. That they did not was a continual source of irritation to Wise. "If so many Negroes had been injured," he wrote with flaming pen, "as were Hebrews by the order of General Grant, the bottomless absurdities of Parson Brownlow, and the heartless agent of the Associated Press, you would have cried as loudly as the people of Sodom and Gomorrah; but for the white Hebrew who gave you a God and a religion, you had not a word to say." [19]

Too often the very clergymen who fired their congregants with appeals to righteousness and justice for the Negro were the same ones who urged that the United States be designated a Christian nation by the insertion into the Constitution of provisions for the acknowledgement of Christian dogma. Wise wrote at a fever pitch on this matter as frequently as it was presented. In 1861 such a proposal was forwarded to Congress by a Pennsylvania Synod of the Presbyterian Church, and Wise waxed furiously eloquent: "O, ye hypocrites and pharisees! You would

trample under your impious feet the rights of the Israelite and
millions of intelligent citizens who believe not in Christ — you
would cast the firebrand of civil war in our midst to slay innocent
women and children . . . [you] embrace the distant negro and
rebuke the distant slave-holder whom you fear not, who can not
come and join your church, increase your salaries, or praise your
superlative wisdom." [20] Nothing the abolitionists did, could
please Wise!

Convinced that the abolitionists were in control of the Republican party, and that only disaster could result from the
Republican victory in '60, Wise had no sympathy whatever for
President-Elect Lincoln. When he visited Cincinnati in his weari-
some series of receptions and parades leading up to the inauguration in Washington, Wise wrote of him most patronizingly:
"Poor old Abe Lincoln, who had the quiet life of a country lawyer,
having been elected President of this country, and now going to
be inaugurated in his office, the Philistines from all corners of
the land congregate around their Dagon and worship him . . .
Why all this noise? . . . Wait till he has done something . . . Some
of our friends might like to know how the president looks, and
we can tell them; he looks . . . 'like a country squire for the first
time in the city.' He wept on leaving Springfield and invited his
friends to pray for him; that is exactly the picture of his looks.
We have no doubt he is an honest man, and, as much as we can
learn, also quite an intelligent man; but he will look queer, in
the white house, with his primitive manner." [21]

In his first inaugural address, Lincoln referred to Christianity
as one of the principle supports of the nation in its days of crisis.
The Israelite shortly thereafter published a bitterly partisan letter from a correspondent in New York, attacking him for this
apparent identification of the United States as a Christian country, and also branding Lincoln a coward for his trip by stealth
from Harrisburg to Washington for the inauguration. Wise edi-

torialized in a note following the letter: "From a dozen of letters on the same topic we publish only the above, because it comes from a particular friend. We have only to say for Mr. Lincoln, that his style of writing is so careless and without any successful attempt at either correctness or elegance that he must not be criticized in using this or that word to express an idea. He takes domestic words, as used in Springfield and vicinity to express familiar ideas. In Springfield religion is called Christianity, because people there do not think of any other form of worship, hence Mr. Lincoln uses the same word to express the same sentiment. Mr. Lincoln received the heaviest vote of infidels ever given to any man in this country. We do not believe there is a German infidel, American eccentric, spiritual rapper or atheist in the northern states who did not vote for Mr. Lincoln. Let us see how much benefit he will derive from their Christianity, or how he will settle the political troubles with such piety. He does not care for words. By and by he will learn the precise use and import of terms." [22] Wise would never have written in this manner had he not been aroused as he always was by careless references to the United States as a Christian country in official documents or speeches. *The Israelite's* pages are replete with attacks on governors, mayors, senators and other officials who apparently believed Christianity was the American state religion. And this was, also, another occasion for Wise, the Democrat, to attack the Republican President!

When the President was murdered, however, Wise spoke, with great understanding, of "the generous, genial and honest man, who stood at the head of our people in this unprecedented struggle for national existence and popular liberty; whose words and deeds speak alike and aloud of his unsophisticated mind, purity of heart, honesty of purpose, confidence in the great cause, and implicit faith in the justice of Providence, which inspired him to consistency, courage and self-denial; this Abraham Lincoln,

135

who endeared himself to so many millions of hearts, and gained the admiration of other millions of people, both at home and abroad; whom the myriads of freedmen consider their savior . . . the man who stood at the head of affairs during this gigantic struggle, his cares and troubles, his sleepless nights and days of anxiety, his thoughts and his schemes, his triumphs and mortifications, his hopes and fears, and ten thousand more sentiments, feelings and thoughts . . ." [23] Between 1861 and 1865 Wise's conception of Lincoln's character and significance swerved from the one pole to the other.

During the years that intervened between Lincoln's inauguration and his assassination, Wise wrote indirectly of the occasion for his new insight into the soul of Lincoln. This was in a letter which he wrote to *The Israelite* on January 8, 1863, after his only personal visit with the President. Wise had been drafted into the delegation of Cincinnati Jews who were going to Washington to protest to the President and their Congressmen against General Grant's notorious Order No. 11. They arrived too late, for their mission had already been accomplished by a similar delegation from Paducah, Ky., who were personally involved in the expulsion order, and who were promised by the President that the order would be rescinded immediately.

"Still we thought proper to see the President and express our thanks for his promptness in this matter," Wise wrote the next day, "and before 8 P.M. we were introduced to the President, who being all alone, received us with that frank cordiality, which, though usually neglected, becomes men high in office so well . . . The President gave utterance to his surprise that Gen. Grant should have issued so ridiculous an order, and added — 'to condemn a class is, to say the least, to wrong the good with the bad. I do not like to hear a class or nationality condemned on account of a few sinners.' The President, we must confess, fully illustrated to us and convinced us that he knows of no distinction between Jew and Gentile, that he feels no prejudice against any nationality, and that he by no means will allow that a citizen in any wise be wronged on account of his place of birth or religious confession. He illustrated this point to us in a very happy manner, of which we can only give the substance at present . . . Now, then, in our traveling habiliments, we spoke about half an hour to the President of the U. S. in an open and frank manner, and were dismissed in the same simple style. Sorry we are to say that Congress did not think proper to be as just as the President is . . ."

Dr. Wise was warmly impressed by "poor old Abe Lincoln," the "country squire," whom, he had predicted in February of '61, would "look queer, in the white house, with his primitive manner." Nothing here, in January of '63, about Lincoln's "primitive manner" or his careless style. Wise, like so many visitors to the large office on the second floor of the White House, fell under the spell of Lincoln's democratic manner, good humor, and disarming frankness. Wise spoke with a President whose sense of justice measured his own, and he came away convinced that the President, for one, would not be among those who delighted in casting barbs at American Jewry. This visit, then, is the key to Wise's understanding of the man "who endeared himself to so many millions of hearts, and gained the admiration of other millions of people . . ." Wise became one of the millions, because he met the President face to face, and saw the true Lincoln.

But Wise held more true to his "silence" resolve than we might expect him to do; once he had done what he could to prevent the war, warning the people against the evils of militarism, against empowering the politicians with greater and greater prerogatives, against the danger to democracy and liberty involved in war, against the bloodshed and tears and pain which would come with the first battle, against the corruption and abuse of position and fanaticism and hatred which would rise with the smoke of the cannon and musket, Wise held to his resolution.

The pages of *The Israelite* contain practically no references to the great military and political events of the war years; the battles, the political struggles for power, the anguish of casualty figures, the threatened invasions, the Emancipation Proclamation, the election of '64, are all passed over in all but silence.

On a few occasions, however, Wise felt impelled to treat of the war from a religious viewpoint. He wrote almost from the isolation of a religious neutrality. In one editorial he wrote of the salvation of the individual soul as more important than all the "political crises and financial panics." "If for a moment," he cautioned, "the popular topics of the day absorb the whole attention of the thousands, you should not forget that topics, events, days and generations pass on the fleet wings of time, and your soul remains, with or without salvation, with everlasting joy or remorse, bliss or torment." He came to believe that the war was a punishment from God, designed to cleanse the American soul of materialism, corruption, the love of luxury, the neglect of culture. "Would to God," he prayed, "the calamity of civil war that has befallen us would lead us to investigate closely the national sins that exist among us, and rouse us to extinguish them for ever." "If the war costs us ten thousand professed politicians," he said bitterly, believing as always that the preachers and politicians were alone responsible for the war, "it will turn out a blessing at last, a blessing to the whole land. . . . We cannot enumerate the ten thousand national vices that exist among us, vices which directly or indirectly brought on us the national calamity under which we now suffer. Let these suffice to establish the fact, that this storm deservedly came upon us, that it will purify the atmosphere, and we shall go forth purified and improved to a great extent." "All the standing armies, navies, national guards, armories, forts and fortresses," he exclaimed, "can not save this republic from ultimate destruction, if the nation comes not to the conclusion that there are more precious and desirable objects, holier and more lasting interests, to be attended to than the one and ever annoying object of making money."[24]

Wise supported the various war efforts, howbeit in a mild fashion. Advertisements to stimulate war loans were printed in the pages of *The Israelite* and were reinforced by editorial notes; charitable campaigns connected with the war were given ample publicity; news of Jewish soldiers and officers was given at great length. None of this was, however, based on a partisan conception of the war, for Wise's interest in and sympathy for southern Jewry remained steadfast. From the beginning to the end he had only friendship to offer to the Jews of the south, never the rancour or resentment or even hatred some of the other rabbis of the time seemed to bear.

The influence of *The Israelite*, before the war, had been strongest in the west and in the south. Wise had created valuable contacts with southern congregations, rabbis, and persons in the pre-war years. Almost half of his subscribers lived in the south. As long as he could, he printed advertisements for southern business firms and congregations, letters from southern subscribers, reports from southern congregations, and lists of his agents in southern cities. Immediately after the outbreak of the war he printed directions for the payment of monies owed to him to two agents in the south; copies of *The Israelite* and *Die Deborah* were mailed to the south as long as it was legal to do so. When, finally, in June '61, the Postmaster General of the United States halted all mails to the Confederate States, except under flag of truce through military channels, Wise complained vociferously. "Thus nearly one half of our list of subscribers is gone without prospect of an early settlement of this affair . . . It strikes us that [it] is unconstitutional . . . We know that we will hardly be able to stand this shock." [25] And for some time *The Israelite* continued to print appeals for additional subscribers and for prompt payment of back subscription monies. The financial crisis was passed, after a while, but for several months Wise had been prepared to accept the eventuality of ceasing publication for the duration of the war.

Financial crisis or not, however, Wise lost those subscribers and the influence he wielded over them and the support they gave to his ideas, projects, and plans for American Jewry. This he could not forget. And it is likely that when, ever and again, there seemed to be a possibility of a final conclusion to the war, his hopes soared for a reintegration of southern Jewry into his fold of *Israelite* readers and supporters.

He always defended their right to support the Confederacy together with their neighbors; he was never willing to disown them for disloyalty to the Union, as were Einhorn and Felsenthal, for instance. When news of southern Jewish congregations filtered through the grape-vine, when southern cities were captured by the armies of the Union, when letters were smuggled or legally delivered across the blockade lines, Wise eagerly printed such tidings as were communicated to him. In 1862, for instance, he obtained information about the congregations in Jackson and Summit, Miss., Atlanta and Columbus, Ga., Montgomery and Mobile, Ala., and was happy to relate that "our informant tells us wonders of the material prosperity of our friends in the far South." [26] Earlier the same year he printed an advertisement for a rabbi for the Charleston Reform congregation and added an editorial word for good measure. The congregation is an excellent one, he says, and therefore competent men, only, need apply. He will recommend none but the finest candidates. But "letters to Charleston," he adds, "must be sent via Fortress Monroe, by flag of truce." There is no other indication that a bitter war is in progress and that the rabbi is to minister to a congregation of the enemy. Wise did not consider them enemies, but friends. [27] In '63 and '64 *The Israelite* printed several letters from Jewish Confederate prisoners at Fort Delaware, appealing for help and assistance; Wise forwarded one of these to the proper authorities at Washington, but to no avail. [28] Once the war had ended, and communications of one sort or another were restored, *The Israelite* printed voluminous reports from the south as rapidly as Wise could obtain them, as though he were consciously trying to erase the four year period during which his contact with southern Jewry had been slight if not non-existent.

There were further demonstrations of his sympathy for the south. Wise preached forgiveness and conciliation as soon as the war was won. In his Victory Sermon preached on April 14, 1865, and printed in *The Israelite* on April 21, 1865, he pleaded for mercy towards the vanquished, asked that they be welcomed back into the Union, and that no spirit of revenge be borne against them. Even after the assassination of Lincoln, when Wise himself realized that the perpetrators of that infamous deed had to be punished severely, he hoped that vengeance would not be exacted from the entire south. In 1867 he attacked those clergy-men who were still calling for revenge against the south, and asserted that, as Christians, they demonstrated very little of the Christian spirit. When the amnesty proclamation was issued in that same year he greeted it with "joyous satisfaction" as "a blessing and an honor to our country," and looked forward to the time when all southern prisoners would be freed. [29] As late as 1873 he was still the champion of the south and wrote in an editorial, "As long as the South is interfered with, any way mo-lested, or denied any rights or privileges which others enjoy anywhere, we will be found to stand with the South." [30] He was ever true to the "dear friends and near relations, beloved brethren and kinsmen" against whom he had never desired the north to go to war.

II

Judging from the available sources[31] there was relatively little anti-Semitism in the United States prior to the Civil War, and that, apparently, stemmed from fundamentalist Christian doctrine and indefinite suspicions carried on from the mediaeval world. From the outbreak of the Civil War and onward, however, a veritable torrent of slander and abuse was loosed upon the Jews, stimulated primarily by economic and political tensions.[32] A detailed study of the growth of anti-Semitism in the United States will undoubtedly demonstrate that, contrary to popular supposition, the Civil War was the period in which modern anti-Semitism began in America, and not the later period of intensive Eastern-European Jewish immigration to the United States. Simon Wolf, who, in after years devoted his career to Jewish defense work in government circles in Washington, wrote in a letter to the editor of the New York *Evening Post* of November 22, 1864, "the war now raging has developed an intensity of malice that borders upon the darkest days of superstition and the Spanish Inquisition." Wise said a year previously, "as Israelites, we were more mortified and outraged during this war than we were in Austria under the Metternich regime, in Russia under Nesselrode, in Bavaria under Mounteufel . . . We feel sorely afflicted and disgusted, and wish nothing more earnestly than peace."[33]

A rising crescendo of libels was hurled at the Jews almost from the very beginning of the war, libels remarkably similar to those with which the Jews were plagued during the Second World War. In both the north and the south, these were the accusations: draft-dodging, the purchase of officer-commissions, war profiteering, bribery, smuggling and black-marketeering, speculation at the expense of the government, and many other types of foul disloyalty. Judah P. Benjamin was a favorite target in the north, but also among his enemies in the south; August Belmont was his northern counterpart. Jews were referred to in prejudicial terms in the Congress of the north, and in the legislatures of the Confederacy. Public heroes, military and civilian, took occasion to accuse the Jews of every kind of treachery and baseness. The notorious General Order No. Eleven, issued by General Grant in late '62, by which all Jews were expelled from the Department of the Tennessee for trading with the enemy, was only one of a number of anti-Semitic statements issuing from prominent quarters. Wise wrote, after the war, and in reference to another libel concerning Belmont, "since the outbreak of the late rebellion we have been used to the outpourings of such persons." [34]

Yes, Wise was used to such outpourings. He took pains to publish them in *The Israelite*, so that his readers might know their enemies, as many as he heard or saw or as were reported to him: dozens and dozens of clippings from newspapers in cities large and small, quotations from speeches by politicians and clergymen prominent and unknown, libels from sources north and south. Wise published them all, together with all the evidence he could gather, and answered them with an unflagging zeal, though with a rising temper. At the same time, he carefully printed many pro-Jewish statements, defenses of the Jews by public newspapers and magazines, comments by gentiles who, also, were zealous to oppose the bigotry of their day.

A few instances will illustrate the character of these libels and the nature of Wise's defense. On November 30, 1863, Major General S. A. Hurlbut issued his Order No. 162, prohibiting 14 Jewish clothing houses in the Memphis, Tenn., area from selling military clothing, and ordering them to send their goods back across the lines. Wise comments, "the goods were bought and shipped on legal permits, and five percent duty was paid thereon, which is a clear loss to the merchants. The cause for the order is not clearly stated, so we cannot tell why it was issued." But his correspondents had given him additional information concerning the case, which he considered reliable enough to offer to his readers. "Most wonderful, however, in this matter, is that two non-Jewish houses, of Memphis, Tickner & Co., and Waggner and Cheek, were not included in this order. On the contrary, it is maintained, on good authority, that Tickner & Co. not only knew in advance that such an order was to be issued, but were given permits to bring military goods to Memphis and monopolize the trade." Wise concludes a tirade against military rule with a quotation from a Washington dispatch, detailing the news of another huge Quartermaster Department fraud involving millions of dollars, perpetrated by high ranking officers, whose religion is of course not mentioned. [35]

On February 16, 1863, an Associated Press dispatch from New Orleans, telegraphed to all the member-newspapers, told of three Jews who had been caught in a fishing smack on Lake Ponchartrain, carrying medicine and letters from New Orleans to the Confederate lines. The letters, the report said, were "from forty or fifty leading citizens of New Orleans to persons high in authority in the Confederate government." The article concluded with the following sentences: "The Jews in New Orleans and all the South ought to be exterminated. They run the blockade, and are always to be found at the bottom of every new villainy." The religion of the "leading citizens" and of the "persons high in authority in the Confederate government" was not specified, of course, nor was extermination urged as the only course of procedure for dealing with them. Wise demanded an investigation of the Associated Press, and quoted editorials to that effect from the Cincinnati dailies, which also defended the Jews and attacked the A.P. reporter responsible for this bitter assault. The *Enquirer* surmised that the report was inspired by Massachusetts Yankees who had been out-smarted by local Jews in their first attempts at carpet-bagging. [36]

Wise admitted that there were Jews who were unscrupulous, but insisted that they be judged as individuals, not as members of the Jewish people. Jews are not a class apart, he believed, but part and parcel of the society in which they live. He pointed to the efforts of Jews in the cause of the Union, pleading as Jews have pleaded before and since his time: "Our sons enlisted in the army, our daughters sew and knit for the wounded soldiers and their poor families, our capitalists spend freely, our hospitals are thrown open to the sick soldiers of all creeds, our merchants represented at every benevolent association contribute largely to the wealth and propserity of the cities, give bread and employment to thousands; we keep from politics, gambling houses, public-offices, penitentiaries, and newspaper publications — what else must we do to heal those petty scribblers from their mad prejudice?" [37]

As the war progressed, congressional committees made periodic examinations into the political and military agencies responsible for carrying on the war, and uncovered mountains of evidence of misappropriation, bribery, waste, corruption, and speculation. Wise printed excerpts from the public reports of these committees. It became more and more obvious to him that many of the libels about Jewish corruption, smuggling, and other dishonesty had been circulated as a smoke screen, to draw attention away from the activities of the financiers, profiteers, incompetent and dishonest office-holders, and bribe-taking politicians. The Jews were then, as always, a convenient scape-goat.

Occasionally a libel could be run into the ground. The Cincinnati *Enquirer* of October 20, 1861, reported that a "combination of Jewish clothing houses in this city" had been organized "to take advantage of the pressing necessity of our Western soldiers for blankets, etc." The Jews of Cincinnati became so aroused that the editors were forced to interview the business men concerned, to examine their records, and then to retract the statement. The apology stated that one clothing man said "that they had made contracts at an early period in the war, when prices were down, and were now uncomplainingly living up to them, since prices had materially raised. His figures were sufficient assurance of his truthfulness." Wise suspected that *The Enquirer* had published the report in an effort to divert the public from inquiring too closely into its own "supposed secession proclivities;" and, further, that the Jews, being defenseless, could not retaliate against the paper whereas the powerful interests, who were actually guilty of such practices, could deal the paper a staggering blow for such an expose. Nevertheless, the retraction was printed. [38]

This did not happen very frequently, however, and Wise reluctantly had to admit that the truth made little impression. Anti-Semitism was now a political and economic weapon. Was it here to stay? Wise could not tell, but he was willing to resort to any measure to nail the lie. In 1868, he fell in heartily with the proposal of the Jews of Chattanooga, Tenn., who determined to build a monument to the Jewish war dead who had fallen in their area. He offered the suggestion to all communities: "The Jews have been outraged during the war by officials, such as Grant, Butler, and others, by many a corporal and many a scribe whose names are not worth mentioning, although Brownlow is now Governor and senator. They always assumed the Jews were idle spectators in the great drama . . . Coming generations may accept the slanderous statements made against our brethren as being true. Therefore, also, we admonish our coreligionists to have every dead soldier exhumed and buried in our cemeteries, and let the monuments to the deceased Soldiers of our persuasion put to shame all those who slandered the Jews in a dangerous and excitable time." A desperate measure, indeed, to counteract anti-Semitism! And yet how modern the need appears, measured by the anti-Semitic libels of World War II. As late as 1891, however, Wise was still defending the Jews against the old accusations he had answered in almost every issue of *The Israelite* from 1861 to 1865, and Simon Wolf was gathering statistics to prove that the Jews had been patriotic during the Civil War. [39]

NOTES

[1] VII, No. 42, p. 334, April 19, 1861. All references, unless otherwise noted, are to volume and number of *The Israelite*.

[2] See Jacob R. Marcus, *The Americanization of Isaac Mayer Wise*, Cincinnati, 1931, pp. 10–18, for a detailed treatment of Wise's political ideas. Wise probably voted for Stephen Douglas in the election of '60, although he supported no candidate in the columns of *The Israelite*. His eulogy of Douglas seems to indicate this: "This is one of our national sins, the bitter consequences of which we now suffer; all parties in this country committed the same sin — they killed their greatest men, and elevated imbeciles to the highest stations of honor . . . Douglas is dead, and his most bitter enemies must admit that the country has lost a great man." VII, No. 49, p. 386, June 7, 1861. On Sept. 5, 1863, Wise himself was nominated for the office of State Senator by the Democratic Party convention at Carthage, but he declined the nomination at the behest of the officers of his congregation and of the Talmud Yelodim Institute. The letter he wrote on that occasion was full of regret: "I certainly feel obliged to decline a nomination so honorably tendered, notwithstanding my private opinion, that I might render some services to my country, not altogether unessential, especially as those who nominated me know well my sincere attachment to this country and government." X, No. 12, pp. 92–3, Sept. 18, 1863.

[3] VII, No. 26, p. 205, Dec. 28, 1860.

[4] VII, No. 27, Jan. 4, 1861 to No. 32, Feb. 8, 1861.

[5] Max Kohler ("Jews and the American Anti-Slavery Movement," *PAJHS*, No. V, (1897), p. 150) and Philip S. Foner (*The Jews in American History, 1654–1865*, N. Y., 1945, p. 60) state erroneously that Dr. Wise endorsed the pro-slavery sermon preached on Jan. 4, 1861 by Rabbi Morris J. Raphall.

[6] IX, No. 34, p. 268, Feb. 27, 1863.

[7] Included in the collection, *Fast Day Sermons*, N. Y., 1861. See *AJCW*, pp. 16–18. Among other things, Raphall insisted that the Bible favored the institution of slavery, and that no Biblical passages could be furnished to defend the abolitionist viewpoint. On the other hand, he was fully aware of the differences between the Biblical conception of the slave as "a *person* in whom the dignity of human nature is to be respected" and "the heathen view of slavery which prevailed at Rome, and which, I am sorry to say, is adopted in the South, [which] reduces the slave to a

thing, and a thing can have no rights." Raphall was a defender of slavery, but not a defender of Southern slavery!

[8] VII, No. 29, p. 230, Jan. 18, 1861. Wise knew, however, that arguments from the Bible are dangerous. Proofs could be cited for almost any point of view. So he also cited refutations of abolitionist arguments based on Biblical passages and events. He believed, for instance, that "the Hyksos of Manetho, who oppressed the Israelites in Egypt, were Negroes." See VII, No. 38, p. 300, March 22, 1861, which concludes with the amazing statement that "the unity of the human race can not successfully be defended either biblically or scientifically."

[9] XIV, No. 52, p. 4, July 3, 1868. Wise was quite unsuccessful. No writer on the subject has ever regarded Raphall as other than a convinced pro-slavery adherent. As late as 1897 Wise himself was forced to print a formal denial that he "shared the opinion of Dr. Raphall . . . that slavery was a divine institution, sanctioned by the Old Testament Scriptures, or that there is on record one paragraph to show that the said Isaac M. Wise ever was a pro-slavery man or favored the institution of slavery at any time." LXVIII, No. 52, p. 4, June 24, 1897, answering the *London Jewish Chronicle*.

[10] VIII, No. 25, p. 196, Dec. 20, 1861.

[11] XI, No. 20, p. 156, Nov. 11, 1864 to No. 26, p. 204, Dec. 23. The series is entitled "On the Provisional Portion of the Mosaic Code, with Special Reference to Polygamy and Slavery."

[12] VII, No. 28, p. 221, Jan. 11, 1861. Wise continues, applying this reasoning to religious radicalism, "As easy as it is by stringent conservatism to drive the intelligent from the Synagogue, so easy it is by radicalism to deprive a man of religion . . . Support the spirit of progress by rational reforms. But forget not, that religion is the most sacred boon God has granted to man and play not with it as a child does with the ball . . . Let us be reasonable in piety and pious in our reasoning. Let us be progressive in improvements and conservative in principles."

[13] VII, No. 7, p. 5, Aug. 17, 1860; VII, No. 28, p. 220, Jan. 11, 1861.

[14] VII, No. 22, p. 173, Nov. 30, 1860; No. 24, p. 188, Dec. 14; No. 26, p. 205, Dec. 28; No. 37, p. 292, March 15, 1861; VIII, No. 30, p. 236, Jan. 24, 1862. See Louis Ruchames, "The Abolitionists and the Jews," *PAJHS*, XLII (1952), No. 2, pp. 131–55, for a rebuttal of Wise's opinion of the abolitionists.

[15] VII, No. 31, p. 244, Feb. 1, 1861; No. 48, p. 381, May 31; VIII, No. 16, p. 124, Oct. 18; cf. X, No. 8, p. 60, Aug. 19, 1864.

[16] Lincoln's adverse opinion of this law and its intention is contained in his letter to Canisius, May 17, 1859, Chicago Historical Society.

[17] VII, No. 30, p. 238, Jan. 25, 1861.

[18] VII, No. 38, p. 301, March 22, 1861; VIII, No. 35, p. 278, Feb. 28, 1862. Senator Henry Wilson, of Mass., quoted above, attacked the Jews several times in Congressional speeches. In 1872, when Wilson was nominated for the Vice-

Presidency, Wise reminded his readers of Wilson's past record and urged them not to vote for a man "whose conceptions of justice, equality, and liberty, are so narrow and ungenerous." XIX, No. 9, p. 8, Aug. 30, 1872; No. 10, p. 8, Sept. 6. Wise overlooked Wilson's liberal championship of Jewish chaplains in 1862; Rabbi Felsenthal thought Wilson the hero of the entire chaplaincy controversy: *Sinai,* VII, 200–201.

[19] IX, No. 34, p. 268, Feb. 27, 1863.

[20] VII, No. 29, p. 229, Jan. 18, 1861. During the war, Wise found yet another reason for hating the abolitionists. He believed that they were responsible, in the final analysis, for the exclusion of rabbis from the chaplaincy provisions of the Act of Congress, passed July 22, 1861. He wrote, in one of a long series of editorials on the chaplaincy controversy running for over a year, that "a score of fanatics, adepts in the act of Salem witch-burning, abolitionists, know-nothings, and detesters of everything except Natick leather and niggers, have, true to their avowed purpose of troubling and pestering the foreigner and the 'Christ-killer' . . . instigated the unconstitutional provision limiting chaplains to ministers of 'a Christian denomination.' " VIII, No. 25, p. 196, Dec. 20, 1861. Believing that the establishment of a Chaplains Corps was unconstitutional, because it provided for the employment of clergymen by the state, Wise accused Congress of violating the Constitution to pay a political debt to the abolitionist ministers who helped elect them; since "the Hebrew Rabbis are no politicians . . . [and] proved to be conservative in politics while Christian clergymen are the most violent abolitionists," there was no need to provide political offices for rabbis! VIII, No. 44, p. 348, May 2, 1862. In his hatred of abolitionists, in this instance, Wise was deliberately forgetting that there were a few abolitionist rabbis.

[21] VII, No. 33, p. 262, Feb. 15, 1861.

[22] VII, No. 37, p. 294, March 15, 1861. Wise, also, believed that Lincoln had been a coward in running away from the threatened assassination. In VII, No. 35, p. 278, March 1, 1861, under the Hebrew title, "Haftoras Lincoln," but without comment, Wise quoted Neh. 6.10–12, where Nehemiah tells of his refusal to flee a threatened assault.

[23] XI, No. 44, p. 348, April 28, 1865.

[24] VII, No. 37, p. 292, March 15, 1861; No. 45, p. 356, May 10; VIII, No. 1, p. 4, July 5, 1861; No. 3, p. 20, July 19. See also VIII, No. 30, p. 236, Jan. 24, 1862; X, No. 2, p. 12, July 10, 1863; XI, No. 8, p. 60, Aug. 19, 1864.

[25] VII, No. 50, p. 396, June 14, 1861; cf. XIII, No. 1, p. 5, July 6, 1866.

[26] IX, No. 19, p. 147, Nov. 14, 1862.

[27] VIII, No. 36, pp. 283, 285, March 7, 1862.

[28] X, No. 16, p. 122, Oct. 16, 1863; XI, No. 16, p. 124, Oct. 14, 1864.

[29] XIV, No. 3, p. 4, July 19, 1867; No. 12, p. 4, Sept. 20. In June, 1867, Wise visited Richmond and was bitter in his reaction to the results of the war, whereby

the negroes seemed destined to assume control of the entire Southland. He wrote of the negroes roaming the streets at will, while the white remained in their homes. Undoubtedly he was absorbing the propaganda line of the defeated Confederates when he predicted that the whites would eventually be forced to leave the South; then the negroes would be in full command and would stimulate a flood of negro immigration from Africa. There was no humanitarianism in his sarcastic comments on the significance of the emancipation of the Southern slaves: "posterity will consider us an admirably generous class of people, who not only expunged the disgrace of slavery at an expense of a million of men and three thousand millions of treasure, and now support a standing army at an expense of two hundred millions a year, to protect the freedmen; but also virtually give them eleven States, to be entirely under their control and safe-keeping." XIII, No. 51, p. 4, June 28, 1867.

[30] XX, No. 8, p. 4, Feb. 21, 1873.

[31] See pp. 59–64, 73 above.

[32] See *AJCW*, pp. 156–175.

[33] X, No. 24, p. 188, Dec. 11, 1863.

[34] XIV, No. 35, p. 4, March 6, 1868.

[35] X, No. 24, p. 188, Dec. 11, 1863.

[36] IX, No. 33, p. 258, Feb. 20, 1863.

[37] VIII, No. 36, p. 284, March 7, 1862.

[38] VIII, No. 17, p. 132, Oct. 25, 1861.

[39] XIV, No. 31, p. 4, February 7, 1868; XXXVIII, No. 23, p. 4, Dec. 3, 1891 ff.

VII

The First American
Jewish Theological Seminary:
Maimonides College, 1867-1873

THE REVEREND ISAAC LEESER, spiritual leader of Beth El Emeth Congregation of Philadelphia, had only four months more to live. At the age of sixty, worn and haggard, his body wracked by over-work and careless attention to his physical health, he ought to have rested and relaxed.

But he would not. His agile, dogged mind was still envisioning projects and programs designed to solve the fundamental problems which plagued the American Jewish community. Single-handed, with a minimum of encouragement from the laity and hardly any cooperation from his colleagues in the rabbinate, Leeser had attempted, during a career which stretched over thirty-eight of the most eventful years in the development of the burgeoning American Jewry, to give form and substance to Jewish cultural and religious life in America. From his pen came the first complete English translations of the Sephardic and Ashkenazic prayerbooks, the first Jewishly-oriented translation into English of the entire Bible, the first series of sermons to be delivered and published by an American Jewish clergyman, the monthly issues of the first successful American Jewish periodical (*The Occident and American Jewish Advocate* of which he was both publisher and editor), and translations of various volumes issued under the aegis of the first Jewish Publication Society of America, of which he was founder and director. His eyes had recognized the crying needs of American Jewry for cultural guidance and religious inspiration; his hands had worked to provide the answers to those needs. In order to fulfill his responsibilities as he saw them, he became the first American rabbi to travel great distances throughout the country; his was the aspiration to give a sense of cohesive togetherness and mutuality to the widely-scattered, isolated Jewish communities throughout the nation. [1]

And now, in October, 1867, he was embarking upon the realization of his most cherished dream, an American Jewish theological seminary, a college for the training and education of rabbinical students. Maimonides College it was to be called, in honor of the man whom many conceive to have been the most erudite and productive Jewish scholar who ever lived. And he, Isaac Leeser, who had devised so many other schemes for the intensification of positive and affirmative Jewish living in the United States, was to be its Provost.

I

THE BACKGROUND OF THE IDEA

Maimonides College was new, but the idea of an institution of higher Jewish learning in the United States was not a novel one. Before Isaac Leeser had even come to the United States, a committee consisting of the Reverend M. L. M. Peixotto, minister of Shearith Israel Congregation of New York City, Mordecai M. Noah, the famous Tammany Hall politician and journalist, and Judah Zuntz, an active member of the New York Jewish community, had circularized a number of American Jews, soliciting their interest in an exciting new educational venture. This was the first documented attempt to attract interest for a Jewish institution of higher education; it would not, however, occasion surprise if an earlier one were to be uncovered, for it was obvious, even then, in 1821, that the study of the Jewish heritage had to be integrated into American life by the creation of an institution dedicated to that purpose. The New York committee was sponsoring a proposal by Moses Elias Levy, one of the earliest Jewish settlers in Florida and the father of Senator David Levy Yulee. Levy's plan called for the purchase of a tract of land for his school, the settlement there of a number of families including the instructors, the assumption of the responsibility of educating the coming Jewish generations by the "Hebrew community at large" and the establishment of local societies for the support of this institution throughout the country. [2]

This project, announced in a circular letter dated May 9, 1821, did not give specific notice to the need for an American-trained religious leadership. But its emphasis upon the teaching of "the Hebrew language and laws, so as to comprehend both letter and spirit," in order to "promote the perpetuity of our religion," leaves little doubt that, if successful, the institution would have produced not only Jewish agriculturalists and artisans, but also Jewish scholars.

According to the printed circular, Moses Levy had planned to travel from city to city, to deliver the proposals in person, and to discuss with Jewish leaders everywhere the practical aspects of his program. There is no record, however, of the result of his discussions, and the project appears to have been abandoned without any further public appeal. Nevertheless, at least one of its proponents, Mordecai M. Noah, was not discouraged; he continued to speak throughout the following decades in favor of the establishment of a national institution "where children of the Jewish persuasion can obtain a classical education, and at the same time, be properly instructed in the Hebrew language; where they can live in conformity to our laws, and acquire a liberal knowledge of the principles of their religion." [3]

Isaac Leeser, however, appears to have been the first to campaign for the establishment of an educational institution created primarily for the training of young men as rabbis, in connection with the 1841 proposal for the organization of an American Jewish religious union. One of the educational objectives of the proposed "religious union" was the creation of a theological institute:

A High School [that is, a *Hochschule*, a university in German educational terminology] for education in the higher branches, is to be established in some central point whenever practicable . . . where young men are to be educated in such a manner, that they may be fit for the office of Hazan, lecturer and teacher; and young women be educated for the high calling of female instructors . . . [4]

Since the congregational union itself was never organized, the creation of the school was never discussed, but Leeser was not so easily discouraged.

He continued, in the pages of *The Occident*, to press for the creation of a rabbinical seminary. He complained bitterly, and with justification, about the inadequate background and training of the men who were then serving as rabbis in American synagogues. Educated abroad, for the most part unordained, they could not adjust easily to American ways and manners. Leeser was convinced that this deficiency in rabbinic leadership was one indisputable explanation for the lack of loyalty of many American Jews to their ancestral faith. "We see but one remedy for the evil," he said, "and this is to establish a HIGH SCHOOL for general education in one central position . . . whence may issue men of ample religious and literary endowment . . . men in whose hands the future destinies of their respective congregations could be placed with safety . . ." [5]

Another voice soon joined Leeser's appeal. Soon after his arrival in America in 1846, Isaac Mayer Wise, who became rabbi in Albany, New York, came to the conclusion that American Jewry could not long survive without a congregational union and a rabbinical seminary. In his call to a national conference of Jewish representatives, issued in December, 1848, as we have already seen, Wise decried the inadequacy of the rabbinate, and asserted that higher Jewish education was a major responsibility of every American Jew. But so few congregations were interested in meeting to discuss such national problems, that the conference was not even held. [6]

A few months later, however, as we have already noted, when the charter of the Hebrew Education Society of Philadelphia was drawn up, Leeser insisted on the insertion of a provision for the eventual establishment of a rabbinical seminary, whenever funds would permit, because he was certain that this was the next logical step in the growth of a self-respecting, self-perpetuating American Jewish community. He had little hope of immediate action, but time and again he pointed to this enabling clause as a portent of the future. [7]

In 1852, Sampson Simson, the eccentric New York philanthropist and founder of the Jews' Hospital of New York (now Mount Sinai Hospital) established an organization which he named the "Jewish Theological Seminary and Scientific Institute," appointing for it a board of trustees, and contributing to it a tract of land in Yonkers comprising some four and one-half acres. Unfortunately he did not give to this board the same amount of time and leadership which he gave to the hospital project. His aggressive and positive policies created the hospital in the face of much indifference and apathy, but when he died in 1857 the seminary was still only a tract of land held in trust by a twelve-man board which took its responsibility to be limited to acting as trustees for the land. [8]

The seven surviving trustees, in 1890, deeded this property to the Jewish Theological Seminary Association of America, with the approval of the New York state legislature. Taxes had accumulated, however, during these long years of neglect, and amounted to one-third of the total value of the land. Negotiations were conducted with the proper officials, and the taxes were reduced to a more reasonable figure. Final disposition of the property cannot be traced, but it was probably sold at the time of the reorganization of the Seminary in 1902. After a lapse of exactly fifty years, then, Sampson Simson's dream found some slight fruition in a contribution to the growth of a great seminary, due in no measure, however, to the unimaginative policies of his appointees. [9]

Time may have passed swiftly for Simson's trustees, but it dragged very slowly for those who agonized over the continuing need for a seminary that was more than a name or a piece of real estate. From 1849 to 1855 Wise was silent, although he had not given up hope for the activation of his idea of a seminary. In 1855 he thought he had found a solution to the knotty problem of organization. He gathered together a group of his close supporters in Cincinnati, numbering perhaps two hundred men, who agreed to constitute themselves as the founding branch of the Zion Collegiate Association. Wise's scheme was to stimulate the organization of local societies throughout the country, societies which would be pledged to support Jewish education and to participate in the founding of a Zion College. Wise felt instinctively that no single community could create and successfully support an institution of national significance; it would have to obtain the cooperation of many Jewish communities. Through correspondence and personal speaking tours, Wise stimulated enough interest in his project for similar associations to be organized in New York City, Philadelphia, Baltimore, Cleveland and Louisville. The plan was working!

If only Wise had followed his own better judgment. But with characteristic recklessness and impetuousness, he led his Cincinnati chapter into the unilateral decision to create a Zion

College in Cincinnati, without any consultation of the other Zion Collegiate Associations and certainly without their approval. Early in November, 1855, the Cincinnatians held an elaborate banquet, attended by some one hundred and fifty well-wishers, commemorating the opening of the new institution. Governor-elect Salmon P. Chase and other distinguished non-Jews came as guests of honor to speak words of congratulation and friendship. Wise's *Israelite* published a detailed announcement of the faculty and program of the College during the weeks after the banquet:

ZION COLLEGE.

Parents and Guardians take notice, that the time of the admitting examination to Zion College, begins the 23d inst., 10 A. M., at the office, Metropolitan Building, corner of Ninth and Walnut streets, and the course of lectures and studies begins the 26th inst., at 9 A. M,

The Directors have elected the following Professors and assistant Professors

Rev. Dr. W. ROTHENHEIM,

Professor of the Hebrew department, including the Bible, Talmud and the languages, History, Geography and Archeology appartaining thereto.

Rev. Dr. M. LILIENTHAL,

Professor of the Classical department and living languages, including Latin, Greek and universal history; Criticism, Rhetoric, practical elocution, Composition and Grammar of the English, French and German languages.

MELVIN M. COHEN, ESQ.

Assistant Professor in this department, for the English branches, the history, geography and constitution of the United States.

Rev. Dr. ISAAC M. WISE,

Professor of the scientific and philosophical department, including mental philosophy, natural history, natural philosophy, chemistry, mathematics, &c.

157

J. Junkerman, Esq., Assistant professor of mathematics, arithmetic and drawing.

S. Thompson, Esq., assistant professor in scientific penmanship.

Arrangements have been made for instruction in bookkeeping, vocal and instrumental music, the Italian and Spanish languages, and gymnastic exercises. Terms of tuition $50 per annum

The Boarding-houses for students are under the control of the Professors.

Students are held to study such branches as required by their parents or guardians; if no directions are given they are held to study all branches.

For particulars enquire of either of the directors, professors, or at the office of the Israelite.

The Board of Directors.

S. FRIEDMAN.

PH. HEIDELBACH,	S. KATZENBERGER,
M. HELLMAN,	V. H. LOVENSTEIN,
CHARLES CAHN,	Dr. A. ROSENFELD,
M. ESCALES,	M. J. MACK.

The New York Association, however, took great offense at the Cincinnatians' uncooperative attitude and severed all connection with Wise's brain-child. Other chapters were not even firmly established, let alone able or willing to support a College they had no part in creating.

Cincinnati and Isaac Mayer Wise had to go it alone. At first the College offered promise of survival. Twenty-eight scholarships were made available, and fourteen students enrolled for the first term, including two Christians. But the College could not compete with established secular schools, and Cincinnati alone (or any other city, for that matter) could not possibly support a Jewish school of higher learning. Wise's high prospects were being pounded into fine dust that year of 1855: the Cleveland Conference of Rabbis for which he had held out great hopes ended in utter and abysmal misunderstanding; the radical reformers in the East and traditionalists everywhere turned down his proffers of cooperation with scorn, wrath or suspicion. Zion

College had been opened as a symbol and a promise. But without the help of other communities and the sympathetic support of other rabbis, neither Cincinnati nor Wise could long maintain the symbol or the promise. Zion College was closed without a word of eulogy some time during 1856 or 1857.[10]

But the need was not to be denied. Each passing year provided further evidence that American Jewish religious life and growth would become altogether stultified without an American-oriented rabbinate which could deal realistically with the problems of second generation American Jews. Outstanding European preachers and theologians continued to emigrate to America, but the barriers of language and habit restricted their usefulness. Lay and rabbinic leaders with vision saw clearly that American Jewish congregations were failing to discharge their responsibilities unless they made satisfactory provision for the spiritual leadership of the future. Isaac Leeser minced no words in his counter-attack on those who liked things as they were:

... We have heard, indeed, some men assert, while indulging in a sneering, vulgar fault-finding, that this is not the country to do this thing; that we are not able to train scholars in America, and that it is an assumption ... to propose doing what hitherto has always been done for us in Europe. It is German civilization, German mind we need here, and can depend on it with perfect safety. Yes, if the question were merely to find a certain number of *superior clergy* (excuse us reader, for employing the phrase) for congregations who understand German, and can afford to pay heavy salaries, the thing would be well enough ...

[I]s it nothing to have a ministry trained on the spot, who can speak the language of the country with all the elegance and correctness that are customary in other societies? must our pulpit always remain German? must natives of this country learn foreign languages first before they can receive religious instructions in the synagogue? We know well enough, that in so speaking we shall be charged with committing treason to our native land, as we are German ourself, and have, whatever information we have, brought it over with us when we crossed the Atlantic ... But after all is nothing due to the *native* population, who cannot speak German? or do our Germanists (to make a new word) expect to maintain the Teutonic tongue for more than two generations in the large cities, unless it be done by excluding Israelites from a general intercourse with society . . .[11]

Leeser's continual campaigning, and Wise's, though they were unfortunately not conducted conjointly or in friendship, were bound to make sense to a gradually widening circle of people.

By 1865, three movements were in progress for the establishment of a national Jewish educational institution.

In New York City, the radical Reformers, led by Rabbis Samuel Adler of Temple Emanu-El and David Einhorn of Temple Beth-El, created the "Emanu-El Theological Seminary Association," on October 8, 1865. Conceived to serve only the interests of those congregations which had made a sharp break with tradition, the Association's meetings bristled with hostility towards orthodoxy. The objective of the Association was to spread only the doctrines of the most extreme Reformers. During the first year a sum of six thousand dollars was collected from one hundred and thirty-three contributing members who paid ten dollars dues a year, and from seventy-five life members who made an endowment contribution of one hundred dollars. During that first year, also, under the aegis of the Association, two students who indicated their desire to study for the rabbinate were granted scholarships to Columbia College and were tutored in Hebrew literature by Isaac Adler, son of the rabbi of Emanu-El.[12]

At the second annual meeting, Rabbi Einhorn delivered a long and impassioned appeal for a change of the Seminary's name, insisting that other Reform congregations would find little interest in supporting a seminary named for and controlled by one single synagogue. Einhorn further asserted that the Association must take action to create a genuine seminary, not one in name only:

. . . Your institution exists only in the imagination; you have a pretty large number of members, an excellent Board of trustees, annual meetings, but one thing only is wanting — the Seminary; you have everything, but neither teachers nor pupils. We have just heard, from the Report of our worthy President, of the existence of two pupils, but these are waiting for a Seminary as for the Messiah. Where is their professor? Dr. Adler, this I know, does not instruct them. Your Seminary is a still-born child, because the noble mother that bore it was pleased to wear a too tightly-laced corset . . . [13]

Einhorn's plea bore fruit. The meeting empowered a committee to change the name of the association. In December, 1866, the Board of the Association announced the adoption of a new name, "The American Hebrew College of the City of New York," and appealed for the support of all sympathetic congregations and individuals. [14] Einhorn was too optimistic about the effect of a change of name, however; little evidence of greater support and interest for the organization was revealed in the president's report at the third annual meeting. [15]

It was not long before the Association readopted its original name and intent. In 1872 several students, including Emil G. Hirsch and Felix Adler, were studying in Germany on fellowships awarded by the Association. That same year the Association transferred its funds (some $10,000) to the congregation's treasurer on the condition that they would be used to defray the expenses of a new "Emanu-El Preparatory School for Jewish Rabbis." [16] This new School was not a school, however; rather it was and continued to be a fund for the awarding of stipends to worthy rabbinical students. In 1953, the moneys (amounting to over $26,168), were contributed by Temple Emanu-El to the Hebrew Union College-Jewish Institute of Religion for the establishment of a Student Loan Fund. So, except for one further abortive attempt on the part of Temple Emanu-El to organize a "Hebrew Theological Seminary Association" in 1876, [17] there came an end to the ambition of the

161

radical Reformers to organize their own theological seminary.

The second movement for the creation of a Jewish institution of higher learning was stimulated within the ranks of the Independent Order of B'nai B'rith by Grand Saar Benjamin F. Peixotto, who said,

> ... The Order of B'nai Berith is the first organization which, by reason of its members and unity, may attempt the task of disenthrallment, of moral elevation, of intellectual advancement. What congregations have failed to do, the Order may accomplish . . . We want teachers, we want preachers, we want publications . . . We want, in a word, an American Jewish University . . . [18]

The Order passed a resolution favoring the project at its annual convention in Cincinnati in October, 1866. The proposals were very specific. Each of the Order's seven thousand members would be expected to contribute an average of ten dollars, the resultant fund of $70,000 being judged sufficient to erect the first building of the university campus. Half that amount would be required to provide the annual budget: therefore each of the seventy-eight lodges would have to raise an average of $500. In return for this sum each lodge would be entitled to designate five scholarship students. This would mean a total of three hundred and ninety students on scholarship, not counting those who could defray their own expenses. Each lodge was requested to ratify the proposal, to commence the collection of funds, and to prepare to send delegates to a national convention which would determine details of organization and elect a board of trustees. [19]

During the following months, B'nai B'rith politicians, rabbis of every religious persuasion, and active lay-leaders in every community discussed little else than the "B. B. University" scheme. Lodges conducted hearings on the subject and held excited elections. Controversy was rife. The Jewish journals printed lengthy communications from supporters and opponents of the plan. Those favoring Peixotto's project seem to have been the more numerous, but the feeling was abroad that controversy might lead to disaster for so young and pioneering an American Jewish organization as the B'nai B'rith, the first successful national Jewish fraternal order. Caution seemed to be advisable. In August, 1867, the Constitution Grand Lodge, the highest authority of the Order, which exercised veto power over convention actions, determined to reject the entire program because "the establishment of a Jewish University of the I. O. B. B. is fraught with danger and injury to the best interests of the Order."[20] Individual lodges were urged to support educational projects, but the Grand Lodge's action withdrew the Order from leadership in the field of Jewish education.

II

The Founding of Maimonides College

The third project which was under discussion in the late years of the Civil War was the Philadelphia program. Stimulated by Isaac Leeser, a group of laymen in that city had determined to take action which would lead to the establishment of a seminary. At their helm were Abraham Hart, the distinguished publisher and civic leader, who was also President of the Board of Delegates of American Israelites; Moses A. Dropsie, prominent attorney and Republican leader; and Isidore Binswanger, successful merchant-manufacturer and philanthropist. These men and their adherents were convinced that the very existence of Judaism was at stake, and that the creation of a rabbinical school could not be deferred much longer.

On November 6, 1864, the Philadelphians met for formal action. They resolved that two members and the president of each of the Philadelphia congregations act as a committee to

163

canvas "their respective congregations in the collection of funds . . . for the purpose of founding a College for the Education of Youth for the Jewish Ministry . . ." [21] The response was far from enthusiastic, but the Philadelphia leaders were not so easily swayed from their determination. Another way had to be found, and eventually it was. Two years later they opened up a subscription book, and solicited and obtained pledges of endowment contributions and annual dues from a respectable number of men. With this evidence of good faith and proof of sincerity, they opened negotiations with the Executive Committee of the Board of Delegates of American Israelites, which since 1859 had been the only national association of representatives of local Jewish communities. That Committee recommended, at its meeting in August, 1866, that the Board enter into a partnership with the Hebrew Education Society of Philadelphia for the establishment of a seminary, thereby obviating the necessity of applying for a new charter. The Committee further urged the membership of the Board of Delegates to assume the responsibility of raising funds for the new institution. [22]

All during the year 1866-1867, details of the project were under continual consideration by the officers of the Hebrew Education Society and the rabbis of Philadelphia, on the one hand, and by the officers of the Board of Delegates and the rabbis of New York City, on the other hand. The entire proposal had to be ratified at the annual convention of the Board of Delegates, held auspiciously in Philadelphia, on May 27, 1867.

At that convention, ample opportunity was afforded for full and complete discussion. A. S. Cohen of New York, representing Congregation Darech Amuno, spoke forthrightly in favor of immediate action: "if we establish such a college, the students will soon be forthcoming . . . [W]e should do something besides agitation." Later he gave emphasis to his statement with the

164

announcement that his congregation had already appropriated one hundred dollars for the endowment fund of the college. The Reverend Samuel M. Isaacs, of Shaaray Tefila Congregation of New York City, said that "the necessity of supplying the American Jewish pulpit with ministers who speak the language of the country" could not be denied. He questioned the continuation of the practice of importing German ministers who would not take the time or make the effort to learn English. Rabbi Marcus Jastrow of Congregation Rodeph Shalom of Philadelphia defended the German rabbis and their knowledge and ability, although he admitted that "for the rising generation in the United States, their influence would be vastly increased by their ability to speak in the vernacular . . ." The Reverend Sabato Morais of Mikveh Israel Congregation of Philadelphia feared that the movement was premature. He thought it well nigh impossible to find students sufficiently advanced in Hebraic studies to become candidates for the rabbinate, and urged a stronger emphasis upon elementary Jewish education. He even dragged in the extraneous matter of a uniform ritual for all American synagogues, a subject which, however, other speakers hardly wished to discuss at that time. Isaac Leeser summarized all the arguments in favor of the establishment of a seminary, but warned the delegates that the one great difficulty would be the procurement of students. He said, however, that even this problem could be overcome, and concluded his appeal by referring to the seminary movement as "the great fight against ignorance."

After all this oratory, a vote was taken and the delegates gave unanimous approval to the resolution which empowered the Executive Board, in cooperation with the Hebrew Education Society, to take all necessary steps to establish the college.[23] No time was lost. By the middle of June the Executive Committee had met and, in counsel with the Hebrew Education Society, designated the seven Trustees who were to preside over the administration of the college. They were Abraham Hart, Isidore Binswanger, Moses A. Dropsie and Mayer Sulzberger of Philadelphia, and Henry Josephi, Alex S. Saroni and Myer S. Isaacs of New York City.[24] Early in July official announcement was given to the press of the forthcoming opening of Maimonides College:

MAIMONIDES COLLEGE.

BOARD OF DELEGATES OF AMERICAN ISRAELITES, OFFICE OF THE EXECUTIVE COMMITTE,

New York, July 1st, 5627, 1867.

The Board of Delegates of American Israelites have, in conjunction with the Hebrew Education Society of Philadelphia, established a college in that city, styled MAIMONIDES COLLEGE, under the charter granted to that Society by the Legislature of Pennsylvania.

The College will for the present be under the charge of seven Trustees.

FACULTY.

The faculty of the College, so far as appointed, consists of the following professors:

Rev. ISAAC LEESER, Professor of Homiletics, Belles Lettres and Comparative Theology.

Rev. S. MORAIS, Professor of the Bible and Biblical Literature.

Rev. Dr. M. JASTROW, Professor of Talmud, Hebrew Philosophy and Jewish History and Literature.

Rev. Dr. BETTELHEIM, Professor of Mishnah with commentaries, Shulchan 'Aruch and Yad ha-Chazakah.

Rev. L. BUTTENWIESER, Professor of the Hebrew and Chaldaic languages and of the Talmud.

The vacant professorships will be filled before the opening of the College.

COLLEGIATE COURSE.

The usual collegiate course will be pursued in addition to the Hebrew course. Students have the option of pursuing simply the Hebrew course.

166

The full course will embrace a period of five years, at the expiration of which the graduates who shall pass a satisfactory examination and be otherwise qualified, will receive the usual degrees. Candidates for the ministry, having the proper theological knowledge, will receive the degrees of Bachelor and Doctor of Divinity.

The branches of instruction are as follows: Greek, Latin, German, French, Hebrew, Chaldaic and their literatures, the Natural Sciences, History, Mathematics and Astronomy, Moral and Intellectual Philosophy, Constitutional History and Laws of the United States, Belles Lettres, Homiletics, Comparative Theology, the Bible with its commentaries, the Mishnah with its commentaries, the Shulchan 'Aruch, Yad ha-Chazakah, Jewish History and Literature, Hebrew Philosophy and the Talmud with its commentaries.

Competent instructors in *Chazanuth* and *Shechitah* will be provided for those desiring to become Chazanim.

ADMISSION OF STUDENTS.

Candidates for admission must be able to translate with facility the historical portions of the Bible. The requisite qualifications in the other branches will be determined hereafter by the faculty.

Those not qualified to enter the College will be received in the preparatory school of the Hebrew Education Society, on the usual terms of that institution.

TUITION FEES.

Tuition fees will be one hundred dollars per annum. Board and lodging will be furnished to students for two hundred dollars additional, yearly.

SCHOLARSHIPS.

There are two classes of scholarships provided for students, the resident scholarship of three hundred dollars per annum, which includes board, lodging and tuition, and the regular scholarship of one hundred dollars per annum for tuition only.

Any congregation or individual contributing the sum of $300, or $100 annually, shall be entitled to nominate a student (qualified as to character and capacity) to fill a resident or regular scholarship respectively, such student to be entitled to all privileges; and any such society, individual or congregation contributing $1500 shall be entitled to a permanent regular scholarship.

OPENING OF THE COLLEGE.

The College session for the first year will commence on the fourth Monday of October 5628 (1867).

Applications for admission to the College, and offers by individuals, societies or congregations to avail themselves of the terms above laid down in regard to scholarships, should be addressed at as early a date as possible, to either of the Trustees:

Mr. ABRAHAM HART, President, 430 Library Street, Philadelphia.
  " MOSES A. DROPSIE, 29 South Sixth Street,   "
  " I. BINSWANGER, 241 Chestnut Street,   "
  " HENRY JOSEPHI, 58 Nassau Street, New York.
  " ALEXANDER S. SARONI, 5 Barclay Street, New York.
  " MYER S. ISAACS, 243 Broadway,   "
  " MAYER SULZBERGER, Secretary Board of Trustees, 29 South Sixth Street, Philadelphia.

Donations to the College Fund and Annual Subscriptions will also be received and acknowledged by either of the Trustees.

ABRAHAM HART, President,
Board of Delegates of American Israelites.

MYER S. ISAACS, Secretary,
243 *Broadway, New York.*

Such was the ambitious announcement of the founding of Maimonides College. [25]

III

THE FACULTY

Who were these men who had volunteered to assist Isaac Leeser as members of the faculty?

Sabato Morais had succeeded Leeser in the ministry of Mikveh Israel Congregation in 1851, after a dispute with the board made Leeser's position untenable. Born in Leghorn, Italy, April 13, 1823, Morais had seized every opportunity for educational betterment. He rose out of a poverty-stricken environment by dint of working during the day and studying at night. As a young man he achieved a notable record in both Hebraic and secular studies. In 1846 he was called to England to become Hebrew tutor at the Orphans' School of the London Spanish and Portuguese Synagogue, a position which he occupied with notable success. In 1851 he yielded to the incessant urging of friends to journey to America for an interview with the Mikveh Israel authorities, and in a general election, was chosen to lead the congregation. Morais brought to the College a wealth of learning and a kindly, fatherly spirit. [26]

Marcus Jastrow had been rabbi of Congregation Rodeph Shalom for only about a year when the College was opened. Born in Rogasen, Poland, he had earned his Doctor of Philosophy Degree at the University of Halle in 1855, and served as Preacher of the German Congregation of Warsaw from 1858 to 1861. In the latter year he became implicated in the Polish uprising against Russia and went into exile after an imprisonment of three months. He was called to Philadelphia while serving as rabbi in Worms, Germany. Jastrow was a passionate and acid-tongued partisan, but his scholarship was unchallengable. He was a man of encyclopedic memory; his great academic career reached its culmination in the publication, in 1903, of his masterly Talmudic Hebrew and Aramaic dictionary. He brought intensity and vast knowledge to the College. After Leeser's death, on February 1, 1867, Jastrow was appointed Provost. [27]

Like Jastrow, Aaron S. Bettelheim had been a resident of Philadelphia for only a brief time. A native of Galgoc, Hungary, where he was born in 1830, Bettelheim had studied for the Doctor of Philosophy degree at the University of Prague while he was pursuing rabbinical studies at the Prague Seminary. From 1848 until 1867, when he came to Philadelphia in response to a call from Beth Israel Congregation, he followed a variegated career as congregational rabbi, political journalist, tutor, school superintendent, and Hebrew book censor. Bettelheim was a voracious student; his hunger for learning went far beyond the boundaries of Jewish scholarship. In Richmond, where he later served as rabbi of Congregation Beth Ahabah, he took a degree in medicine at the Richmond Medical College. [28]

Laemmlein Buttenwieser was born in Würzburg, Germany, in 1825. Reared from early childhood to aspire to follow a family tradition of Jewish scholarship, he emigrated to America in 1848. He occupied teaching positions in Boston and Cincinnati before coming to Philadelphia in 1861, to teach for the Hebrew Education Society of Philadelphia. After demonstrating his superior abilities, he was appointed Principal of the Hebrew Department of the Society's school. Buttenwieser was the only original member of the faculty who was paid for his services; he earned his living not as a rabbi but as a teacher. [29]

Others who joined the faculty during the following years were the Reverend George Jacobs, the Reverend Hyman Polano, and Mr. William H. Williams. Jacobs came to Philadelphia in 1868 as Leeser's successor in the pulpit of Beth El Emeth Congregation, which had been organized in 1857 by Leeser's friends and supporters. Born in Kingston, Jamaica, in 1834, he had originally earned his livelihood as a merchant, serving gratuitously in the rabbinic office in Kingston and later in Richmond. In 1857, however, Beth Shalome Congregation of Richmond persuaded him to undertake rabbinical duties on a full time basis, and he ministered to that congregation until he was called to Philadelphia. Jacobs' academic background was, perhaps, less thorough than that of his colleagues, but he more than bridged the difference with his keen intellectual acumen and broad cultural interest. [30]

Hyman Polano was born in Maasluis, Holland, in 1830. He was trained from childhood for the calling of *hazan* in the Sephardic rite, but an injury to his throat prevented his pursuing that career. He came to Philadelphia in 1848, and served as Hebrew teacher both for the classes of the Hebrew Education Society and for a host of private pupils. He was the author of *Selections from the Talmud* and of an elementary Hebrew primer. [31]

Williams, the only non-Jew on the faculty of the College, and its highest paid instructor, was head of the English Department of the Hebrew Education Society. He had previously been a member of the faculty of Central High School of Philadelphia, and Principal of the Milton Academy. [32]

That the faculty was more than adequate cannot be denied. No complaint was ever heard that the professors and instructors were unfaithful to their duties. Each had a capacity for teaching (they all were instructors for the Hebrew Education Society or in their own synagogues) and each had knowledge to impart.

IV

THE STUDENTS

But if the ability of the faculty was a known quantity when the College's opening was announced, the student body remained the major question-mark. Leeser had asserted that it might prove difficult to attract students; Morais had stated his conviction that American boys were not sufficiently advanced in Hebrew learning to undertake rabbinic studies. Both were proven by experience to have judged the situation accurately.

When the College opened for classes, eight students were approved for matriculation by the committee on admissions: Emile S. Levi; Robert Bren (or Baum); a son of the Rev. Isaac Marks; a son of H. Friedlander of Dubuque, Iowa; and students named Zemanski, Messing, Kramer and Kantrowitz, whose first names and cities of residence were not noted in the minutes of the Board of Trustees. These students had not been interviewed; their parents had written to the authorities to discuss their admission. Several of the boys or their parents, however, changed their minds during the summer of 1867, and the following did not appear for registration: Marks, Messing, Kramer and Kantrowitz. Bren and Zemanski withdrew after attending classes for only two weeks. Levi and Friedlander were the only two of the original eight applicants who remained during the entire academic year. They were joined by three late-comers who registered during the period from October to February: Marcus E. Lam, Nathan Hamburg (or Hamberger) and David Levy (or Levi). These five were the original student body of the College, but of their number, two did not return in the autumn of 1868: Emile Levi, the only paying student of the five ($25 a quarter-term) for reasons not stated in the Minute Book of the Board; and the Friedlander boy because "the distance was too great" and he had no intention of pre- paring for the rabbinate, but had come to the College only out of a desire to develop his knowledge of Judaism. Three students, then, the late-comers of the first year, returned to the classes of Maimonides College at the opening of the second year. [33]

To say that this response to the opening of the first Jewish theological seminary in America was unenthusiastic would run the risk of inviting ridicule. Three students from the total Amer- ican Jewish population of perhaps one hundred and seventy-five thousand souls!

Equally revealing was the lack of interest in the first full scholarship to be offered to a New York youth who aspired to study at the College. Congregation Shaaray Tefila, whose rabbi, the Reverend Samuel M. Isaacs, was one of the strongest sup- porters of the College, advertised the availability of a "resident scholarship" in eight successive issues of the *Jewish Messenger* of New York, during January and February of 1868. There appear to have been no applicants whatever. [34] The scholarship was not awarded until the following winter when it was granted to

Ignatz Klein, a fatherless inmate of the Hebrew Orphan Asylum of New York, whose deficiencies in Hebrew studies, commented upon by the faculty at the time of his admittance, demonstrated how desperate the College was for students. [35] In August, 1869, Klein went swimming in the Delaware River with a fellow-student and was drowned, despite the efforts of his friend and a policeman who went to his rescue. The Reverend Isaacs had the unenviable duty of conveying the news to Ignatz' widowed mother, rendered doubly difficult because he had undoubtedly been the one who had convinced her of the desirability of sending her son to the College. The authorities of the institution defrayed the expenses of the funeral. [36]

With Klein's death, then, the student body was reduced to the original three. In an unofficial poll, the faculty ranked Levy first and Lam second. Of the third pupil, the faculty said, "Nathan Hamberger despite his efforts can equal neither of the two just named." All three students were granted free tuition; in addition, both Levy and Lam were boarded and clothed at the expense of the College in the home of one of their teachers, Hyman Polano. [37]

In November, 1869, a new student appeared at the College. He was Hyman Saft, a Polish immigrant who had been serving as Cantor and *Shochet* at Leavenworth, Kansas. His arrival was welcomed by both faculty and board. Here was a specific opportunity for the College to realize its objective of raising the standards of the Jewish ministry. Saft was not a boy, like the others. He was twenty six years old. The faculty said of him, in a communication to the board:

[His] attainments in Hebrew are comparatively proficient — in English and German very small; in order to devote himself exclusively to these he wishes to be exonerated from an attendance upon any of the classes except the Rev. Dr. Jastrow's, Rev. Mr. Morais' and Mr. Williams' — Rev. Dr. Jastrow and Rev. Mess. Morais and Jacobs have volunteered to give him private instruction, Mr. Morais in the Book of Creeds by Albo; Dr. Jastrow in German and Moreh Nebuchim; and Mr. Jacobs in composition. The young man is incapable of supporting himself for want of means and we have written to Rev. Mr. Isaacs, in New York, inquiring if he could induce some congregations in that city to afford him assistance; the answers so far have not been favorable, and we add our solicitations to his to provide some way for his continued attendance upon the College. [38]

By the following March, Saft had withdrawn from the College, probably because neither the Philadelphians nor the New Yorkers had been able to raise the necessary maintenance funds. But Isaacs was able to help Saft; he secured for him an appointment as Reader at his synagogue. Saft subsequently served congregations in Denver, Colorado, Marshall, Texas, and Alexandria, Louisiana, before going to St. Louis where he died in 1897. [39]

In June, 1870, Congregation Rodeph Shalom of New York agreed to contribute funds for a scholarship (there is no indication that any student other than Klein was awarded the Shaaray Tefila grant). Four months later Samuel Mendelsohn, a twenty year old Russian immigrant who had been in the United States for just two years, was designated as its recipient. Because of his background, Mendelsohn was assigned special lessons in English grammar, literature and composition, in addition to the regular course of study still being pursued by Levy and Lam. (The exact date of Hamberger's departure from the College's classes is not known, but there is no further mention of him in the faculty reports after Mendelsohn's admission). [40]

The applications of only two further prospective students were considered during the lifetime of the College. A boy named Abramson from Hartford, Conn., was provisionally admitted on the condition that his expenses would be defrayed by the Hartford congregation. The congregation being unwilling or unable to assume the burden, Abramson was not heard from again. [41] The second was an inmate of the Cleveland Orphan Asylum, on whose behalf the Superintendent, L. Aufrecht, wrote a letter of inquiry. Financial difficulties were also the reason for his failure to make an appearance in Philadelphia. [42]

A little less than two years after he commenced his studies at Maimonides College, and about four years after his arrival in America, Mendelsohn and his fellow-student, David Levy, inaugurated a most ambitious enterprise: the publication of a weekly Jewish journal, named *The Index*. Perhaps they were tired of living off the bounty of the supporters of the College and hoped in this way to earn their livelihood; perhaps they thirsted for some manner in which they could express their maturity (Mendelsohn was now twenty two and Levi eighteen — but the latter had been a student at Maimonides for almost five years); perhaps they saw portents of the approaching demise of the College — how long could an institution survive with only three students! At any rate, there was great need for a Philadelphia Jewish periodical — the venerable *Occident* had ceased publication in 1869 after Mayer Sulzberger had fulfilled his pledge to Leeser to continue the journal for at least a year after its founder's death; and another two years were to come and go before Alfred Jones commenced publication of the Philadelphia *Jewish Record*.

After a trip to New York to seek advertisements and to gain the support and good-will of Isaacs' *Messenger*, Mendelsohn brought forth the first issue of *The Index* on October 1, 1872. It was published by S. Pincus and printed by H. La Grange. The reviews were more than favorable. Isaac M. Wise commented in his *Israelite*:

It is a neatly printed sheet, of orthodox tendencies, edited in good taste, and promising quite fair to become a journal of many merits. [43]

The *Messenger* went into some detail in its description of the first issue:

The new paper, *The Jewish Index*, presents a neat appearance, and will fill a void in the community. The Jews of Philadelphia are surely numerous enough to support a paper of their own, and we trust they will give it a hearty and liberal patronage. A story by an old favorite (Mrs. Hartog) is commenced. There are other continued articles, neatly written editorials, and crisp news items. Rev. Mr. Morais is to be a regular contributor to this journal, his first installment being a translation of Luzzato's Jewish Moral Theology. The *Index* opens under favorable auspices. We wish it every success. [44]

Unfortunately, no copy of *The Index's* issues has been preserved, and we are therefore unable to judge its merits for ourselves. Indeed, we do not even know how long it survived. The only notation of its passing was Isaacs' comment in the *Messenger* of December 27, 1872, that he had not seen the journal "of late."

The only words from the *Index* which have been preserved were a paragraph reprinted in the *Messenger*. The paragraph editorializes on the question of "The Jewish Vote," an important issue at the time when Grant was running for his second term as President, because there were still many Jews who believed that they should not vote for the author of the intolerant General Order Number Eleven of 1862. [45] This is the quotation from *The Index*:

Politicians will make up their minds at once that whichever way Jews will vote, they will be governed by considerations of public duty. Like other citizens, they have a lively interest in the solution of national problems, and, like them, they will vote for the candidate who represents their views, regardless, in the main, of personal predilections. It is only when no vital interest is at stake that individual preferences may decide, and a question can arise as to Jewish votes. But when will such an event happen? Even now, with politics in a greater muddle than ever, the large majority of citizens honestly believe that the success of this or that party is fraught with great danger to the country. The Jews being no wiser than their neighbors, are swayed by the same passions and inflamed with the same prejudices; wherefore they will doubtless adhere to their respective political parties. Those, however, who may determine that there are no great issues involved in the coming contest are differently situated. They are prepared to vote against any candidate who is hostile to them on account of their religion. Such a course need not be referred to a desire of revenge, but to the conviction which every liberal man must share, that one so narrow-minded as to entertain religious prejudices against the civil rights of fellow-citizens is unfit to execute the laws of a free people. [46]

These opinions were by no means unique . . . but they are all that remain of the short-lived *Index*.

Perhaps the journal's career was brought to a hasty conclusion because its editors decided to leave the college; or, vice-versa, perhaps the *Index's* failure to attract sufficient interest compelled Levy and Mendelsohn to look elsewhere for the next stage of their careers. In December, 1872, or January, 1873, both left the College to occupy positions of Jewish leadership. Levy accepted an invitation to become Assistant Superintendent of the Hebrew Orphan Asylum of New York City, and Mendelsohn consented to serve as rabbi of Congregation Beth El of Norfolk, Va. [47] Both were in dire financial straits, and the College Board had to lend them enough cash to enable them to purchase presentable suits of clothing. Peculiarly enough, however, neither Levy nor Mendelsohn received any kind of certificate or diploma attesting to his training and qualifications; no formal graduation ceremonies were conducted in signification of their departure from the College. Both pursued long and honorable careers of service in the rabbinate, but the College had neither graduated nor ordained them.

This marked the end, to all intents and purposes, of the College's student body. Lam, who was serving as a Hebrew instructor for the Hebrew Education Society, continued to study with Jastrow and Morais, for at least two more years. In May, 1875, another young man, named Rubenstein, undertook private studies with Morais and other Philadelphia rabbis, but Maimonides College had long since ceased to exist for want of a student body. [48]

V

THE CURRICULUM

How much of the ambitious course of study which was outlined in the prospectus had been imparted to these students?

On May 13, 1868, at the end of the first year, the students who had been enrolled in the College were subjected, in keeping with a time-honored American practice, to a public oral examination, in the presence of the faculty, the board, and other interested persons. This was the first of a series of annual public examinations during the life of the College. The reporter for *The Jewish Messenger* felt that the students had acquitted themselves with distinction:

... The students appeared to have a thorough comprehension of the general principles laid down by Rambam; they read the Talmud with a fluency which would have surprised the doubters in American ability, and they displayed such a through knowledge of the Bible, from the easiest passages of Genesis to the most difficult in Isaiah, together with Rashi's commentary thereon, that no doubt lingered in the minds of the auditors of the entire capability of the College to produce first-class scholars. In Latin, Greek and the ordinary branches, the progress was, of course, satisfactory ... [49]

A more detailed description of the nature of the studies was provided by Mayer Sulzberger, Secretary of the Board of the College, in a published report which was dated May 22, 1868:

... Rev. Dr. Jastrow commenced the course by giving students a general knowledge of the Bible, the number of its books, their chronological order, the historical events detailed therein, and the influence which those events and the actors in them exercised on Judaism. He also initiated them into the Yad ha-Chazakah of Maimonides, not confining them so much to the study of the text, as to a proper knowl-

178

edge of the principles. Rev. Dr. Bettelheim devoted his time entirely to teaching the Shulchan Aruch, and during the term went over quite a number of chapters with the students . . .[50]

The Faculty, however, was not so enthusiastic about the ability or fluency of the students as were these public spokesmen. At a long and serious meeting of those gentlemen on November 16, 1868, it was decided that a request be submitted to the Board for permission to change the course of study:

> . . . On account of the mental condition of the pupils and the want of scholars of advanced grade [we desire] to simplify the course of instruction and abridge the number of studies; with this view.
>
> Dr. Jastrow instead of delivering lectures on Israelitish History to read the Historical parts of the Bible with the pupils, making verbal comments on the same, they not being sufficiently advanced for lectures.
>
> Dr. Bettelheim to teach Mishna instead of Shulchan Aruch.
>
> Rev. Mr. Buttenwieser to dispense with Greek, giving the time to German.
>
> In the English department to devote the time now occupied by Elocution to Composition. The time given to Physical Geography to be used for Rhetoric. To substitute in place of the Silliman's Chemistry, Familiar Science.[51]

The permission was granted without objection. From nine in the morning until half past four in the afternoon, with one and a half hours off for lunch, the students labored over this far more realistic course of instruction.

By March 16, 1869, according to a further report by the Faculty to the Board, the students had made measurable progress. Dr. Jastrow's classes had studied twenty-five chapters of the First Book of Samuel "in a cursive reading interrupted by historical, linguistical etc. explanation," and, in addition, some twelve scattered passages of Maimonides' *Mishneh Torah*. Under Morais, the students had completed (in almost two years of study) some forty chapters of Isaiah, and the Rashi commentary to fifteen chapters of Exodus. In grammar, Morais had concentrated on the field of composition and was certain that his pupils

179

were "able to write Hebrew sentences with the vowel points correctly."

Bettelheim had little confidence in the preparation of his students. At the 1868 annual meeting of the Board of Delegates he said that the students were "even in the reading of Hebrew, very little advanced . . . American boys [are] not used to sit at the feet of their teachers." [52] He attempted to suit his course to the capacity of his pupils:

In teaching Shulchan Aruch I have selected those rules which are of practical application, omitting such as seemed better for a subsequent part of the course. The method of teaching has been . . . to acquaint the scholars more with the spirit than with the body of the Jewish law; nevertheless I lead them to understand every paragraph as far as possible. I began Shulchan Aruch paragraph 1 to 24; 24 to 45; 45 to 57; 157 to 168; 242 to 266.

I thought that it was advisable by commenting on the Holy-days and Festivals to make the scholars acquainted with the rules of those Festivals, for this reason I taught them some paragraphs from 625 to 670 and following, 686 and following and so I hope that the scholars will make better progress in Hebrew and Talmud, as the ground upon the Shulchan Aruch is built, and by becoming acquainted with the spirit of the Laws, by reviewing the next year the result will be the best . . .

Mr. Buttenwieser had taught the students fourteen sides of Talmud, in addition to ten during the first year. He had completed, with them, fifty-two pages of Harkness' first Greek reader, before abandoning the subject in favor of concentration on German. In the latter field, twenty-five lessons in the Ollendorf *German Grammar* had been studied.

Mr. Williams listed the areas which had been completed in text-books which he had used during the first two years:

First year. — Alsop's Algebra, entire; Davies' Legendra entire; Gummere's Surveying entire; Mahan's Civil Engineering — Fifty Pages. — Latin. Sallust — Forty Pages.

Second Class — Alsop's Algebra. first part; Weber's Universal History to the end of 5th Century. Silliman's Chemistry to non-metallic elements 150 pp. Physical Geography 225 pages. — Andrew's Latin Lessons entire. — Elocution twice a week.

Second Year to date. — Weber's Universal History from 5th to 16th century. Familiar science 200 pp. Algebra to Quadratic equations. — Roger's Mensuration, the mensuration of Superficies. — Latin — 1st Book of Caesar — Composition — once a week. [53]

Professor Williams had obviously undertaken an impossible task. His fellow members of the Faculty had retreated from their visions of a highly advanced and complex curriculum, and were pursuing the most elementary kind of courses, while Williams himself was still burdened with almost a complete schedule of secular subjects. It was to take another year, however, before the Faculty recommended that the Board take definite action in this regard:

The Faculty of the College suggest that some change be made by which the pupils would have the benefit of a greater variety of English [secular] studies, and the opportunity of devoting a longer time each day to this department. They need the contact with more boys of their own age to stimulate them to greater exertions and excite more emulation in their studies than the paucity of members in the College at present can supply. These advantages might be obtained by entering them in some other College . . . [54]

The Board promptly appointed a committee to confer with the authorities of the University of Pennsylvania to discuss the possibility of the matriculation of the Maimonides College students in that institution. The Pennsylvania officials were quite willing to admit them if they could meet the entrance requirements in Latin and Greek. Such not being the case, the Faculty set about preparing the students in those subjects. By the Fall of 1871, Levy and Lam were able to enter the freshman class of the University. Thenceforth the College classes were held only from half past three to quarter to six, Monday through Thursday, and from two to three o'clock on Sunday. Williams abandoned his catch-all curriculum, but he was retained on the staff as special tutor in English to Samuel Mendelsohn. [55]

It is, at this date, well nigh impossible to evaluate the training which was given to the students of Maimonides College. The only direct witness is a testimonial Hebrew poem which the students presented to the Board of the College on March 17, 1871, a pedantic routine composition which might well have been indited by Samuel Mendelsohn, who made the speech of presentation, and who obviously came to the College already well versed in Hebrew learning. [56] But Mendelsohn and Levy did serve long years in the rabbinate, and Lam was a well-known and highly respected Hebrew teacher in Philadelphia until his death. [57] Their studies at Maimonides, though obviously not of the most systematic and advanced type, did prepare these young men for active service. In this regard, certainly, the members of the Faculty had fulfilled their promise. There is, however, no indication in the Board's Minute Book or elsewhere, that Levy and Mendelsohn left the College with the approval of a Faculty convinced that its students had reached the end of their academic careers.

VI

The Library

No sooner had the Trustees determined the date for the opening of the College, and accepted the applications of prospective students, than they authorized the establishment of a Library.

A public plea was made for contributions of books, the Board offering to defray shipping expenses for such donations. Within a year, about one hundred volumes of Hebrew classics and various works of Judaica in English, French, German and Latin, had been sent to the College. These included standard sets of the Mishna, Talmud, Midrash and various Biblical commentaries. Their donors included the Reverend Messers. E. M. Myers of Wilmington, N. C., and Abraham De Sola of Montreal, Messers. Michael M. Allen and E. M. Ellinger of New York, Moses A. Dropsie, A. P. Schoneman and E. S. Linse of Philadelphia, and a Mrs. Spanier of New York. Only one contribution in funds was received, one hundred dollars from John D. Phillips of New York, in 1868.[58]

In December, 1869, the Board authorized Mayer Sulzberger, Secretary, who was to become one of the great modern collectors of rare Hebrew books and manuscripts in the prime of his career as lawyer, jurist, and Jewish communal leader, to spend up to five hundred dollars in bids for a collection of Hebrew volumes from Amsterdam, which were to be sold at auction in New York City the following month. Sulzberger purchased the major portion of the collection, numbering some three hundred and eighteen volumes, for the sum of $184.73.[59] This was the only serious effort to obtain desirable volumes for a planned College library.

There was some confusion, after Isaac Leeser's death, as to the disposition of his library, a fine collection numbering over eight hundred volumes. Some sources say that it was bequeathed to the College, others that it was left to the Hebrew Education Society in trust for the College. At any rate, the Leeser Library was not catalogued until 1883 — long after the closing of the College — and the College had no benefit from it, although Faculty members continually inquired as to its whereabouts, on the presumption that they were to enjoy its use.[60]

Although the Board continued to authorize the expenditure of small sums of money for the purchase of specific volumes required by the instructors and students for classroom assignments ($28.34 in 1869 and $32.21 in 1870),[61] the Library itself was not augmented by any further acquisitions, either through outright purchase or through donation. Indeed, the appeal of 1867, which had been printed in *The Jewish Messenger*, was never again repeated, nor were any other public steps taken to obtain books as gifts for the College. Here we meet with an evidence of laxity and apathy on the part of the administrators of the College which could not but point to eventual collapse; for its library is the very soul of an academic institution.

As a matter of fact, the Board demonstrated a reprehensible indifference to all practical problems connected with the Library. In early 1868, Mayer Sulzberger, the Secretary, was requested by the Board to take custody of the Library until such time as a Librarian should be officially designated. No one was ever appointed to the position, and, as a result, the Library remained a step-child until the very end. In February, 1868, the Board resolved to institute a catalogue for its collection of books; but no one was assigned to the task! Over three years later the Trustees were still discussing the project, despite the appeal of the Faculty in June, 1870, "that they be furnished with a list of the books belonging to the College in order to select such as may be needed for their use." That the Faculty of an institution of higher learning should be compelled to request that such a basic tool for teaching be provided was a serious indictment of the Board's understanding of its responsibilities. [62]

Actually, however, the failure of the Board to provide a catalogue was not its worst offense; the books themselves were unavailable to instructors or students! From the very beginning, the College itself had no permanent home. It was living temporarily in the basement of the Hebrew Education Society's building; rooms were available only for class time, and those rooms, according to the President, were "prejudicial to the health of the professors and students!" [63] Except for an eight months' period of experimentation during 1871 when classes were held in the Rodeph Shalom Synagogue's vestry rooms,

these temporary quarters in the H.E.S. became permanent —
but with no change in the conditions of their use. If no rooms
belonged to the College, where could the Library be stored?
In 1870, Isidore Binswanger who was Hart's successor as President of the College, offered a "room in his house with the
privilege of shelving the same and possession of a key, for the
purpose of being occupied by the library." [64] Although Binswanger's offer was gratefully accepted, no action resulted, for the
books remained in Sulzberger's possession. Six months later the
Trustees were inquiring whether the United Hebrew Charities
Society might not have room for the Library in its office, and,
a short time later, when classes were moved to Rodeph Shalom
Synagogue, the Faculty expressed its hope that the Library too
might be located there. [65] Apparently, however, both Trustees
and professors tired of wondering and hoping, for no more was
heard of the Library. If reference books were ever made available
to the students, they came from the professors' own personal
libraries, for the books owned by Maimonides College were
never available for consultation.

An indication of the effect of this condition on the teaching
methods of the College is to be discovered in a letter which the
Reverend L. Buttenweiser wrote to the Secretary:

Philad[a] January 14th 1868.

Mayer Sulzberger Esq.

    Dear Sir,

    The want of at least one more copy of Tract. "Baba Metziah" is so
keenly felt by both pupils and myself, that I think myself justified in
asking you most politely, to please and see that the Gemara which you
have among the books of the College will be rebound and sent here
into the College with as little delay as possible.

Yours respectfully

L. Buttenwieser [66]

One wonders if even this modest request was honored.

VII

FINANCES

The financial condition of Maimonides College at its opening was probably more auspicious than that of any other institution in American Jewish life up to that time. Pledges totaling $6635 had been made by forty-three persons, all of whom were residents of Philadelphia and New York with the exception of two contributors from St. Louis and one from Norfolk. Twenty-eight of these gentlemen, moreover, agreed to become annual supporters of the College in amounts totaling $437.50.[67] This was prior to the opening of the institution!

In addition, Myer S. Isaacs of New York City, one of the Trustees appointed by the Board of Delegates, reported at a Board meeting on October 24, 1867, that "there had been established in New York, three $300 scholarships and five $100 scholarships; that the New York delegates had held a meeting & intend to hold another for the purpose of securing the endowment of the College."[68]

Had this financial well-being continued and even expanded, there can be little doubt that the College's situation would have been greatly enhanced. A building, even a house, might have been rented, to offer attractive quarters for the class-rooms; a physical Library would have been created for the shelving of the books owned by the College; visitors might have been induced to support the institution after seeing something tangible.

But all of the enthusiasm would seem to have been concentrated into the months prior to the opening of the College. No further endowment contributions were secured, and, as late as 1869, the Trustees were still attempting to collect pledges which had been made during the summer of 1867.[69]

Isaacs' report had been not only exaggerated, but misleading. After his glowing description of scholarships already secured, a letter which he wrote to Isaac Leeser on December 2, 1867, was hardly calculated to increase the College's confidence in his ability to secure funds:

Respecting the College, I am sorry not to have the power of transmitting *substantial* news from New York. We have *promises*, but not much benefit can accrue from these unsupported by practical aid. Our meeting was held on the 28th but there being no quorum, we were able to do nothing then & were compelled to await another meeting.

Our people here will help the College when they *see* it successful — they appear to be so deeply absorbed in local interests as not to have time or thought for national good . . .[70]

Isaacs must have been deeply chagrined at the lack of activity on the part not only of New Yorkers in general, but more particularly on the part of the members of the Board of Delegates. Indeed, beyond accepting reports about the College from its representatives and making brief notation of the College's need for students and funds in its long, dull annual reports, the Board did nothing to warrant its privilege of appointing seven members of the College's Board of Trustees and of being a co-sponsor of the institution. Actually, the Board of Delegates had in most ways already become a letter-head organization; its lack of activity was a drag on the progress of the College.[71]

By 1870, Myer Isaacs had taken refuge in wishful-thinking and doggerel. He wrote to Sabato Morais,

> Lives there a Jew
> With soul so great
> That really to himself did state,
> Maimonides I will endow?
> Is there, Patrick, tell me now?

For a Yankee in Mass. has given $40,000 for the Hebrew Professorship at Andover![72]

187

Isaacs had more of a conscience that this would indicate. In August, 1868, he had written to Morais that "I feel personally that I ought not to be a trustee because I lack the time & means to push the work of money-getting. I'll make another effort these holydays." He was not very optimistic, however. Moses A. Dropsie had sent to him some letters of appeal for funds for the College which he wished him to transmit to the wealthier congregations of New York City: "I have despatched his notes to our leading congregations, with more misgivings than hopes. We must be unusually patient, & persevere with the College notwithstanding our limited success with the public." [73]

Dropsie was one of a very small number of the Trustees who took seriously the task of fund-raising. He wrote letters to many congregations throughout the country, with little or no success, and made a personal trip to Baltimore with Isidore Binswanger "to secure promised subscriptions and procure new ones." [74] Though on their return they reported "having gone to that city & to have been received in a flattering manner & that the leading Israelites were profuse in their promises to forward the object of the visit," [75] they seem to have been too sanguine in their expectations. There is no record that any Baltimorean ever sent one penny for the College.

Dropsie took to heart the failure of the New York Jews to support the College. When, in 1886, Doctor Morais and a group of New Yorkers determined to establish the Jewish Theological Seminary Association, Dropsie refused to support the effort. The memory of the frustrations of 1867–73 was too strong for him again to be willing to join hands with some of those who had turned an indifferent ear to his pleas for help. Perhaps, also, that was in his mind when he decided, in his will of 1895, to bequeath a large sum of money for the establishment of a new College for Hebrew and Cognate Learning in Phila-

188

delphia, rather than make any contribution for the support of the Theological Seminary of New York.[76]

By the academic year 1872–3, only four of those who had pledged annual contributions in 1867 were still among the College's benefactors, and altogether only nine persons were supporting its budget. Of these nine, five were Officers or Trustees. They contributed $525 out of a total of $855 which had been collected during the nineteen months beginning with June, 1872.[77]

In December, 1873, when the Treasurer made his final report, and the College authorities ceased pretending that they were still a functioning institution, the College had assets of $6.64 and $100 allocated for the purchase of books (the gift of John D. Phillips of New York . . . still unspent in 1873!)

VIII

L'ENVOI

Meanwhile, the initiative in Jewish religious affairs had passed to the West. Isaac M. Wise had finally succeeded in bringing together twenty-eight congregations who determined, on July 8, 1873, to create a new Union of American Hebrew Congregations. Two years later the Union opened the Hebrew Union College, which was to live and thrive and thus become the first successful American Jewish theological seminary. An effort was then undertaken by some Philadelphia Jews and others to convince the Union that Maimonides College should be re-opened as an eastern branch of the Cincinnati institution,[78] but the subject was not even brought up for formal consideration. So Maimonides College drifted off into oblivion.

Why had it failed to survive? What went wrong?

Firstly, the problem of leadership. Any educational institution must, at first, be the shadow of its professional leader, its president who devotes his time and effort, his enthusiasm and talents, to its welfare. The early years of a seminary must, perforce, depend on the energy of its head. So, Isaac M. Wise was to confess, in a letter to A. A. Jones of Philadelphia, that the future of the College was in his hands; if he abandoned his responsibility because of personal attacks upon himself, the Hebrew Union College could not survive:

> All talks in regard to my humble self are absurd. I must do the work, as nobody else here will do it. If I give up the thing is gone. Whether I am lauded or insulted, paid or taxed, makes no difference; the work must be done, and I must do it or it will never be built up. Hence it is a waste of words to write about me . . .[79]

Isaac Leeser had been the one persuasive champion for the creation of a seminary in the East. Had he lived for a few more years, the future of the College might have been secure. He had succeeded, against all manner of indifference and opposition, in accomplishing much. He was the best known American rabbi at the time of his death. He had traveled further than any other rabbi, visited more cities and towns, dedicated more synagogues, and made the acquaintance of more Jews than any other rabbi in his time, with the possible exception of Wise. His very popularity and vast following would have galvanized more support for the College throughout the country, if not in New York, which was, even then, *sui generis*, and offered little cooperation to institutions and organizations which it did not control.

But Leeser died. With him died the major potentiality for the College's growth. Only he would have devoted the time and energy necessary for its success. Only he would have scouted the country for prospective students, as did Isaac M. Wise, arguing away the objections of parents who wanted their sons to enter the business field.

Who was his successor? A Provost who did not even believe the College could succeed, and who had been in the United States for so brief a period of time that he could not wisely deal with American conditions. Marcus Jastrow was a great scholar and a forceful rabbi, but the Board had no justification for its decision to appoint him as Leeser's successor; this indicated a sit-back-and-wait policy which expected no leadership, no dynamism from the professional head of the institution. The officials who presided over the reorganization of the Jewish Theological Seminary in 1902 and called Solomon Schechter to its presidency understood full well a principle which seems not to have entered the minds of the Trustees of Maimonides College: the president shapes the future of a small educational institution.

A second reason for the failure of the College was, of course, the lack of students. Had dozens of students entered during the first year, and dozens more the second year, perhaps the Trustees would have awakened to their administrative responsibilities of finding a permanent building and appointing a more dynamic and able Provost. But the scarcity of potential students was one indication of the seriousness of the problem of the survival of Judaism in America: the lack of interest in the synagogue, the lack of respect for learning and spirituality, the failure of parents to imbue their sons with the aspiration to pursue the rabbinical calling. Part of the need for Maimonides College was the hope of overcoming these weaknesses. It was all well and good for the *Messenger* to say, in explanation of the failure of the College, that boys were not interested in a profession which was so poorly paid, which subjected its practitioners to the "whims and caprices of members of the congregation," which offered no certain future or security.[80] But all that this explanation really accomplished was to state in negative terms the tremendous challenge faced by those who were determined to arouse the interest of the American Jewish community in the state of its spiritual health. Yet, no young man from a congregation presided over by one of the College's professors was induced to enter the College by his rabbi!

A third reason for the failure of the College was that its supporters represented a waning influence in American Jewish life: the British-Dutch amalgam which crossed the lines of the Ashkenazic and Sephardic rites, but which was gradually falling back before the overwhelming numbers of recent German immigrants. True, Isaac M. Wise and his adherents in the West and in the South were bitterly scornful of the Board of Delegates and the College,[81] but their opposition was damaging only because Wise represented a segment of the American Jewish community which was gradually reaching the height of its power and maturity. In 1866, Rabbi Henry S. Jacobs, then in New Orleans, wrote a revealing letter about conditions among the New York synagogues to his friend Isaac Leeser:

... I place a great deal of the blame for this wretched [religious] state of affairs on the shoulders of our so-called orthodox chiefs, who are idle and selfish, and contribute nothing to the *general* good of Israel. All their efforts seem concentrated on little aims which begin in their own synagogues and end there. And then there is no unity of action. Look for instance at the several large congregations at the North. At the 19th St. Synagogue, everything seems to have been attained in Mr. Lyons's cadences, & his choir's artistic performances. The pulpit is silent. — and does not seem to be needed. Our worthy brethren there are apparently contented with the order of things as they are, and are either so pious as not to require exhortation or so wicked as to fear denunciation. At Dr. Raphall's & Mr. Isaac's, I hear trumpet-tongued praises of the *choir* in the former, it is said, led by a Xian! Do you not remember my feeble and unsuccessful effort in Com[mittee] at the first Session of the Board of Delegates to have its scope of a character which might feed our wants: — a College, — preparatory Schools, — a supervising Board to examine into the qualifications & personal worth of those coming to this country for office etc? But no: it seemed that the assembly of Delegates from various parts of the Union looked only to the aggrandisement of New York, and we Dummies had only to listen with wrapt attention to the Delphic Oracles, & play the meek parts of "makeweights" . . . [82]

These rabbis and their lay-leaders had neither the ability nor the strength to establish and support a seminary. Even their Board of Delegates expired within a few years.

A futher reason for the College's failure was its organizational structure. Its fate was in the hands of the leaders of two important societies which had primary responsibilities other than the support of the College. The Hebrew Education Society of Philadelphia, created for the more dramatic purpose of educating the children of the community was, itself, on shaky financial ground; in 1872 its officers were discussing the possibility of closing their school. [83] The Board of Delegates had, long since, demonstrated its inability to collect sizable funds or stimulate action for any purpose, charitable or otherwise; its leaders were content with high-sounding pronouncements and exhortations. [84] It was a mistake, at the very beginning, for Maimonides College to accept the sponsorship of these two organizations; they could not maintain it. Significantly enough, even board meetings were frequently postponed, because the required quorums were not on hand. Isaac M. Wise had learned his lesson well enough to know that a seminary could only be properly supported if it were created by a national organization which, in turn, was composed of many local affiliates pledged to participate in the national activities. The creators of the Jewish Theological Seminary also understood this practical consideration. Maimonides was all but doomed, when it was founded without this basic requirement.

And, finally, the College was a victim of that shameful insularity and isolationism in American Jewish life which still riddles virtually every effort to build constructive national programs. Loyalties were limited to specific groups and ob-

193

jectives. Once the B'nai B'rith abandoned its own educational program, its lodges ignored outside appeals. No single contribution to Maimonides College was ever made by one of the Order's lodges, although thousands of dollars had been pledged towards their own contemplated institution. The Eastern radical reformers would not think of helping Maimonides College; neither would the Western and Southern groups who followed Wise. The New York Jews were indifferent to a Philadelphia institution, and so, with few exceptions, were residents of other large cities. It was not so much a matter of principle or theological integrity, as of allegiance to objectives which fell far short of catholicity. No one was directly at fault; Dropsie and other Philadelphians later demonstrated their own capacity for narrowness. American Jewish leaders, lay as well as rabbinical, were still too immature to see that the welfare of the entire group was reason enough to compromise and cooperate.

*   *   *

What has been the justification for this extensive study of a failure? Why should we concern ourselves with an institution which is all but forgotten?

This story of Maimonides College has indicated the difficulties, problems and obstacles which were faced by any group which sought to create an American Jewish seminary, and which were so strong as to preclude the possibility of Maimonides College's survival. These same obstacles, in varying strength, also faced the Hebrew Union College, the Jewish Theological Seminary and the other institutions of higher Jewish learning which today grace the American Jewish scene. We take them for granted. We accept their brilliant faculties, their hosts of scholarly and talented alumni, their great libraries, as though they were created without effort. Perhaps this story of the era of frustration,

194

chaos, indifference, disunity, and lack of imagination which preceded their foundation and out of which they arose, may awaken within us a sense of gratitude for their existence and achievements. Had it not been for the ability and devotion of their leadership, and a greater response on the part of certain segments of the community, even they might not have succeeded.

In addition, although the proof is difficult to discover, there is little doubt that the creators of the Hebrew Union College and of the Jewish Theological Seminary, profited directly and indirectly from the mistakes and failures of Maimonides College. Wise, we know, followed every step of its progress (or lack of progress) with keen, though jaundiced eyes. When the time came for Morais to gather the conservative forces together for the creation of a rival to the Hebrew Union College, he undoubtedly recounted, in memory, the motives and shortcomings which led to the collapse of the Maimonides effort. Even failures have a kind of immortality.

Appendix

I THE CAREERS OF THE THREE GRADUATES.

A. DAVID LEVY

David Levy, born in Philadelphia, October 9, 1854, had been an inmate of the Jewish Foster Home of that city before taking up his studies at Maimonides College. He left the College in January, 1873, to become Assistant Superintendent of the Hebrew Orphan Asylum of New York; after a year he went to Montreal, Canada, to teach. At the age of twenty-one, in 1875, he was elected rabbi of the venerable Beth Elohim Congregation of Charleston, S. C. There he served until 1893, endearing himself to the members of the community. He pursued his flair for art under professional painters in Charleston, and designed a new Ark for the synagogue after a disastrous earthquake. In 1879 he published his own prayer-book, *The Service of the Sanctuary*. He was a member of the Central Conference of American Rabbis' Committee on Hymns, and wrote a number of poems for its first hymnal. In 1893 he accepted a call to New Haven where he remained until 1913. There he achieved a splendid reputation as preacher and educator. From 1913 to 1917 he officiated in Bridgeport, Conn., and from 1917 to 1921 in Easton, Pa. After his retirement in 1921, he returned to Charleston, which he always regarded as his home, and where he passed away in 1930. Levy, like his colleague Mendelsohn, though trained by men of conservative bent, was a thorough-going Reformer. An indication of his liberalism was his practice of preaching regularly every summer in a Methodist Church in Bethlehem, N. H., where he vacationed. [85]

B. MARCUS LAM

Marcus Eliezer Lam was born in Amsterdam on April 4, 1854. His family emigrated to Philadelphia when he was four years old, and it was there that he received his early education prior to his matriculation at Maimonides College. Apparently Lam had never aspired to follow the rabbinate as a career; rather he loved the pursuit of Jewish learning for its own sake. After the closing of the College, he continued to study with several of the professors, although he soon entered into a mercantile career, serving as a salesman for tailors' trimmings. Because of his training at Maimonides College, he was an able and beloved volunteer instructor for the Hebrew Education Society for many years; in addition to this public service, he also acted as private tutor in Hebrew for many of the leading Jewish Philadelphia families. Occasionally he would translate articles of Jewish significance from Dutch into English for publication in the Jewish periodical press of the city. He was also proficient enough to act as assistant and substitute *hazan* at Mikveh Israel Synagogue from time to time. He was a co-founder of the YMHA of Philadelphia, and for many years carried heavy responsibilities in the conduct of the affairs of Mikveh Israel's Federal Street Cemetery. At the time of his death on July 28, 1934, he was the oldest living member of his beloved synagogue, the last living link with Maimonides College in the city of its founding. [86]

197

C. Samuel Mendelsohn

Samuel Mendelsohn, who had been born in Russia, March 31, 1850, was rabbi of Congregation Beth-El of Norfolk, following his studies at Maimonides College, from 1873 to 1876. In the latter year he was called to minister to the Temple of Israel, Wilmington, N. C., through the instrumentality of his teacher, Dr. Marcus Jastrow, who had served as a kind of advisor to the congregation since its founding in 1872. Mendelsohn officiated at the dedication of the first synagogue in North Carolina, on May 12, 1876, which the congregation had already begun constructing before his election. In 1879, he was married to Esther Jastrow, the rabbi's niece. For many years the congregation, because of Mendelsohn's loyalty to his teacher and his wife's uncle, used the Jastrow prayer book, although it had become affiliated with the Union of American Hebrew Congregations in 1878; eventually, however, it adopted the Union Prayer Book. Mendelsohn, who joined the Central Conference of American Rabbis when it was founded in 1889, served his congregation faithfully until his death in 1922. In addition to his translation of the Book of Haggai for the Jewish Publication Society, and his index of Biblical citations in the Jastrow Talmudic Dictionary, he was the author of a work on *Criminal Jurisprudence Among the Ancient Hebrews*. [87]

In the writer's collection of American Jewish memorabilia is a set of two volumes of Isaac Leeser's *Discourses on the Jewish Religion* (1867) autographed by Samuel Mendelsohn to "Mr. Marcus Lam;/presented/by/his colleague & friend/S. Mendelsohn/Philadelphia,/January 20th, 1873." This set of books encompasses the history of Maimonides College: two volumes of its founder's presented to a student who became a Hebrew teacher by one of two fellow-students who entered the active rabbinate.

198

II THE MOSES ELIAS LEVY PROJECT, 1821.

Sir,

Mr. Levy will present you with the foregoing Resolutions, and explain at length the important objects which we trust will grow out of the Institution, and solicit your co-operation.

We are, respectfully,

M. M. PEIXOTTO
M. M. NOAH
JUDAH ZUNTZ
M. E. LEVY

To

MESS. MOSES MYERS ⎫

JO. MYERS ⎬ Norfolk Va.
PHILIP J. COHEN ⎭

CIRCULAR.

WHEREAS, Mr. M. E. Levy has submitted to us a plan for the education of Jewish youth, and ameliorating the condition of the Jews generally, which, among many advantages, promises to promote the perpetuity of our religion, and prove in a high degree beneficial to our brethren, we have, in the furtherance of such an object, associated ourselves with Mr. Levy, and have adopted the following Resolutions:

1. *Resolved*, That to carry into effect the important objects of this Institution, the education of Hebrew youth of both sexes, should be the care and concern of the Hebrew community at large.

2. *Resolved*, As a cardinal object of this Institution, that Hebrew youth are to be instructed in the Hebrew language and laws, so as to comprehend both letter and spirit, and duly to estimate their character and principles.

3. *Resolved*, That in addition to a course of religious instruction, the scholars and students of this Institution shall be taught the elementary branches of education, and such branches of the useful arts and of science, as their capacities may warrant.

4. *Resolved*, That a portion of time of such students shall be devoted to practical lessons in agriculture and horticulture, with a view of promoting health and industry, and in order to qualify them for such pursuits.

5. *Resolved*, That suitable persons shall be selected to preside over the various interests and duties of this Institution, who are distinguished for their intelligence, integrity, and moral and religious virtues.

6. *Resolved*, That the observance of simple and economical habits, the love of truth, and all virtues, religious and moral, which tend to ennoble the Israelite and the man, shall be inculcated in the minds of the Students of this Institution. That they be instructed in the universal love of mankind, in principles of patriotism, and the defense of their Country.

7. *Resolved*, That a tract of land of suitable magnitude shall be purchased in a healthy and central part of the Union, for the accommodation of a certain number of families, and the establishment of this Institution; and that each Scholar, after having completed his Studies, shall be entitled to a piece of land, if he thinks proper to settle thereon.

8. *Resolved*, That three distinguished persons of religion and morality shall be appointed Inspectors of this Institution, whose duty it shall be to see that the laws for its government are faithfully executed, that religion in its purity is promoted, and to do all which to them may seem proper for its interest, safety, and permanency, and in their character of Censors, to see that no measure is adopted, which may even remotely have a tendency to injure the character and spirit of the Institution.

9. *Resolved*, That the name of this Institution shall be (CHENUCH) or (PROBATIONARY;) and efforts shall be made to establish societies in different parts of the union, with a view of carrying it into successful operation.

10. *Resolved*, that the members of this Institution must be Israelites, men who have confidence in the covenant, and are zealous in support of their religion and its perpetuity, as a sacred duty; who will take an interest in forwarding the Institution, and promoting harmony and good will among its members.

11. *Resolved*, that the societies in the different cities in the Union, shall consist of only four members each, and who shall at an appointed time meet (by delegates) in order to devise suitable plans for carrying the institution into operation, and each society shall appoint a corresponding secretary from its members.

12. *Resolved*, that Judah Zuntz be Corresponding Secretary.

M. L. M. PEIXOTTO.
M. E. LEVY.
M. M. NOAH.
JUDAH ZUNTZ.

New-York, 7 Eaar, 5581 — May 9, 1821.

III   The Philadelphia Project, 1864.

Sir:

At a meeting of the Jews of this city, for the purpose of founding a College for the Education of Youth for the Jewish Ministry, held on Sunday, November 6th, 1864, at the National Guards' Hall, it was

Resolved, "That the President of the meeting be authorized to appoint two gentlemen from each of the Jewish Congregations in this city, in connection with the President thereof, to form a Committee for canvassing their respective congregations in the collection of funds for the foundation of the College."

In accordance with the above, yourself and the following named gentlemen have been appointed to form said Committee.

A meeting of the Committee will be held on Sunday, November 13th, 1864, at 10 o'clock in the morning, at the Office of Moses A. Dropsie, No. 29 South Sixth Street, up stairs.

Very truly yours,

J. Solis Cohen, M. D. ⎱
Mayer Sulzberger, ⎰ *Secretaries.*

To

Committee.

L. J. LEBERMAN,	ELIAS WOLF,	HENRY MARCUS,
A. HART,	H. WEILLER,	S. ALEXANDER,
S. W. ARNOLD,	S. SILBERMAN,	H. DE BOER,
A. T. JONES,	M. GOLDMAN,	ISAAC GOLDSMITH,
LAZARUS MAYER,	ISAAC ROSENBAUM,	R. BRUNSWICK,
CHAS. BLOOMINGDALE,	JOSEPH M. ASCH,	G. WOLF,
JOSEPH EINSTEIN,	B. ABELES,	M. ROSENBAUM.

IV THE BEGINNING OF MAIMONIDES COLLEGE, 1866.

BOARD OF DELEGATES OF AMERICAN ISRAELITES,
OFFICE OF THE EXECUTIVE COMMITTEE,

New York, August 1st, 5626, 1866.

To the President: —

The Executive Committee desire to call the attention of the Israelites of the United States to the steps that have been taken towards establishing Hebrew High Schools and a Seminary for training ministers and teachers of our faith.

They do not propose to dwell upon the reasons that induced them to undertake the furtherance of an object whose vital importance all are prepared to acknowledge. A few words of explanation are, they apprehend, all that is needed to enlist the active co-operation of their co-religionists in a movement promising to be of enduring benefit to the community at large.

At two successive sessions of the Board of Delegates, the question of Hebrew education of a higher order than that proposed and maintained in the ordinary schools, was earnestly discussed. At the session in 5625, a Committee was appointed to devise measures for carrying into effect the express desire of the Board. At the session of 5626, the preliminary report was received. The following resolutions were unanimously adopted on the 28th of May, 5626 — 1866:

RESOLVED, That the Delegates now present be requested to use their best energies in behalf of Hebrew and religious education in the various cities they represent throughout the Union; and to collect funds for the establishment of a College in the city of Philadelphia for the rearing of Jewish Divines: — the Legislature of Pennsylvania having already granted to the Hebrew Education Society of that city a charter, with the privilege of conferring degrees of scholarship, equal with those of Harvard, Yale, or Rutgers Colleges.

RESOLVED, That this Board will, through its Executive Committee, take immediate measures to engraft upon preparatory schools in such cities as the congregations may deem advisable, and upon free schools where now established, Hebrew High Schools, the pupils of which shall hereafter be eligible to the College to be organized by the Board.

Accordingly, the Executive Committee, desiring that action upon these resolutions may not be delayed, forward this statement, requesting that it may be submitted to your members, and their active interest in this educational movement be excited by your personal effort in co-operation with this Committee.

202

I. — HIGH SCHOOLS.

With reference to High Schools, the Board have in view: their encouragement and erection as preparatory to the College. The College is confessedly of national importance, but its substantial success cannot be justly anticipated in the absence of introductory institutions. The Board must necessarily rely upon the active co-operation of local organizations in sustaining efficient High Schools. Such a school has been inaugurated at Philadelphia, and another has commenced its sessions at New York. The Executive Committee propose to adopt regulations by which uniformity in the course of preparatory studies may be secured, and graduates of the High Schools be qualified to enter the College. It is not alone for those who will become ministers and teachers that these High Schools are required. The study of the Hebrew language has been too generally restricted to that which is purely elementary. The Committee most earnestly impress upon you the necessity of establishing and maintaining Hebrew High Schools, wherever the population will permit. Without these, the College cannot, indeed, be successfully initiated. These schools must prepare the pupil for the higher branches of Hebrew study, which, in connection with subjects directly incidental to theology, will be pursued at the College.

II. — THE COLLEGE.

It has been deemed expedient to avail themselves of the opportunity presented by the Hebrew Education Society of Philadelphia for the establishment of the Seminary in that city.

The charter of the Society enables it to establish a college, with all the powers incident to similar institutions throughout the country; such as conferring degrees, &c., as the following extract will show:

"SEC. 3. It shall also be lawful for said corporation to establish, whenever funds will permit, a superior Seminary of learning within the limits of this Commonwealth, the faculty of which Seminary (or College) shall have power to furnish graduates and others the usual degrees of *Bachelor of Arts*, *Master of Arts* and *Doctor of Laws* and of *Divinity*, as the same is exercised by other colleges established in this Commonwealth."

The advantages offered by Philadelphia as the seat of the proposed College, are: its central location, the convenient access of students to the excellent libraries, the facilities for attending the undergraduate course of the University of Pennsylvania, and the moderate terms upon which students may obtain board.

The College will be controlled and governed by Trustees elected by the Board of Delegates, and, with the co-operation of the Hebrew Education Society: — individuals and societies endowing the institution, as hereafter provided, to have a voice also in the selection of Trustees. The Faculty shall be chosen with reference to entire fitness for the important functions entrusted to them. The course of study at the College is intended to include the higher branches of Hebrew learning and cognate studies, fitting candidates for the ministry and for teachers of Hebrew.

It is intended that the tuition fees shall be as moderate as the endowment will allow, and adequate means will be provided for free scholarships, to which nominations may be made by contributing congregations, societies and individuals. The details are still undetermined and will form the subject of a further communication, as soon as they shall be completed. The Executive Committee now desire to leave the matter in your hands, earnestly trusting that promptitude and liberality will be exercised in providing funds for the endowment of the College. There should be an amount of at least fifty thousand dollars pledged to warrant the Committee undertaking its establishment. Surely, the Israelites of the United States will cheerfully respond to the appeal of the Committee, and speedily place it in their power to open the College. The alacrity and noble liberality displayed by the Jews of the United States on former occasions, when addressed by the Board of Delegates, in assisting the distressed and suffering of Morocco and the Holy Land — inspire the Committee with confidence that this communication, made in behalf of a cause so vitally important, will elicit a cordial and munificent response, and encourage the hope that this College may be rendered free to all, and a monument of the intelligent public spirit of American Israelites.

The following form of subscription list is submitted as meeting the views of the Committee, having been already adopted in Philadelphia, and resulting in these subscriptions:

WE, the undersigned, hereby give the sums set opposite to our respective names as donations for the founding and annual subscriptions for the support of a College to be established under the charter of the Hebrew Education Society for the Education of youth for the Jewish ministry —

	Donations.	Annual Subscriptions.
I. Binswanger.	$500 00	$50 00
A. Hart.	500 00	50 00
Geo. Cromeline.	500 00	50 00

	Donations.	Annual Subscriptions.
M. A. Dropsie	500 00	50 00
S. W. Arnold	500 00	50 00
L. J. Leberman	250 00	50 00
Chas. Bloomingdale	200 00	25 00
Lazarus Mayer	200 00	25 00
Jos. Newhouse	200 00	25 00
Abraham Kahn	200 00	25 00
M. Rosenbach	200 00	25 00
S. Abeles	100 00	
B. Abeles	100 00	25 00
H. Marcus	100 00	25 00
Miss Gratz	100 00	
C. Johnson	100 00	25 00
Mayer Arnold	100 00	25 00
M. Reinhart	50 00	5 00
Joseph Einstein	25 00	10 00
S. Alexander	25 00	10 00
H. De Boer	25 00	10 00
J. A. Ephraim	25 00	10 00
Moses Nathan	20 00	10 00
Augustus Mailert	20 00	5 00
R. Brunswick	20 00	10 00

It will be seen that annual subscriptions are contemplated, as well as donations to the endowment fund. Further lists will be statedly published.

Every member of the Board of Delegates is *ex officio* one of the Collection Committee, and will be happy to take charge of donations for transmission to the Treasurer. Subscriptions may be paid at once or may be made payable when demanded by the Executive Committee.

The Committee will be happy to receive suggestions upon this important subject, desiring that, when they establish the College, it shall be on a perfectly satisfactory and substantial basis, and with a prospect of entire success, and assured usefulness to Israel. They especially solicit your prompt attention to the collection of funds, so that they may be prepared to commence the college sessions without delay.

Communications may be addressed to any officer of the Board:

> ABRAHAM HART, President, Philadelphia.
> HENRY JOSEPHI, Vice-President, New York.
> ISAAC LEESER, Vice-President, Philadelphia.
> ALEX S. SARONI, Treasurer, 5 Barclay Street, New York.
> MYER S. ISAACS, Secretary, 78 Nassau Street, New York.

V   THE MAIMONIDES COLLEGE PROSPECTUS

CHARTER & BY-LAWS OF THE HEBREW EDUCATION SOCIETY

OF PHILADELPHIA.

TOGETHER WITH RULES AND REGULATIONS
FOR THE GOVERNMENT OF MAIMONIDES COLLEGE.

Philadelphia: Stein & Jones, Printers, 321 Chestnut Street 1868

RULES AND REGULATIONS
FOR THE GOVERNMENT OF
MAIMONIDES COLLEGE.

The faculty of Arts is composed of the following Professorships:
A Professorship of Homiletics, Belles Lettres and Comparative Theology.
 " " The Bible and Biblical Literature.
 " " Talmud, Hebrew Philosophy, Jewish History and Literature.
 " " Mishnah with Commentaries, Shulchan Aruch and Yad ha-Chazakah.
 " " Hebrew and Chaldaic Languages.
 " " Greek and Latin "
 " " Rhetoric and English Literature.
 " " Mathematics.
 " " Natural Philosophy and Chemistry.
 " " German and French Languages.

OF THE FACULTY.

1. The Professors shall constitute "The Faculty of Arts," to whom, as a body, shall be committed the immediate regulation and government of the Collegiate Department, subject to the rules and statutes and the control of the Board of Trustees.

2. The College shall be under the supervision of the Provost, who shall make report in relation to it to the Board at least once a year.

3. Stated meetings of the Faculty shall be held every month, for the purpose of administering the general discipline of the College; and special meetings, as often as the business of the institution may require, to be called by the Provost or a majority of the members. At all meet-

ings of the Faculty, the Provost shall preside, or in his absence a chairman can be elected.

4. The Faculty shall appoint a Secretary from its own body whose duty it shall be, to keep the minutes of their proceedings, which shall be, at all times, open to the inspection of the Trustees.

5. No proceedings of the Faculty shall be considered as valid, unless passed by a majority of the members at a meeting formally constituted.

6. It shall be the duty of the Faculty to make reports to the Board at their stated meetings, upon the state of the Collegiate department, stating particularly the names and residences of such students as have been admitted into, or have left the institution since the last report, with such remarks as they may deem expedient.

7. It shall be the special duty of the Provost, to visit and superintend the various departments; to see that the rules and statutes are duly carried into effect, to report to the Board every instance of refusal and neglect to comply with such rules and statutes, and to advise and suggest such alterations and improvements as he may deem best calculated to promote the welfare and usefulness of the institution.

Of The Classes.

1. The students shall be distributed into five classes.

2. No applicant shall be admitted into the Freshman class under the age of 14; any special exception shall be decided by the Board, upon the application of the Faculty. His fitness must appear on examination, to be conducted by the Professors, who must concur in opinion that he is qualified in such branches as shall be prescribed by the Board.

3. The requisites for entering the Freshman class shall be as follows:

LATIN — Caesar, Virgil, Sallust, Odes of Horace.

ENGLISH — The elements of English grammar and of modern Geography.

HEBREW — The translation of the historical portions of the Bible with facility.

ARITHMETIC, including fractions and extraction of roots.

4. The Faculty shall keep a book called the Matriculation book, in which every candidate for entrance into this College shall, on his admission, have his name, age and residence entered, and the name and residence of his parent or guardian.

5. No student shall be admitted to advanced standing, without being as fully instructed as the class to which admission is asked, in all the studies in which the class has been instructed.

6. Vacation shall be from the 10th of July to the 31st of August.

Course of Instruction.

1. The subjects of instruction in the institution shall be the following:— Greek, Latin, German, French, Hebrew, Chaldaic and their literatures, the Natural sciences, History, Mathematics and Astronomy, Moral and Intellectual Philosophy, Constitutional History and Laws of the United States, Belles Lettres, Homiletics, Comparative Theology, the Bible with its commentaries, the Mishnah with its commentaries, the Shulchan 'Aruch, Yad ha-chazakah, Jewish History and Literature, Hebrew Philosophy and the Talmud with its commentaries.

2. At the close of each yearly term there shall be held an examination of all the classes in the presence of a Committee of the Board, and of such other Trustees as shall attend; after every examination the students who are distinguished in each class shall be arranged in the order of merit.

3. No student shall be suffered to proceed to a higher class who shall not, on examination show himself to be master of the studies of the proceeding year, but he may be allowed the privilege, (if the faculty shall judge it expedient to grant it,) of a second examination for admission thereto, at the opening of the next succeeding year.

4. Punishment shall be exclusively directed to a sense of duty, and the principles of honor and shame, and shall consist of private admonition by a Professor — admonition in the presence of the Faculty — admonition in the presence of the Faculty and of the class of the offender — removal to a lower class — suspension for a limited time from college — dismissal — expulsion.

5. No punishment except private admonition shall be inflicted, unless ordered by a resolution of a majority of the whole of the Faculty; nor shall the punishment of expulsion be inflicted unless it be first sanctioned by a vote of the Trustees. In case of dismissal, the offender may be re-admitted, but the effect of expulsion shall be an utter disqualification of the individual for re-admission into this institution, or of receiving any of its honors.

6. The fees for tuition of each year shall be one hundred dollars, payable at the commencement thereof; and no student shall be considered as entitled to his seat in the class for the term, until such payment is made. Notice that the tuition money is due, and that the Treasurer will at times attend (the time then to be stated) shall be given by the Secretary.

7. The Board sanction the institution of a Literary Society, to consist of the students and alumni of the college, or such of them as shall be

admitted members thereof, when suitable rooms can be appropriated for their use. The said society to be under the general control and supervision of the Faculty.

Of Commencements and Conferring Degrees in the Arts.

1. There shall be an annual commencement of graduates in the arts on the last Thursday morning of each term, at 10 o'clock.

2. Candidates for the degree of Bachelor in the Arts or Divinity shall be publicly examined by the Faculty in the collegiate departments, in the presence of the Committee of Examination and such other members of the Board of Trustees as may attend.

3. The Provost shall report the names of those who shall have been found worthy of receiving such degree to the Board, who shall, if the report be approved, confer such degree accordingly. But no degree shall be conferred unless by the vote of the Trustees; and every student, before he can be recommended for the degree of Bachelor of Arts or Divinity, shall settle his account with the Treasurer.

4. The Degree of Master of Arts may be conferred on the Alumni of the College, who shall have been Bachelor in the Arts of three years standing, and shall apply for that honor.

5. The order of the commencement shall be directed by the Faculty.

Notes

[1] Henry Englander, "Isaac Leeser," *Yearbook, The Central Conference of American Rabbis*, Vol. XXVIII, 1918, pp. 213–52; *DAB*, XI, pp. 137–8.

[2] Circular addressed to "Mess. Moses Myers, Jo. Myers, Philip I. Cohen — Norfolk, Va.," Moses Myers Collection, American Jewish Archives. Reprinted in the Appendix.

[3] *OCC*, I, No. 6, pp. 303–7, Sept., 1843.

[4] Buchler, "The Struggle for Unity: Attempts at Union in American Jewish Life, 1654–1868," p. 42.

[5] *OCC*, IV, No. 10, p. 475, Jan., 1847.

[6] See pp. 35–8, above.

[7] See pp. 44–5, above.

[8] Grinstein, *The Rise of the Jewish Community of New York, 1654–1860*, pp. 252, 448.

[9] *ASM*, XV, No. 4, p. 29, Nov. 7, 1856; *Proceedings of the Second Biennial Convention of the Jewish Theological Seminary Association, Held in the City of New York, Sunday Adar 24, 5650, March 16th, 1890*, New York, 1890, pp. 15, 21; *Proceedings of the Third Biennial Convention . . ., Adar 28, 5652, March 27th, 1892*, New York, 1892, p. 22; Cyrus Adler, "The Standpoint of the Seminary," *Lectures, Selected Papers, Addresses*, Phila., 1933, p. 252.

[10] Buchler, *op. cit.*, p. 32; *OCC*, XII, No. 12, pp. 615–6, March, 1855; *ASM*, XII, No. 7, p. 52, June 1, 1855; No. 25, p. 196, Oct. 5; No. 26, Oct. 12; XIV, No. 11, p. 86, June 27, 1856; *ISR*, II, No. 14, p. 108, Oct. 12, 1855; No. 16, p. 132, Oct. 26; No. 18, pp. 148–51, Nov. 9; No. 19, p. 156, Nov. 16; Wise, *Reminiscences*, pp. 324 ff.

[11] *OCC*, XXV, No. 7, pp. 324–5, Oct. 1867.

[12] *OCC*, XXIII, No. 9, pp. 389 ff., Dec., 1865; *MESS*, XVIII, No. 5, p. 117, Oct. 20, 1865; *HL*, IX, No. 3, p. 4, Oct. 26, 1866.

[13] *HL, op. cit.*

[14] *ISR*, XIII, No. 32, p. 5, Feb. 15, 1867.

[15] *HL*, XI, No. 6, p. 4, Nov. 15, 1867.

[16] Nathan A. Perilman, "One Hundred Years of Congregation Emanu-El," *Moral and Spiritual Foundations for the World of Tomorrow*, New York, 1945, p. 206. But some time during this period, according to Richard J. H. Gottheil, *The Life of Gustav Gottheil, Memoir of a Priest in Israel*, Williamsport, Pa., 1936, pp. 49, 55, classes were actually held by the Emanu-El Seminary. It has been impossible to ascertain further details.

[17] *Hebrew Union College-Jewish Institute of Religion Bulletin*, Oct., 1953, p. 7; *The Hebrew Theological Seminary Association: Proceedings of the First Convention Held at the City of New York. May 24th and 25th, 5636–1876*, New York, 1876.

[18] *HL*, IX, No. 3, pp. 4–5, Oct. 26, 1866.

[19] *Ibid.*

[20] *MESS*, XXII, No. 8, p. 5, Aug. 23, 1867. For discussion of the problem, see *HL*, IX, No. 4, p. 5, Nov. 2, 1866; No. 11, pp. 4–5, Dec. 21; *MESS*, XXI, No. 1, p. 5, Jan. 4, 1867; No. 12, pp. 4–5, March 22.

[21] Printed Circular, signed by J. Solis-Cohen, M.D., and Mayer Sulzberger, Secretaries. Morais Collection, Dropsie College Library. Reprinted in the Appendix.

[22] Printed Circular, dated August 1, 5626, 1866, files of the Board of Delegates of American Israelites, Library of the A. J. H. S. Reprinted in the Appendix.

[23] *MESS*, XXI, No. 21, p. 5, May 31, 1867.

[24] *MESS*, XXI, No. 24, p. 5, June 21, 1867.

[25] *OCC*, XXV, No. 5, pp. 228–30, Aug., 1867.

[26] *Commemoration of the One Hundredth Anniversary of the Birth of the Reverend Doctor*

Sabato Morais, by the Congregation Mikveh Israel in the City of Philadelphia, Wednesday Evening, April 18, 1923, Iyar 2, 5683, Phila., 1924.

[27] Edward Davis, *The History of Rodeph Shalom Congregation, Philadelphia, 1802–1926,* Phila., 1926, pp. 81 ff.

[28] *UJE,* II, p. 256; Rebekah Kohut, *My Portion,* New York, 1927, pp. 13–8.

[29] It has been difficult to ascertain many details of Buttenwieser's life. Several have been supplied by his grandson, Benjamin J. Buttenwieser, former U. S. Assistant High Commissioner for Germany, in a letter to the writer, Sept. 17, 1951. In a letter in the Leeser Collection, Dropsie College Library, dated Jan. 7, 1859, Buttenwieser requested Leeser's help in obtaining a position at Rodeph Shalom of Philadelphia, but whether this was as *hazan,* preacher or teacher is not indicated. In a Hebrew Education Society circular, published on Oct. 22, 1866, in the H.E.S. Collection, Dropsie College Library, Buttenwieser is described as "a profound Hebrew scholar, a thorough Talmudist, and a graduate of one of the most celebrated Universities of Germany." Coincidentally, later on, Buttenwieser also taught for the Emanu-El Seminary, according to Gottheil, *op. cit.,* p. 52.

[30] Morais, *The Jews of Philadelphia,* pp. 105–6.

[31] Data furnished by the Rev. Leon H. Elmaleh, Minister Emeritus of Mikveh Israel Congregation, of which Polano later became Sexton.

[32] Hebrew Education Society Circular, *op. cit.*

[33] *Minute Book of the Board of Trustees of Maimonides College* (=*MB*), pp. 6, 7, 10; *Jewish Record* (Phila.), II, No. 22, p. 4, Sept. 8, 1876.

[34] *MESS,* XXIII, No. 1, p. 2, Jan. 3, 1868, through No. 8, p. 2, Feb. 21.

[35] Letter, M. S. Isaacs to Sabato Morais, Sept. 8, 1868, Morais Collection, Dropsie College Library; *MB,* p. 19; a Rev. Mayer wrote on March 16, 1869, about the possibility of sending his son, but nothing came of this, *MB,* p. 26.

[36] *MESS,* XXVI, No. 6, p. 5, Aug. 6, 1869; *HL,* XIV, No. 17, p. 4, Aug. 6.

[37] *MB,* pp. 23–4, 35.

[38] *MB,* p. 30.

[39] *MB,* p. 30; *MESS,* XXVI, No. 19, p. 4, Nov. 12, 1869; *Seventy-Fifth Anniversary Booklet, Temple Emanuel,* Denver, 1949, p. 10; letters from Saft's daughter, Mrs. Hattie Saft Levy, Denver, to the writer, Feb. 17, April 12, 1950.

[40] *MB,* pp. 36, 39. But Mendelsohn's naturalization papers, in the author's collection of Jewish Americana, state that he arrived in the United States on April 20, 1870.

[41] *MB,* p. 39.

[42] *MB,* p. 45. Nowhere in the sources is the name of Julius T. Loeb mentioned as a student at the College. Dr. Joshua Bloch gives no source for his reference to such a student in *PAJHS,* No. XLII, Pt. 1 (Sept., 1952), p. 103.

[43] *ISR*, XIX, No. 17, p. 8, Oct. 25, 1872; for the background see *MESS*, XXXII, No. 9, p. 6, Aug. 30, 1872; *ISR*, XIX, No. 8, p. 2.

[44] *MESS*, XXXII, No. 15, p. 2, Oct. 11, 1872.

[45] *AJCW*, pp. 121–55, for details of the Order's background, and the Jewish reaction to Grant's campaign in 1868.

[46] *MESS*, XXXII, No. 16, p. 3, Oct. 16, 1872.

[47] *MESS*, XXXIII, No. 2, p. 5, Jan. 10, 1873.

[48] *Jewish Record*, I, No. 5, p. 5, May 21, 1875.

[49] *MESS*, XXIII, No. 20, p. 5, May 23, 1868. See also *HL*, XII, No. 10, p. 1, June 12, 1868; *MESS*, XXVI, No. 1, p. 4, July 2, 1869; No. 2, p. 4, July 9; *HL*, XIV, No. 7, p. 4, May 28, 1869; No. 12, p. 4, July 7.

[50] *MESS*, XXIV, No. 6, pp. 2–3, Aug. 7, 1868.

[51] *MB*, pp. 18–9.

[52] *HL*, XII, No. 7, p. 4, May 22, 1868.

[53] The report of the meeting of Nov. 16, 1868, is in *MB*, pp. 24–6

[54] *MB*, pp. 37–8.

[55] *MB*, pp. 38 ff.

[56] *MESS*, XXXI, No. 13, p. 5, March 29, 1872.

[57] See above, pp. 196–8, for the later careers of these students.

[58] *MB*, pp. 7, 10–11; *MESS*, XXII, No. 20, p. 5, Nov. 22, 1867; XXIII, No. 3, p. 5, Jan. 17, 1868; No. 7, p. 6, Feb. 14; No. 20, p. 2, March 27; No. 22, p. 2, June 5.

[59] *MESS*, XXVII, No. 5, p. 5, Feb. 4, 1870.

[60] *MB*, pp. 21, 30; Minute Book of the Executive Committee of the Board of Delegates of American Israelites, p. 131, Library of the A. J. H. S.; *MESS*, XXIV, No. 6, p. 6, Aug. 7, 1868.

[61] *MB*, p. 43.

[62] *MB*, pp. 11, 38, 41.

[63] *MB*, p. 43.

[64] *MB*, p. 31.

[65] *MB*, pp. 36, 43.

[66] Sulzberger Collection, Dropsie College Library.

[67] Circular of Board of Delegates, Aug. 1, 1866; *MESS*, XXII, No. 7, p. 5, Aug. 16, 1867; No. 8, p. 5, Aug. 23.

[68] *MB*, p. 7.

[69] *MB*, p. 28.

[70] Leeser Collection, Dropsie College Library.

[71] Truly significant, in this regard, is the fact that the correspondence files of the Board contain neither out-going nor in-coming communications concerning the College.

[72] Letter, Oct. 25, 5630, Morais Collection, Dropsie College Library. "Patrick" is a reference to an article which Morais had recently published under that pseudonym.

[73] Letter, Aug. 27, 1868, Morais Collection.

[74] *MB*, p. 31.

[75] *MB*, p. 33. Morais also seems to have attempted to solicit subscriptions, see letter, Louis Strasburger, New York City, to Morais, Jan. 3, 1869, promising to help, Morais Collection.

[76] Cyrus Adler, "Moses Aaron Dropsie," *Lectures, Selected Papers, Addresses*, pp. 54–5.

[77] Financial Report, filed loosely in *MB*.

[78] *Jewish Record*, II, No. 22, pp. 4–5, Sept. 8, 1876; No. 24, p. 5, Sept. 22.

[79] *Ibid.*, Sept. 22.

[80] *MESS*, XXIX, No. 8, p. 4, Feb. 24, 1871.

[81] *ISR*, XIV, No. 7, p. 405, Aug. 16, 1867, the first of a long series of attacks.

[82] Letter, July 5, 5626, Leeser Collection.

[83] *Fifty Years' Work of the Hebrew Education Society of Philadelphia, 1848–1898*, Phila., 1899, p. 72.

[84] *AJCW*, pp. 75–7.

[85] *Yearbook, The Central Conference of American Rabbis*, Vol. XLI, 1931, pp. 241–2; *New Haven Register*, Oct. 19, 1913; letter from Dr. Rollin G. Osterweis to the writer, Aug. 1, 1949; *Jewish Record*, I, No. 32, p. 5, Nov. 26, 1875; No. 44, pp. 2–3, Oct. 18, 1876; *MESS*, XXXVIII, No. 22, p. 3, Dec. 10, 1875; Charles Reznikoff and Uriah Z. Engelman, *The Jews of Charleston*, Phila., 1950, pp. 162, 167–8, 231–2, 320; Joshua Trachtenberg, *Consider The Years*, Easton, 1944, pp. 204, 326.

[86] *Jewish Exponent*, Aug. 3, 1934, p. 8; interview with Mrs. Alvin Levi and Mrs. Marcus E. Lam, Phila.; *Jewish Record*, I, No. 17, p. 5, Aug. 13, 1875.

[87] *Yearbook, The Central Conference of American Rabbis*, Vol. XXXIII, 1923, p. 157; *MESS*, XXXIII, No. 11, p. 2, March 14, 1873; No. 18, pp. 4–5, May 9; *Jewish Record*, I, No. 6, p. 5, May 19, 1875; No. 43, p. 5, Feb. 11, 1876; No. 45, p. 4, Feb. 25; No. 50, p. 4, March 31; *Seventy-Fifth Anniversary Booklet, Temple of Israel*, Wilmington, N. C., 1951.

VIII

Jewish Welfare Activities for the Military during the Spanish-American War*

Wहen PRESIDENT HARRY S. TRUMAN sent American forces into action, in June, 1950, against the North Korean invaders swarming across the 38th parallel, the National Jewish Welfare Board, whose facilities, resources and techniques had been tested and perfected over a period of almost thirty-five years of wartime and peacetime service, was immediately prepared, in cooperation with Jewish chaplains serving in the Army, Air Force and Navy, to activate a well-rounded program of religious and welfare ministration to Jewish men serving their country.

In April, 1898, when the United States declared war on Spain, there was no National Jewish Welfare Board, nor was there any other national Jewish service organization which could potentially meet the needs of thousands of Jewish servicemen away from their homes. Local Jewish communities were well organized; but none of their synagogues or cultural, social and philanthropic groups had a plan for emergency ministration to soldiers and sailors. Nor were any Jewish chaplains serving the military forces. Four had been appointed thirty-five years previously during the Civil War, but their commissions were granted only for the duration of hostilities, as stipulated in temporary war-time legislation, which was not intended to apply to chaplaincy service in

* Read at the Annual Meeting of the American Jewish Historical Society, New York, February, 1952, and originally published in *Publication of the American Jewish Historical Society*, Vol. XLI, No. 4 (June, 1952), pp. 356–80, thereafter reprinted in the 1952 New Year's editions of a number of Anglo-Jewish periodicals, without notes, as distributed in mimeographed form by the National Jewish Welfare Board.

the regular military and naval establishments, nor in any future conflict.[1] There was no automatic provision for the appointment of Jewish chaplains in proportion to Jewish servicemen when war was declared.

One of the first to recognize the need for religious guidance for Jewish soldiers and to publicize that need was fifty-five year old Rabbi Edward Benjamin Morris Browne of Columbus, Ga., but the only thanks he received for his foresight was ridicule and scorn. Shortly after the war began, Rabbi Browne made application for a commission as chaplain;[2] the Army apparently considered him too old for military duty, but several American Jewish periodicals pilloried him for his action. Said the editor of the *American Hebrew*:

It is a long time since we have heard of Rabbi E. B. M. Browne, but the war has given him an opportunity to come to the front again. He has tendered his services to the President as chaplain to the Jews in the army, in case no younger rabbi should seek the place. We hope that Dr. Browne will be permitted to remain in the quietude of his home.[3]

Rabbi Isaac Mayer Wise, editor of *The American Israelite*, who was never reticent in public statements about his colleagues, wrote with even greater sarcasm:

Up till very recently the people of the United States have had a vague feeling that the war with Spain was not quite in proper working order, that something, they did not know just exactly what, was lacking to make our army and navy perfectly effective. The trouble has fortunately now been located: the "Hebrews" in the army lacked a chaplain of their own faith, and President McKinley was delaying the invasion of Cuba until a proper one could be secured. The country was scoured from end to end, but none of those available answered to the requirements. The President was in despair and was about to discharge all the Jews from the service, rather than imperil their immortal souls by having them go forth to battle without a proper spiritual guide, when help came. There was one who could save, and only one. His extreme modesty had hitherto kept him in the background . . . We are not prepared to say what the President is going to do in the matter any further than to call attention to the significant fact that the invasion of Cuba has actually begun, and that the order for the forward movement was not given until the Rabbi of Columbus, Ga., had been heard from . . . By a terrible wrench, the violence of which only those who are fortunate enough to know the Rabbi well can appreciate, he has overcome his shrinking modesty, his lifelong aversion to anything that approached even remotely to notoriety, and announced his presence and readiness to sacrifice himself. Now let the war proceed. [4]

Admittedly, Rabbi Browne was not one of the leading lights of the American rabbinate. He was noted for his travels — from one congregation to another, in various parts of the country. During his career he served in Milwaukee, Wisc., Montgomery, Ala., Evansville, Ind., New York City, Toledo, Ohio and Columbus, Ga. Between several of these rabbinical peregrinations, he branched off into other fields of endeavor, including journalism, medicine, teaching and lecturing on the public platform. On several occasions, he was accused of scandalous conduct, but the charges were slanderous, said Rabbi Browne, and he produced witnesses to prove his innocence. [5] But such a clergyman, frequently embroiled in public controversy and hardly to be described as successful in any of his pulpits, could not earn the admiration or respect of his colleagues.

Nevertheless the attack on "the Rev. Dr. Alphabetical Bob-up-serenely on all occasions Browne" by *The Israelite* and the *American Hebrew*, personal as it was, can only be regarded as unfortunate and ill-timed. No one could gainsay the need for Jewish chaplains. The periodicals were assembling lists, which grew every week, of Jewish men who were joining the ranks. They needed the ministrations and moral support of a chaplain of their own faith. Wise had been a leader, in 1861–1862, of the movement to have Congress modify or abolish its undemocratic provision which limited the appointment of chaplains to clergymen of Christian denominations. [6] It ill-behooved him to ridicule the effort of any rabbi to secure adequate ministration by rabbis in uniform for men of their faith. Wise should have seconded the motion and urged the public to support the effort by Rabbi Browne, ignoring the personal element for the sake of the principle at stake.

Valuable time was lost while the editors were laughing at Rabbi Browne. It was not until July that the Central Conference of American Rabbis met in convention in Atlantic City and requested that McKinley appoint a suitable number of rabbis as chaplains:

... Holding at the disposal of our country all the material and spiritual needs in our possession, the Central Conference of American Rabbis also desires to assist the Government in maintaining the moral and religious tone of the army. To achieve that end we will furnish an adequate supply of religious literature to the Jewish soldiers and sailors in the various camps and at the front.

For the more effective performance of this duty we respectfully ask the President of the United States to appoint two or more Jewish chaplains at large to minister to the spiritual needs of the soldiers and sailors of our denomination in the army and navy of the country. [7]

It was already too late, however; neither the Central Conference's resolution nor the tardy recognition of the problem by such periodicals as the Philadelphia *Jewish Exponent*, the New York *Jewish Messenger*, and the Cleveland *Jewish Review*, could anticipate the cessation of hostilities in early August. [8] American Jewry was too late in awakening to the religious needs of its men in uniform during the war.

Several rabbis were, however, elected to serve as chaplains of local military organizations. One of these was Rabbi J. Leonard Levy, Associate Rabbi of Reform Congregation Keneseth Israel of Philadelphia, who, late in May, 1898, received the following letter from Charles M. Keegan, an ambitious young tobacco salesman who had begun organizing a Volunteer Brigade in March:

May 25, 1898.

Dear Sir:

Keegan's Brigade of Pennsylvania Volunteers are, at the present moment, without a chaplain. From our acquaintance with you, and from the patriotic sentiments you have from time to time uttered, the members of the Brigade will feel happy if you will accept the position of Chaplain. The men have banded themselves together for the protection of the Fatherland, and will feel happy if they can receive spiritual ministrations at your hands in the broad and liberal spirit for which you have become known in this community and throughout the country.

Hoping we may be favored with a reply in the affirmative, believe me,

Yours very truly,

C. M. KEEGAN [9]

Rabbi Levy immediately referred the matter to the Board of Trustees of the Congregation, writing that "the post of chaplain in this Brigade has been entirely unsought by me, and has been tendered voluntarily by Col. Keegan and his men. I am personally satisfied to accept the offer . . ." [10] To Colonel Keegan he wrote that "I have referred your letter to the Board of Trustees of my Congregation & am willing to act in harmony with their decision . . ." [11] The Board met on May 29th and unanimously resolved that "Rev. Levy be given permission to accept position of Chaplain tendered to him by Col. Keegan's brigade & that during his absence his salary be paid him as usual." [12] Rabbi Levy had, meanwhile, left Philadelphia for an extended lecture tour throughout the West, and it took several weeks before he received news of his Board's action. On June 10th he telegraphed his acceptance to Colonel Keegan, and several days later the Philadelphia papers published the news, together with Rabbi Levy's pledge that he would devote any salary received from the Government for his military service "to the relief of all cases of distress occasioned in the families of men who go as volunteers." [13] This patriotic gesture received the hearty approval of the press and public, and within a brief time other officers of the Brigade had followed his leadership. [14]

Meanwhile, about 900 men had enlisted for service with the First Regiment of Keegan's Brigade, while about 500 had joined a similar regiment created by John Wanamaker. The men and officers of both regiments were impatient for official recognition by the War Department, and a call to active service. But government policy now frowned on such informal, civilian formation of "volunteer" military units as had been popular and acceptable during the Civil War; state officials preferred to create new regiments of the Pennsylvania National Guard, rather than accept into the National Guard units whose officers were self-appointed and frequently without military experience or ability. As time dragged on, more and more of the men who had enlisted in Keegan's Brigade, some 1,000 according to newspaper reports, withdrew and joined the National Guard or enlisted in the Army itself for immediate active duty; Keegan did not attempt to restrain his men for the sake of his own ambitions, but seems to have borne his snubbing by Army officers and state authorities with as much grace as possible under the circumstances. In all this complicated military and political maneuvering and the attendant melting away of Keegan's Brigade, Rabbi Levy, of course, had no opportunity to be Chaplain in anything but name. The war came to a close with the Colonel and his Chaplain still in civilian garb. [15]

Despite the fact that he never saw active service, Rabbi Levy's election as Chaplain of the Brigade was a tribute to his reputation as a civic leader in Philadelphia. That he supported the war effort was obvious. Immediately after the declaration of hostilities he had not only announced his approval of the President's action, but also indicated his desire to do something tangible: ". . . I hope it may be my privilege to lend my support to my country in the hour of trial. I hope it will be my privilege to be able to undertake some service compatible with my calling during the present difficulty . . ." [16]

In a city-wide rally to stimulate support for the Brigade, and before his election as its chaplain, he had declared that, ". . . when . . . murdered men and outraged women and children look to this great nation for aid, shall we refuse their appeal? No, not if we are Americans, the children of the heroic Washington and lovers of the martyred Lincoln . . ." [17]

That his fervent advocacy of the Administration's stand against Spain was only partly responsible for his election as Brigade Chaplain is apparent from the fact that it was not a Jewish Brigade. Of the thirteen men appointed to company command, only one, George Levy (the Rabbi's brother), was Jewish. The only other Jewish officer was Joseph J. Snellenberg, a leading member of Rabbi Levy's congregation, who was elected major of the Brigade and served as chairman of its finance committee. [18] These two could not have been powerful enough to secure the appointment for Rabbi Levy unless a majority of their fellow-officers shared their respect for him as a clergyman of broad sympathies and superior talents. That a rabbi should have been chosen chaplain for the entire Brigade, rather than chaplain only for the men of his faith, at that date in American history, was testimony not only to his own character and ability, but to the liberal, democratic instincts of the men who did the voting. [19]

The other rabbi who was elected chaplain on a local rather than a national level was Dr. Emil G. Hirsch, spiritual leader of Sinai Congregation of Chicago, one of the most influential clergymen of his time. [20] Dr. Hirsch was appointed Chaplain in the Illinois Naval Reserve, with the rank of Lieutenant, by the Governor of Illinois, on June 8, 1898. [21] State Naval Reserve units were similar in character to the National Guard, and many men who had enlisted in such units were called to active duty with the United States Navy during the Spanish-American War.

Rabbi Hirsch was not called to active duty, however, and, although it is reported that he once appeared in his pulpit in Naval uniform,[22] the only record of any service her endered as chaplain is that which concerns a trip which he made to Newport News, Va., in October, 1898, to participate in the ceremonies attendant upon the launching of the Battleship *Illinois*.[23] After less than two years' service, he resigned his commission. Meager as his service was, Dr. Hirsch's appointment must be counted as yet another military honor to a rabbi at a time of national emergency, another vote of confidence in the American rabbinate, and another indication that Judaism received equal regard and respect with Christianity as an American faith.

The only rabbi actually to tour the fighting front in Cuba was J. Leonard Levy's senior rabbi, Dr. Joseph Krauskopf[24] — not in the capacity of military chaplain, however, but of Field Commissioner for the National Relief Commission, an organization whose activities resembled those of the Sanitary Commission during the Civil War and of the United Service Organizations during World War II. During June, July and August, 1898, Krauskopf, nationally known as an orator, administrator and public servant in many fields of human endeavor, toured military camps in Washington, D. C., Jacksonville, Fernandina and Tampa, Florida, Chickamauga and Atlanta, Montauk Point, Long Island, and Cuba. His reports on the poor sanitary and medical conditions in the camps, the failings of the Red Cross, and the morale of the soldiers were an especially important contribution to the campaign for reforms in the armed forces. Though his particular mission was devoted to the welfare of all the men, and though he moved most frequently with high ranking officers, Dr. Krauskopf was always conscious of his calling as a rabbi, seeking out Jewish men and conducting services for them, taking messages from them back home to their families.[25]

The trip to Cuba was a heavy responsibility. Krauskopf and his fellow Commissioners were charged not only with the task of investigating conditions among the troops, but also of distributing tons of medical and food stores as a voluntary contribution from the American people to their sons at the front. In addition, Dr. Krauskopf conveyed the personal offer of Oscar S. Straus to provide a $10,000 ice-plant for the American headquarters in Santiago, and also undertook the obligation of distributing 1,000 Union Prayer Books, a gift of the Central Conference of American Rabbis, and sundry Jewish magazines, tracts and newspapers, to Jewish servicemen. [26]

In his diary of the trip, a fascinating record of his experiences, Rabbi Krauskopf told of the service he conducted aboard ship:

Sunday, July 24, 1898:

. . . Last evening, the captain of the vessel approached me and asked me to conduct the Sunday service. I hesitated at first but finally consented, and so at 10:30 crew and passengers assembled in the large marines's mess room, and I conducted the entire service, using my Prayer Book and our Relief Commission Song and Hymn Book, copies of which having been previously distributed, and then I preached the sermon, which was very much appreciated. Found four Jewish men among the crew. This is indeed history. A rabbi conducting services for a Gentile audience in an auxiliary U. S. cruiser, along the coast of of Cuba, at the request of a Gentile U. S. commander. I claim the honor of having conducted the first Jewish service in Cuba, or in that part of it that has recently surrendered to the United States . . . The Jewish boys have just asked me for paper and stamps to write home. I shall look after their interests . . . [27]

Once arrived in Cuba, he set about his numerous tasks, touring the fighting fronts on horseback, experiencing all the filth, privation and exhaustion of the men who had been there for weeks on end, inspecting villages, camps, warehouses, hospitals, driving himself day after day. But always there was time to visit with the Jewish "boys:"

. . . General [Joseph Wheeler] asked me if I would not like to see some of the Jewish boys in his division. Assenting, of course, he sent an order to the different brigades for all Jewish boys to assemble at his tent. It was not long before they appeared, quite a goodly number of them, and as soldierly looking a set of men as one could wish to see. Those of the Rough Riders came accompanied by their colonel, Theodore Roosevelt. He came to tell us personally how proud he was of his Jewish Rough-Riders, of whom he had eight. One of them, Sam Green-wald, of Prescott, Ariz., had entered April 30th, as a private, and has since been promoted by the president, through the recommendation of Col. Roosevelt, to second lieutenant for his gallant and heroic service; for two days and nights he fought alongside his colonel, under the hottest fire, and in the most imminent danger, and never wavered.

Another, Sam Goldberg, of Albuquerque, N. M., 22 years old, was struck by a bullet in his hip and continued fighting for two days before he stopped to have the bullet extracted. The story of the bravery of these holds good of a number of others. I was told that fifteen Jewish boys were killed in the battles in and about San Juan Hill and El Caney . . . Roosevelt was overflowing with enthusiasm and pride . . . [28]

Then, of course, after the chat, a religious service — at the suggestion of the rabbi's host: "General Wheeler then, of his own accord, asked me to hold a service for the Jewish boys, and give them a talk, and offered me his own tent for that purpose. He then withdrew to the adjoining tent, where his son lay dangerously ill, so that I could have a private chat with the Jewish boys . . ." [29]

Here and there Rabbi Krauskopf met young men from his own congregation, including several whom he had blessed at Confirmation; one can imagine their feelings when they saw his familiar figure in that unfamiliar environment. [30] Even after he left Cuba, and returned home to file his reports, Dr. Krauskopf maintained his contacts with the boys he met in Cuba and with Theodore Roosevelt who became his devoted admirer. Sam Greenwald visited him on furlough and stayed over in Philadelphia for a few days as the rabbi's house guest. Krauskopf was not a chaplain, officially, but he came as close as any American rabbi to fulfilling the duties of that position in 1898.

A few other rabbis, however, endeavored to do whatever they could for men who were stationed nearby. Rabbi David Marx of the Hebrew Benevolent Congregation, Atlanta, Ga., was given an unofficial appointment as visiting chaplain by the officer in command of Fort McPherson, Atlanta, when it was temporarily converted into a hospital for the care of sick and wounded soldiers. Rabbi Marx writes:

I visited the sick, cheered them, wrote to their folks at home and tried to meet the needs as they arose . . . Members of the congregation did what they could to make the discharged (from the hospital) men know that they were amongst friends. As far as I can recall their religious contacts were adequately met. We never lacked in willingness on the part of our men and women to render service. [31]

Rabbi Isaac E. Marcuson performed similar services for the men stationed at the camp which was located at Ocmulges Park, outside of Macon, Ga. Rabbi Marcuson describes his experiences in an interesting letter:

I spent much of my time out at the camp, particularly when the war ended. Everybody left, but a hospital, a couple of nurses and a doctor or two and a pile of patients. There wasn't a soul to look after the poor devils with no one to provide any comforts or anything else for them. I undertook the job as the civilian chaplain. For two or three months I had to serve as Red Cross, and every other organization which should have given them attention. [32]

Arnold E. Stern of New York, a veteran of the Spanish-American War, recalls some help from Rabbi M. S. Levy of Beth Israel Congregation of San Francisco:

On arriving in San Francisco on Rosh Hashanah eve (about 3 p. m.) we dropped our knapsacks. There were 3 of us in one Co. Jacob Solins (deceased) Henry Amsel NY address unknown. We went to the city. We had a letter to Rev. M. S. Levy, Geary St. Temple. The rabbi came to the camp and he was refused passes to about 45 of the Regt. Telegraphed to Wash DC and I collected all the boys. Also for Yom Kippur. We remained in Shule all day. The hospitality was wonderful. The Ladies Aux'ly of the Temple provided us with a Banquet dinner.

Families were asked to entertain us. We were with the best in San Francisco. [33]

This was not the only service Rabbi Levy performed. According to the recollections of Isidore Weill of Kew Gardens, N. Y., now Adjutant of the Hebrew Veterans of the War with Spain, not only Rabbi Levy, but also Rabbi Jacob Voorsanger of Temple Emanu-El and Simon R. Cohen, then a student at the Hebrew Union College, conducted embarkation services for Jewish soldiers about to leave for the Philippine Islands. [34]

After the war had ended, Rabbi Adolph Spiegel, who resided in Ponce, Puerto Rico, for nine months during 1899, conducted religious services for the American Jewish soldiers stationed there and ministered to their needs as a civilian chaplain. After organizing a civilian congregation for the few American and French Jews living there, however, he decided to return to New York, and his work among the soldiers came to an end. [35]

The services which Krauskopf conducted during his brief stay in Cuba seem to have been unique; data about divine worship conducted overseas by the soldiers themselves has not been located. Only one source, a Jewish weekly, reported that "our Jewish soldier boys have frequently held religious services in the camp;" but it provided no details. [36] Soldiers at several military camps in the United States were given permission to leave the barracks to attend services in near-by communities. The *American Hebrew* addressed a vote of thanks to the officers at Camp Lee, Va., for this courtesy, [37] and the *Jewish Messenger* told its readers that on June 10th "the neat synagogue at Jacksonville held quite a contingent of soldiers who had come to say Kaddish." [38] A soldier stationed at Camp Cuba Libre, just outside Jacksonville, on the other hand, complained that

it is a painful yet truthful fact that out of a number of about three hundred Jewish young men in the camp I am positive that no more than five out of the entire number attend services at the temple in

225

Jacksonville. Yet the opportunity is afforded them by the military officers and camp, and especially so by the generous Jewish people of Jacksonville . . .[39]

Although the congregation in Tampa had only been organized four years previously, its spiritual leader or a layman, according to one source, went out to the huge army transit center outside town to conduct services.[40]

Some veterans of the war[41] do not recall ever having seen a rabbi in a camp or hospital, nor were they ever invited to attend services in a synagogue or extended home hospitality by a Jewish community.[42] Dozens of veterans said they had no contact whatever with Judaism during their period of service. No rabbi ever came to camp; no Jewish layman ever indicated interest in their welfare. Typical is the comment of Mark S. Harris of New York, "To my knowledge no . . . hospitality was ever offered by our own people during the period of the war." M. J. Mendelsohn states flatly, "my religious contacts at that time were nil." Others, however, though fewer in number, have warm recollections of Jewish contacts brought about by the exigencies of military service.

Abraham W. Eckstein of Jamaica, Long Island, who was stationed at Fort Adams, near Newport, R. I., recounts that he and about fifteen other Jewish soldiers went to services at the Touro Synagogue from time to time, and that the community made special efforts to give them home hospitality during the holiday seasons. When one of his fellow soldiers was killed in a fire at the camp, Eckstein was successful in enlisting the community's cooperation and arranged to have the man's remains interred in the Newport Jewish cemetery at the expense of the congregation.[43]

Isidore Weill remembers with pleasure the hospitality which was extended to him and a soldier friend, Harry Sylvester, the only Jews in their company, by the Dreyfuss family of Washington, D. C., when they attended Rosh Hashanah services at the Washington Hebrew Congregation in 1898. Weill has maintained a continuing correspondence with the Dreyfuss' through all the years since the war. [44]

Herbert Loeb Dreifus, now of Philadelphia, but then of Danville, Pa., while stationed at Camp Meade in 1898, attended Rosh Hashanah and Yom Kippur services at Ohev Sholom Congregation in Harrisburg, Pa. The Marks family took him and some of his fellows home from services; this was the inception of a lifetime friendhsip with their son Edgar Marks. [45]

The writer has been unable to locate any men who conducted their own services in camp, and only an occasional soldier like Herman Weberblum [46] or Ralph Cohen [47] who continued to lay *Tefillin* and recite daily prayers. Weberblum, the only Jew in his entire regiment, was invited to attend services at the synagogue in Huntsville, Ala., while stationed nearby, but Saturday inspections always interfered. He was welcomed into many Huntsville Jewish homes, however, and enjoyed the feeling of being among home folk. Harry C. Weinstock, then of Philadelphia, now of St. Cloud, Fla., had the hard luck of being stationed out in the wilderness somewhere; he was able to obtain relief from duty on holidays, but there was no synagogue within reach. [48]

Samuel H. Taylor, now of Venice, Calif., relates a Yom Kippur experience of 1898:

On the Atonement Day in 1898, we were encamped in Athens, Ga., preparing to embark for Cuba. Since no religious representative had come near us we requested the Colonel to excuse us from duty on that day. His reply was that since he had no orders from Washington, and since we were in the process of making hasty preparations to reach Savannah to board a transport for Cuba he could not excuse us from continuing with our assigned duties on that day. We performed our duty as ordered, but to show our sincerity we abstained from eating of any food or drink on the Holy Day . . .

Passover, however, fell at a more propitious time for religious observance:

On our return to Savannah, in April 1899, during the Passover season, committees from both the Reformed and Orthodox communities had prevailed on the Colonel to excuse the Jewish soldiers to enable them to visit the Houses of Worship. Invitations to visit various Jewish homes to participate in Seder Services had likewise been extended to us, which had been taken advantage of . . .

. . . [M]y recollection is that all the boys in Company "E" (my company) attended synagogue services, and later went to the respective homes assigned to us for Seder Services. The synagogue selected by the soldiers was, presumably, for sentimental reasons, based on their ancestral background. Those who had been born of Germanic, French or English parents, selected the Reform Temple, and also observed the Seder Service at the homes of Reformed (or reform, whichever is correct) Jews. As to myself, with three others, being of plebeian origin, having first seen the light of day in the Russian Ukraine, to our regret, selected an Orthodox synagogue, and ate the Seder meal at the home of a Polish Jew, who, at the conclusion of the meal, as we were departing for camp, stationed himself at the door, and collected 50 cents from each of his invited guests, in payment of the food. The 50 cents at that time represented one day's pay . . .

So much for the only sour note registered by either a veteran or an observer. [49]

Overseas, Manila offered the only opportunities for Jewish contacts, although not many soldiers were conscious of them. There were more than a few Jewish families in residence there, and some kind of synagogue, though recollections as to its name, officers or location are very uncertain. Morris Richards[50] and Samuel C. Mendell,[51] both of New York, recall being invited to attend services and thereafter taken to homes for Sabbath and holiday dinners. Paul Wollenberger of Omaha, Neb., however, had a different kind of experience in connection with Manila:

During my service with the sixth Infantry in the P. I. the regiment was split up into batalions [sic!] and I was stationed at Dumaguete,

Negroes Island, the only Jew in the Battalion. One day was ordered to report to the Commanding Officer and informed that an order had been issued at Washington to let all Jewish soldiers go to Manila for the high Jewish Holidays, the Order arrived in the Philippines long after the Holidays, but I was given to understand that since the order was issued, I had to go to Manila on a leave of absence, a four day trip by boat, attend religious services and return when ready, I was compelled to get on that boat, had a very good time, reported to the Adjutant in Manila, spent a few days there and then received return transportation to my post at Negroes Island, a fine two weeks vacation without ever seeing a Chaplain or Rabbi. [52]

Back in the United States, during those Holy Days, an especial effort was made by military officers and civilians alike to assure the proper opportunity for their celebration by Jewish soldiers. Camp Meade granted permission to 500 Jewish servicemen, including twenty-four officers, to go to the synagogue at Middletown, Pa., on Rosh Hashanah and Yom Kippur; [53] and those men of the First and Second Mississippi Regiments who were unable to reach home by Rosh Hashanah were given a cordial welcome in the synagogue and Jewish homes of Meridian, Miss. [54] In the New York area it was orginally planned that rabbis would be designated to conduct services for the High Holy Days at Camp Wikoff; when it was learned, however, that permission had been granted for all Jewish men to leave camp on furlough, they were merely notified of the location of synagogues in New York City and Philadelphia where they could be accommodated, if they were not able to reach home in time. [55] It was also announced that the Young Men's Hebrew Association would provide home hospitality for officers on furlough in New York, and that Dr. Krauskopf would make similar arrangements for those in the Philadelphia area. [56]

For the first time in American history, those High Holy Days of 5659, religious furloughs were to be granted freely to Jewish men in uniform. [57] The newly organized Orthodox Jewish Congregational Union, whose first meeting had just been held in

June,[58] through its President, the Reverend Dr. H. Pereira Mendes, and its Secretary, Max Cohen, appealed to the War Department for a general order enunciating a national policy which would recognize the right, rather than the privilege, of Jewish servicemen to request Holy Day furloughs.[59] Adjutant General H. C. Corbin's answer was the first such policy statement in American history:

> War Department,
> Adjutant General's Office,
> Washington.
>
> September 11th, 1898.
>
> Mr. Max Cohen, Secretary,
> 66 Liberty Street,
> New York City.
>
> Dear Sir:
>
> Replying to your letter of September 8th, I have the honor to state that in so far as it is possible the wishes expressed in your letter will be complied with. Furloughs will be granted to soldiers of your religous [sic!] faith, making application therefor, to celebrate the holidays set forth, and instructions will be given accordingly.
>
> Very respectfully,
>
> H. C. CORBIN
> *Adjutant General*[60]

It ought to be noted, however, that the subject of Holy Day furloughs continued to be unsettled. Either the Adjutant General did not fulfill his promise (for no such "instructions" can be located in the files of the War Department archives), or, at the very least, the order was regarded as applying only to the year 1898. For several years to come, petitions and letters similar to the Orthodox Union's were directed to the proper officials, and such notables as Dr. Mendes, Congressman Henry M. Goldfogle of New York City, and the Hon. Simon Wolf of Washington (long-time unofficial Jewish ambassador in the nation's capital) appealed for a definitive general order. [61] Finally, to cut the red tape and to light a fire under military bureaucrats who seemed to be unwilling to do what was obviously required, President Theodore Roosevelt took matters into his own hands and instructed his secretary to send the following memorandum to the War Department:

Oyster Bay, N. Y., Sept. 8, 1904

Wm. Loeb, Jr.,
  Secy. to the President, U. S.

The President directs that Commanding Officers be authorized to permit Jewish soldiers to be absent for attendance at service, on the Jewish Holidays. Also that Hon. Simon Wolf and Rev. H. Pereira Mendes of N. Y. be notified of action taken by W. D. [62]

When the President "directs" an order to the War Department, it must be accepted, published and obeyed. Four days later the Secretary of War notified Dr. Mendes that

orders have this day been issued to the Commanding Generals of all military departments in the United States and of the Philippines Division to permit such enlisted men of the Army of the Jewish faith as may desire to avail themselves of the privilege to be absent from their duties for such length of time as may be deemed necessary to enable them to attend divine services on the forthcoming Jewish holidays. [63]

Another milestone in the American Jewish struggle for equal treatment before the law had finally been passed.

Aside from several campaigns to organize separate Jewish companies, [64] and an unsuccessful effort to create a National Jewish Cemetery for the reinterment of all fallen Jewish servicemen [65] these are the only recorded or remembered details of Jewish welfare activities in behalf of Jewish servicemen during the Spanish-American War. Jews as individuals and as organized groups gave their full support to non-sectarian activities in connection with the war effort, [66] but, perhaps because of the very brevity of the war itself, and, also, undoubtedly, because of its chaotic disorganization, its lack of genuinely representative spokesmen, and its inability to plan for self-service, the American Jewish community as a whole neglected the religious and cultural welfare of its own men — over 4,000 according to the most reliable estimates — who served their country in 1898. Fortunately American Jewry has come a long way in the intervening years. More reason for gratitude to the National Jewish Welfare Board and its hundreds of local branches and affiliates.

NOTES

[1] Korn, *AJCW*, pp. 56-97.

[2] Report of the Office of the Adjutant General, United States Army, to the writer, November 21, 1950, according to which Rabbi Browne "applied for commissions as Chaplain at various times between 1898 and 1901." The pertinent file does not contain a copy of the Army's answer to Rabbi Browne's first application; it is entirely possible that there was none, considering the fact that he was only volunteering "in case no younger rabbi should seek the place" according to the *American Hebrew's* report. His birthdate was August 22, 1843; information supplied by his granddaughter's husband, Rabbi Jacob M. Rothschild of Atlanta.

[3] *American Hebrew*, June 17, 1898, p. 197.

[4] *ISR*, June 7, 1898, p. 7. *The Jewish Sentiment and Echo* of Atlanta (June 17, 1898, p. 3) berated Wise for his attack on Browne.

[5] Schappes, *op. cit.*, p. 733, for a few biographical data; *ISR*, July 12, 1872, p. 8; July 26, 1872, p. 6; August 9, 1872, p. 6, for some of Rabbi Browne's troubles.

[6] Korn, *op. cit.*, pp. 57, 65.

[7] *Yearbook, The Central Conference of American Rabbis*, Vol. VIII, (1898), p. 53. There is no record of any answer to the Conference's request.

[8] *Jewish Exponent*, July 15, 1898, p. 4; *MESS*, July 22, 1898, p. 4; *Jewish Review*, July 22, 1898, p. 4. The *Exponent* reacted not only to the Conference resolution but also, and even more energetically, to a report (published in the Philadelphia *Ledger*) that a Catholic priest had baptized a Jewish soldier at Camp Alger, Washington, D. C., on July 4th. This caused the *Exponent* to beg for "protection for Jews" in the armed forces: "There is a pressing need for Jewish chaplains, and the Central Conference of Rabbis having recognized this should secure their prompt appointment and aid them in every way in their tasks . . ." The Baltimore *Jewish Comment*

(August 26, 1898, pp. 7–8) was still hoping for action on the Conference's request after the war had ended; this was somewhat unrealistic in view of the rapid demobilization already in progress.

9 Carbon copy of letter in Scrapbook, p. 1, kept by C. M. Keegan, in the author's personal collection of historical documents [courtesy of Bernard C. Carlitz, Philadelphia].

10 *Jewish Exponent*, June 17, 1898, p. 3.

11 Keegan Scrapbook, p. 1.

12 Reform Congregation Keneseth Israel Board of Trustees' Minutes, Vol. III, p. 357, May 29, 1898.

13 Keegan Scrapbook, pp. 32, 59. According to the *Jewish Exponent*, May 6, 1898, p. 9, an unnamed New York congregation, whose synagogue was located at 31 Suffolk Street, voted to support the indigent families of its members who volunteered for military service.

14 Keegan Scrapbook, p. 59.

15 *Ibid.*, pp. 25, 57, 76.

16 Sermon preached at Keneseth Israel Temple, April 24, 1898, printed in *Jewish Exponent*, April 29, 1898, p. 6.

17 *Philadelphia Item*, May 8, 1898, clipping in Keegan Scrapbook, p. 21; *Jewish Exponent*, May 6, p. 7. The only similar instance of such participation in a military rally by a rabbi during the war which has been located in the periodical press concerned Rabbi Leon Harrison of St. Louis who gave an address accepting colors presented to the First Missouri Regiment and Artillery Battery A at a demonstration attended by over 15,000 people; *St. Louis Republic*, quoted in *Jewish Exponent*, May 6, 1898, p. 9.

18 Joseph J. Snellenberg (1849–1898), prominent department store executive and philanthropist, also donated ground for Brigade drill sessions; *Philadelphia Times*, June 28, 1898, clipping in Keegan Scrapbook, p. 69.

19 Joseph Leonard Levy (1865–1917), was born in London, came to the United States in 1889 and occupied the pulpit in Sacramento, Calif., before his call to Keneseth Israel in 1893. Eight years later he was elected Rabbi of Congregation Rodeph Shalom of Pittsburgh, where he remained until his death. He was known as an active leader in Philadelphia and Pittsburgh in virtually every civic welfare movement. *DAB*, XI, pp. 201–2.

20 Emil Gustav Hirsch (1851–1923), was born in Luxembourg, came to the United States in 1866 when his father was elected Rabbi of Congregation Keneseth Israel of Philadelphia, studied for the rabbinate in Germany, and, after three years in Baltimore and Louisville, became Rabbi in Chicago, where he sprang to the forefront as preacher, scholar, and champion of unpopular causes. *DAB*, IX, pp. 67–8; Emil G. Hirsch, *My Religion*, New York, 1925, pp. 11–23.

[21] *Reform Advocate*, June 11, 1898, p. 277; report of the Military and Naval Department, State of Illinois, to the writer, Sept. 14, 1950, which also states that Rabbi Hirsch resigned the commission on April 24, 1900. Hirsch was apparently one of the first clergymen of any denomination to be appointed a chaplain in the Naval Reserve of any state. The first Naval Militia to be organized was in Mass. in 1888. See Clifford N. Drury, *The History of the Chaplain Corps, United States Navy*, Vol. I: 1778–1939, Washington, n. d., p. 152.

[22] Letter from Rabbi Lee J. Levinger, San Francisco, to the writer, February 5, 1948, to whom the writer wishes to record appreciation for his interest in this essay.

[23] *Reform Advocate*, Oct. 1, 1898, p. 105.

[24] Joseph Krauskopf (1858–1923), was born in Prussia, came to the United States in 1872, studied at Hebrew Union College, Cincinnati, and was a member of its first graduating class. He occupied pulpits only in Kansas City and Philadelphia, where his reputation still marks him as one of the pre-eminent clergymen of his time. *DAB*, X, pp. 500–1; Abraham J. Feldman, "Rabbi Joseph Krauskopf," in *The American Jewish Year Book 5685*, Philadelphia, 1924, pp. 420–47.

[25] *Jewish Exponent*, June 17, 1898, p. 3; June 24, p. 2; July 1, pp. 4, 7; July 8, p. 7; July 15, p. 3; July 22, p. 8; Aug. 5, p. 6; Aug. 12, pp. 3, 6; Aug. 19, pp. 3, 6; Aug. 26, p. 6; Sept. 9, p. 6. See the *Jewish Messenger's* sarcastic comments on the spiritual welfare of a congregation which could permit its rabbis to travel all over the country and the world (Levy in California, Krauskopf as far as Cuba), Aug. 12, 1898, p. 4.

[26] *Jewish Exponent*, July 22, 1898, p. 8, and *Reform Advocate*, July 16, 1898, p. 357.

[27] *Jewish Exponent*, Aug. 15, 1898, p. 6. "My Prayer Book" was either the *Service Manual* or the *Service Hymnal*, both of which were written and compiled by Krauskopf, published and used for worship by Reform Congregation Keneseth Israel. A Sunday service was not a new experience for him; he was notorious as one of the first rabbis to introduce a successful Sunday morning service into a synagogue program, notorious among more traditional Jews who opposed him bitterly in this and many other synagogue reforms.

[28] *Reform Advocate*, Aug. 20, 1898, pp. 3–5. This description of the bravery of Greenwald and Goldberg is authenticated by records in the office of the Adjutant General, Department of the Army, report to the writer, dated 25 September 1951. For other Jewish heroes of the war see J. George Fredman and Louis A. Falk, *Jews in American Wars*, New York, 1943, pp. 49–53. For the only available listing of the thousands of Jewish men who served, see Cyrus Adler, "Preliminary list of Jewish Soldiers and Sailors who served in the Spanish-American War," in *The American Jewish Year Book 5661*, Philadelphia, 1900, pp. 525–622.

[29] *Jewish Exponent*, Aug. 12, 1898, p. 6.

[30] *Ibid.*, Aug. 26, p. 6.

[31] Letter from Rabbi Marx to the writer, Nov. 28, 1951.

[32] Letter to the writer, Dec. 31, 1951.

[33] Letter to the writer, Nov. 14, 1951.

[34] Letter to the writer, Oct. 14, 1951.

[35] Rabbi Spiegel has been mistakenly called an Army chaplain in Charles Weiss, "Jews in the Upbuilding of Puerto Rico," *Emanu-El and the Jewish Journal* (San Francisco), Sept. 19, 1941, p. 11, and *American Hebrew*, March 27, 1942, pp. 32–39. Weiss was not at fault, for Spiegel had written to him, in a letter which is quoted in the article, "I was stationed at Ponce, P. R. for nine months during the year 1899 and conducted there divine services during the Holy Days for some of the Jewish soldiers and laymen . . ." The use of the word "stationed" was unfortunate. This misinformation is also printed in *Who's Who in American Jewry*, New York, 1926. War Department records, however, contain no mention of Rabbi Spiegel, and the writer is certain that he was never a chaplain.

[36] *Jewish Review*, Sept. 30, 1898, p. 4.

[37] *American Hebrew*, June 17, 1898, p. 197.

[38] *MESS*, June 17, 1898, p. 5. The Jacksonville synagogue, Ahavath Chesed, had been built in 1882. B. Babbino was the rabbi in 1898 (*UJE*, VI, pp. 4–5).

[39] *MESS*, July 1, 1898, p. 5.

[40] This occurred at least once, on June 26, 1898, according to *Jewish Messenger*, July 1, 1898, p. 4. Samuel Olkin, Los Angeles, Calif., remembers going to services in the synagogue in Tampa, but does not recall the Rabbi's coming to camp. The Tampa congregation, Schaarai Zedek, was organized in 1894 (*UJE*, X, pp. 168–9).

[41] The writer has made an intensive effort to contact and question Jewish veterans of the war for information about their Jewish experiences. Altogether over one hundred and fifty veterans have assisted the writer; some of their recollections are embodied in various parts of this essay. The writer wishes to express especial appreciation to Mr. E. K. Inman, Editor of the *National Tribune*, a paper published in Washington, D. C., in the interests of Spanish-American War veterans; Mr. Edward Grusd, editor of the B'nai B'rith's *National Jewish Monthly*; and Mr. David Galter, Editor of the *Jewish Exponent* of Philadelphia, for publishing requests for information, each of which brought interesting results; and to Mr. James A. Dwyer of the Pennsylvania Dept. of the Sons of Spanish-American War Veterans, and Mr. Isidore Weill, Adjutant of the New York Hebrew Veterans of the War with Spain, both of whom furnished the writer with helpful lists of Jewish veterans affiliated with their organizations.

Although recollections stretching over a period of more than fifty years are sometimes inaccurate and hazy, it will be recognized that most, if not all, of the material here used can be regarded as trustworthy. Time, be it remembered, is fast running out for veterans of the conflict which occurred over fifty years ago, and in a matter of a few years most of them will have passed away. It is the appeal of the writer, therefore, that readers of this essay urgently request veterans of their acquaintance to contact him for the purpose of helping make this, his store of information, as authentic as possible.

[42] Most of the men who commented at length noted the paucity of religious emphasis in the Army and Navy altogether. Some of them never saw or met a chaplain of *any* faith. They have the feeling that the Armed Forces stressed religious worship and relationships far more during World War II than they did during the Spanish-American War.

[43] Letter to the writer, Nov. 15, 1951.

[44] Letter to the writer, Oct. 14, 1951. The Hebrew Veterans of the War with Spain, of which Mr. Weill is Adjutant, was organized Dec. 11, 1899, by the Hebrew Union Veterans Association in order to help combat anti-Semitism. In 1919, it was absorbed into the newly organized Jewish War Veterans. In 1935, it was reorganized and, in 1951, claimed 78 men as members.

[45] Telephone conversation with the writer, Nov. 4, 1951.

[46] Letter to the writer, Oct. 26, 1951.

[47] Letter from his brother, Isidore, to the writer, Nov. 21, 1951.

[48] Letter to the writer, Oct. 23, 1951.

[49] Letters to the writer, Oct. 13 and 30, 1951.

[50] Letter to the writer, Oct. 20, 1951.

[51] Letter to the writer, Nov. 3, 1951.

[52] Letter to the writer, Nov. 20, 1951.

[53] *Reform Advocate*, Oct. 15, 1898, p. 136. The statistics, unverifiable, would seem to be somewhat inflated.

[54] *Ibid.*, Sept. 17, 1898, p. 90.

[55] *American Hebrew*, Sept. 9, 1898, p. 533.

[56] *Ibid.*

[57] See *AJCW*, pp. 93-5, for details of the efforts of Rabbis M. J. Michelbacher of Richmond and Benjamin Szold of Baltimore to obtain such furlough orders, during the Civil War.

[58] See *Jewish Exponent*, April 29, 1898, for the announcement of the organizational meeting.

[59] Letter, Mendes and Cohen to Corbin, Sept. 8, 1898, Records of the War Department, Office of the Adjutant General, Document File no. 239692. It is important to note that a new group took the initiative to submit this request; there is no indication in its minutes that the forty-year-old Board of Delegates of American Israelites, then a commission of the Union of American Hebrew Congregations, representing the Reform wing of Judaism, even considered the subject; *Proceedings of the Union of American Hebrew Congregations*, Cincinnati, 1903, V, pp. 3948-53.

[60] Records of the War Department, Office of the Adjutant General, *supra*. Corbin's letter was highly publicized in the Jewish press; see, for instance, *Reform Advocate*, Sept. 17, 1898, p. 80.

[61] Records of the War Department, Office of the Adjutant General, *op. cit.*

[62] *Ibid.*

[63] *Ibid.*

[64] In Chicago, Ill., Richmond, Va., and Newport, R. I., according to *Jewish Comment* (Baltimore), May 6, 1898, p. 6; *Jewish Sentiment and Echo*, April 29, 1898, p. 3; New York *Times*, Jan. 25, 1950, obituary of Samuel Mason, commander of Touro Cadets of Newport; *MESS*, June 3, 1898, p. 3. All but ignored by the Jewish press, these feeble efforts were vigorously opposed by the editor of *Jewish Comment* who believed that Jews "should enter the ranks like any other American citizens" and denounced demonstrations of "Jewish patriotism" such as published lists of Jewish soldiers and the effort of some Cincinnati Jews to purchase a battleship for the Government; May 6, 1898, p. 6; May 27, pp. 7–8.

[65] *Reform Advocate*, Oct. 8, 1898. Most of the periodicals published the public letter addressed to American Jewry by the Society Agudath Achim Chessed shel Emeth of New York City, but the *Jewish Review* was the only one to give it editorial support (Sept. 23, 1898, p. 1). American Jews were as reluctant during the Spanish-American War as their fathers and grandfathers had been during the Civil War, to organize separatist military facilities, hospitals, companies, and cemeteries; *AJCW*, *op. cit.*, pp. 113–120. It was with obvious relish that *MESS* published a letter from a wounded sailor recuperating in the Convent Hospital in Key West, Fla., dated May 28, 1898, in which he said, "I am treated very well here by the Sisters and priests. I told them I was a Jew, but it makes no difference to them . . ." (June 10, 1898, p. 5). The soldier involved, Samuel Olkin, recalls that "my name was in the Jewish newspaper amongst the wounded and all the Jewish people [in Key West] came with the N. Y. Jewish journal to see me. They entertained me lavishly and gave me some money."

[66] One of the most notable acts by the Jewish community for non-sectarian welfare work was the offer of the facilities of the Jewish hospitals of Baltimore and Philadelphia for the care of sick and wounded soldiers. Although gratitude was expressed by the proper authorities, neither hospital was utilized. *Jewish Comment*, May 6, 1898, pp. 5, 12; *Jewish Exponent*, Sept. 2, 1898, p. 2.

The Council of Jewish Women, through its national officers, Hannah G. Solomon and Sadie American, urged its local sections to organize Army-Navy Committees for non-sectarian service, and to support other local welfare activities. Sections in Philadelphia, New York City, Baltimore and Washington, to name only a few cities, sent members to camps as Red Cross volunteers; collected funds, relief and medical supplies, and foodstuffs, to be sent to Florida and Cuba; supervised the wrapping of bandages, knitting and other such activities. Sisterhoods of congregations performed similar services. *Jewish Exponent*, June 3, 1898, pp. 2–3, 9; June 10, p. 3; June 17, pp. 7–8; June 24, p. 8; July 15, p. 10; *Jewish Comment*, May 27, p. 18; June 3, p. 15; June 10, pp. 15–16; June 17, p. 15.

Index